Rightist Multiculturalism

For nearly two decades, E. D. Hirsch's book *Cultural Literacy* has provoked debate over whose knowledge should be taught in schools, embodying the culture wars in education. Initially developed to mediate against the multicultural "threat," his educational vision inspired the Core Knowledge curriculum, which has garnered wide support from an array of communities, including traditionally marginalized groups. In this groundbreaking book, Kristen Buras provides the first detailed, critical examination of the Core Knowledge movement and explores the history and cultural politics underlying neoconservative initiatives in education.

Ultimately, *Rightist Multiculturalism* does more than assess the limitations and possibilities of Core Knowledge. It illuminates why troubling educational reforms initiated by neoconservatives have acquired grassroots allegiance despite criticism that their vision is culturally elitist. More importantly, Buras argues understanding that neoconservative school reform itself has become a multicultural affair is the first step toward fighting an alternative war of position—that is, reclaiming multiculturalism as a radically transformative project.

Kristen L. Buras is Assistant Professor of Multicultural Urban Education in the Division of Educational Studies at Emory University. She has written on school reform in *Harvard Educational Review* and is co-editor of *The Subaltern Speak: Curriculum, Power, and Educational Struggles*.

The Critical Social Thought Series
Edited by Michael W. Apple,
University of Wisconsin—Madison

Rightist Multiculturalism

Core Lessons on Neoconservative School Reform

Kristen L. Buras

Routledge
Taylor & Francis Group

NEW YORK AND LONDON

First published 2008
by Routledge
270 Madison Ave, New York, NY 10016

Simultaneously published in the UK
by Routledge
2 Park Square, Milton Park, Abingdon, Oxon OX14 4RN

Routledge is an imprint of the Taylor & Francis Group, an informa business

© 2008 Routledge, Taylor and Francis
Typeset in Minion by EvS Communication Networx, Inc.
Printed and bound in the United States of America on acid-free paper by Walsworth Publishing
Company, Marceline, MO.

Library of Congress Cataloging in Publication Data
Buras, Kristen L.
Rightist multiculturalism : Core lessons on neoconservative school reform / Kristen L. Buras.
p. cm. — (Critical social thought series)
Includes bibliographical references and index.
1. Education—Curricula—United States. 2. Curriculum change—United States. 3. Education—
Political aspects—United States. 4. Multiculturalism—United States. I. Title.
LB1570.B887 2008
375'.001—dc22
2007033795

ISBN 10: 0-415-96264-1 (hbk)
ISBN 10: 0-415-96265-X (pbk)
ISBN 10: 0-203-93186-6 (ebk)

ISBN 13: 978-0-415-96264-3 (hbk)
ISBN 13: 978-0-415-96265-0 (pbk)
ISBN 13: 978-0-203-93186-8 (ebk)

For Joe, Always

CONTENTS

SERIES EDITOR'S INTRODUCTION

IF YOU WALK INTO ANY LARGE BOOKSTORE and find yourself looking at the section on Education, you are apt to notice that considerable space is taken up by books with titles such as *Cultural Literacy*, *A Dictionary of Cultural Literacy*, *The Schools We Need and Why We Don't Have Them*, and similar titles. You'll also probably find an entire series of books that detail "everything your first (or second or third, etc.) grader needs to know." Each of these books will list E. D. Hirsch Jr. as author or editor. And each shows the influence of a significant movement that aims to save our schools and our children by changing curricula and pedagogy and giving children the knowledge they supposedly need to get ahead in our society. While there can be no doubt about the influence of Hirsch and the Core Knowledge movement with which he is associated, the key word in the previous sentence is "supposedly." *Rightist Multiculturalism* demonstrates in no uncertain terms why that word must be taken very seriously. Already well known for her earlier critical analysis of Hirsch and his followers (Buras, 1999b), Kristen Buras goes even further here, showing again why she is an educator whose insights must be taken very seriously.

One of the guiding questions within the field of education is a deceptively simple one: What knowledge is of most worth? Over the past four decades, an extensive tradition has grown around a restatement of that question. Rather than "*What* knowledge is of most worth?" the question has been reframed. It has become "*Whose* knowledge is of most worth?" (Apple 1996, 2000, 2006a) There are dangers associated with such a move, of course, including impulses toward reductionism and essentialism. However, the transformation of the question has led to immense progress in our understanding of the cultural politics of education in general and of the relations among educational policies, curricula, teaching, evaluation, and differential power.

Kristen Buras's book is clearly situated in this tradition. But it extends its scope and sophistication in powerful ways that are deeply relevant to the current debates over school reform nationally and internationally. Both the words national and international are important in the previous sentence. Indeed, on a recent trip to give a series of lectures in Australia, it became strikingly clear to me that the ways in which we in the United States deal with questions of the relationship between knowledge and power and the reforms we put in place have an immense impact not only here but in other nations as well. Thus, the "culture wars" over what counts as important knowledge and over who should decide it that have gone on for so long in the United States are alive and well in Australia. The current government's policies there have been strongly influenced by the neoconservative positions that are also powerful here. Ideological attacks on critically democratic educational policies and practices are growing, even in the face of evidence that the alternatives proposed by the government there are more than a little problematic (Apple, 2006a). This makes the debates over what we present to our children in the schools here even more significant. And it makes Kristen Buras's critical examination of E. D. Hirsch Jr. and the Core Knowledge movement even more crucial.

I personally had the opportunity to debate Hirsch face to face at a seminar at the Brookings Institution, hosted by Diane Ravitch (Ravitch, 2005). His positions combined both populist appeals and elitist understandings, as well as a profound misunderstanding of the arguments of Antonio Gramsci, something Buras demonstrates eloquently in this book.

But, to be fair, I found Hirsch to be passionate and articulate. I have few doubts about his commitment to the improvement of educational policy and practice. However, seemingly populist passion doesn't necessarily mean that one is correct educationally. Underneath the rather stipulative nature of his arguments are some assumptions that are questionable at best and often wrong at worst. His claims are based on the following sorts of general propositions. Our schools have turned away from a clear focus on important subject matter. Higher standards must replace those that now dominate education. We harm our most disadvantaged children by not "returning" to a rigorous academic curriculum for all children. Along with others such as Diane Ravitch, he believes that schools are no longer seriously academic (Ravitch, 2000a). These institutions now do too much; they have become social work and health agencies. We have asked schools to reform society or create "well-adjusted" children. This must stop; and the way to stop it is to basically take power from the professional educators and colleges of education (those all-powerful "progressives") who have controlled schools throughout the last century.

There are deeply worrisome problems and downright historical and current inaccuracies in this set of claims, as I have documented elsewhere (Apple, 2005). These problems are even more clearly illuminated by Buras's powerful analysis of the historical roots and current status of Hirsch and the Core Knowledge movement. Buras's position is based in an argument that curriculum coherence must be the result of long-term democratic and substantive discussions, and it must also be grounded in an honest and searching appraisal of the structures of inequalities in this society. A "core" cannot be imposed from the outside and legitimately claim to be based on the "knowledge of all of us." Nor can it be legitimate if—as in all too much of Hirsch's material—it is simply based on, say, test-driven content that has not been itself subject to the kinds of intense debates that must go on if that "knowledge of all of us" is to be truly representative.

Rightist Multiculturalism is crystal clear about the fact that the curriculum has always been the result of tensions, struggles, and compromises. What counts as "core knowledge" has all too often been *someone's* core, not everyone's core (Apple, 2000). Most often the rhetoric of common intellectual heritage is simply that—rhetorical. The hard questions—what and whose knowledge should be taught, who should decide, through what mechanisms, how success should be determined in the short and long term—are not easily dealt with. *Rightist Multiculturalism* insightfully demonstrates that Hirsch's answers to these questions are more than a little inadequate, in part because of the history out of which the movement has arisen and in part because of the very ways it looks at the issues of what and whose knowledge should be considered official.

But the book is not simply a critical assessment of the movement, although it is very good at that. It is also a sympathetic reading of the elements of good sense in the issues raised by Hirsch and by those who find value in his proposals. In doing this, Buras is able to portray the complexities and contradictions in a movement that is attempting to deal with real problems in schools. Buras does justice to these complexities and contradictions, a fact that gives more credibility to her concerns and criticisms.

Buras rightly knows that the solutions that Hirsch proposes have been the subject of a rich tradition of empirical research—much of which actually gives rather less support for his position that such a return to his stipulated definition of core knowledge is socially neutral and gives people the power to fully understand and act on their world (see, e.g., Bourdieu, 1984). She is equally insightful in her argument that although E. D. Hirsch legitimates his position by saying that he is the inheritor of Gramsci's arguments that the working class must know high status knowledge, he is being a bit disingenuous. We do have much to learn from Antonio Gramsci's position that high status knowledge does need to be taught. But Gramsci didn't stop there, he was very clear that such knowledge also needed to be *reorganized and closely connected* to the pressing social and intellectual problems faced by those who have the least economic, social, and cultural capital in this society (Apple, 1996). This is where Buras, rightly, stands.

Hirsch is correct when he recognizes that we do not do poor children any favors by denying them access to what this society has ordained as high status knowledge. But unless we ask "to what should this knowledge be connected?" and "what social purpose does it serve in terms of the collective struggles of those to whom this society has been less responsive?" it is of little benefit.

Since there is sincere and long-standing disagreement about what counts as core knowledge, one of the major reasons for its existence is to stimulate an ongoing and educative debate over what and whose knowledge should be declared "official" in every nation, region, community, and school (Apple 1996, 2006a). Of course, this is based on a very different conception of what counts as the "common" or the "core." Here we can learn something essential from the great cultural critic Raymond Williams. As Williams reminded us, the wisest way to think about a common culture is not necessarily the content that makes it up, but as the very process of democratic deliberation over what should be taught (Williams, 1989).

This is Buras's vision as well. In *Rightist Multiculturalism*, content and process are organically joined. In this book, the combination of rich historical, empirical, and conceptual analysis—and a clear recognition of both the realities of schools and the nature of this society—is coupled with an equally rich vision of what schools should be doing to counter the neoconservative policies and practices now so dominant in education. Kristen Buras has set the stage for the kinds of debate that are essential to an education worthy of its name.

Michael W. Apple
John Bascom Professor of Curriculum and Instruction
and Educational Policy Studies
University of Wisconsin, Madison

ACKNOWLEDGMENTS

I WOULD LIKE TO THANK Michael Apple, Diana Hess, Gloria Ladson-Billings, Bill Reese, and Simone Schweber for their ongoing interest in and support of my work. Our many conversations over the years have formed and inspired me. In particular, I want to convey my gratitude to Michael, whose friendship and scholarship have shaped me in lasting ways and whose political work exemplifies what it means to be a public intellectual.

I also appreciate the political energy, intellectual rigor, and insightful feedback of past and present friends in the Friday Seminar at the University of Wisconsin, Madison. Sharing such a space with kindred spirits should never be taken for granted.

More specifically, I want to express my genuine appreciation to the following colleagues, who have supported this work in a range of ways: Wayne Au, Catherine Bernard, Anthony Brown, Keffrelyn Brown, Ross Collin, Mary Jane Curry, Mary Ann Doyle, Maisha Fisher, David Gabbard, Luís Armando Gandin, Magnia George, Carl Grant, Carole Hahn, Marianne Larsen, Sonia Mehta, Tony Michels, Paulino Motter, Bekisizwe Ndimande, Thomas Pedroni, Kenneth Saltman, Jen Sandler, Vanessa Siddle Walker, Katy Swalwell, and Keita Takayama.

I likewise wish to acknowledge my supportive colleagues in the Division of Educational Studies at Emory University and the many graduate students there with whom I have had spirited discussions. Thanks especially to Taharee Jackson, my research assistant, who diligently helped me to prepare the index for the book.

Finally, I am indebted to my husband, Joe Aguilar, for his confidence in all that I do. It is impossible to measure the contribution that his unconditional support has made to this project. With love, I extend a few simple words to my parents, Christine and Michael Buras: Thank you for our decision on "college night." That decision and all of the decisions that you have made, made me. My passion is your doing.

It should be noted that some of the chapters in this book are adapted from previously published material:

Chapter 1, part of which originally appeared in 2007 as "Neoconservatism" in *Knowledge and Power in the Global Economy: The Effects of School Reform in a Neoliberal/Neoconservative Age,* a book edited by David Gabbard through Lawrence Erlbaum. Reproduced by permission of Taylor and Francis Group, a division of Informa plc.

Chapter 2, part of which originally appeared in 1999 as "Questioning Core Assumptions: A Critical Reading of and Response to E. D. Hirsch's *The School We Need and Why We Don't Have Them*" in *Harvard Educational Review,* Volume 69, Number 1, pp. 67–93, Copyright by the President and Fellows of Harvard College. All rights reserved.

Chapter 3, part of which originally appeared in 2006 as "Tracing the Core Knowledge Movement: History Lessons from Above and Below" in *The Subaltern Speak: Curriculum, Power, and Educational Struggles,* a book co-edited by Michael W. Apple and Kristen L. Buras through Routledge. Reproduced by permission of Taylor and Francis Group, a division of Informa plc.

Chapter 4, part of which originally appeared in 2006 as "Tracing the Core Knowledge Movement: History Lessons from Above and Below" in *The Subaltern Speak: Curriculum, Power, and Educational Struggles,* a book co-edited by Michael W. Apple and Kristen L. Buras through Routledge. Reproduced by permission of Taylor and Francis Group, a division of Informa plc.

Appendix B, which originally appeared as Correspondence in 1999 in *Harvard Educational Review,* Volume 69, Number 4, pp. 467–472, Copyright by the President and Fellows of Harvard College. All rights reserved.

INTRODUCTION
Rightist Multiculturalism as the New Hegemony

Multiculturalism of some kind there is, and there will be. The fight
is over how much, what kind, for whom, at what ages, under what
standards.... That was the reality [in the late 1980s], and remains
the reality. What impressed me was...the apparent inevitability
of multiculturalism. This had to moderate one's response: Simple
denunciation, it seemed, would no longer do.

> **Nathan Glazer in *We Are All Multiculturalists Now***
> **(1997, pp. 19, 33)**

Multiculturalism comes in different guises.... There's a progressive
form that will be helpful to all students, and a retrogressive kind
that...tends to set group against group.... Both seem to...express
admiration for diversity. But in their philosophical and practical
implications, the two conceptions are polar opposites. One version
is the universalistic view [that stresses membership in humanity
as a whole].... The other is a particularistic view that stresses loyalty to one's local culture. It could be called..."ethnic loyalism."

> **E. D. Hirsch in "Toward a Centrist Curriculum"**
> **(1992b, pp. 1–2)**

COMING TO YOUR NEIGHBORHOOD...AND OTHERS

WHEN E. D. HIRSCH WROTE *Cultural Literacy: What Every American Needs to Know* in the late 1980s, the cultural and educational left
articulated forceful critiques. Then there seemed to be silence. It was

1

as if many believed the book was the beginning of the end. What has less often been recognized is that *Cultural Literacy* was just the beginning. Over the past two decades, a curriculum reform movement—first inspired by that book—has taken shape across the nation and includes nearly 1,000 schools. It is perhaps the most enduring and widely appealing school initiative forwarded under the leadership of cultural conservatives and it goes by the name *Core Knowledge*. More than likely, it has come to your neighborhood, the one down the road, or both.

Imagine this educational reform effort described by its leader, E. D. Hirsch, as the "new civil rights frontier." By this, he means that its content compensates for knowledge gaps between "culturally literate" students and their "deficient" peers, thereby promoting equality by repudiating "segregated knowledge." What could be more "democratic," he asks, than broadly disseminating the "shared knowledge" crucial to a stable national culture (Hirsch, 1987, 1996, 1999b, 2006)? It all sounds good—no doubt—greater equality and a more unified democratic community. Consider next, however, that early critics characterized this same educational reform as an elitist attempt to marginalize the voices and cultures of subordinate groups (Aronowitz & Giroux, 1991).

Envision this Core Knowledge curriculum in a diverse array of schools—suburban, urban, and rural—across the nation. Touted as the "Great Books" tradition by a parent associated with a mainly European American, suburban school in the Midwest, the curriculum is concurrently viewed as "multicultural" by a teacher in a poor and isolated rural school, largely white, in the Appalachians (Buras, 2004). Meanwhile, teachers in a predominantly Latino/a school in the urban South embrace the "common content" offered by Core Knowledge, while they stress the importance of supplementing the curriculum with material on "Hispanic culture and traditions" (Mentzer & Shaughnessy, 1996). What is more, a principal in a low-income, African American community in another city appreciates that students in her Core Knowledge school—unlike those who are studying African- and African American-centered curricula in a similarly populated, nearby school—are "listening to Mozart and Beethoven, speaking French and reading classics like 'Robinson Crusoe'" (Donsky, 2005, A1). At the same time, yet another urban school administrator reports that the strength of the Core curriculum is its "expansive" content and coverage of "real world" issues (Buras, 2004). These illustrations only begin to skim the surface of the complex alliance around the most steadfast and popular school reform headed by neoconservatives in the last two decades: Core Knowledge.

Finally, reflect for a moment on this. In two other schools guided by Core—one predominantly white and suburban, the other predominantly black and urban—students in the former learn that Thomas Jefferson is a hero while those in the latter study that he was a slaveholder (Datnow, Borman, & Stringfield, 2000).

These contradictions point toward a host of questions. What do we make of such disparate understandings of Core Knowledge? What exactly constitutes the official content of the Core Knowledge curriculum? How does Core actually take shape in various classroom contexts, and what does this reveal about tensions and competing interests within the broader movement? The most important question and the one on which so much of this book is focused, however, concerns *why* Core Knowledge—early criticized as elitist and Eurocentric—has come to appeal to such a wide array of communities, including those traditionally marginalized. Much of this, I argue, has to do with what I am calling *rightist multiculturalism*, or the new hegemony that neoconservatives have been slowly building over the last several decades. Before I say more about Core Knowledge and the way in which an examination of this reform movement offers a deeper understanding of the cultural politics and dynamics of neoconservatism, let me first say more about the multifaceted rightist bloc at the helm of conservative modernization (Apple, 1996, 2006a; Apple & Buras, 2006).

THE PROJECT OF CONSERVATIVE MODERNIZATION

A complex network of conservative forces has been developing in the United States and in other nations across the globe. This rightist formation consists of several different but not totally distinct groups engaged in a politics of restoration aimed at undermining the limited, progressive gains of the past several decades and delegitimizing the political demands of oppressed groups for cultural recognition and economic redistribution. Michael Apple (1996, 2006a) defines this hegemonic project as the collaborative, although frequently conflicted, work of four major groups: neoliberals who wish to advance the free market and privatization at the expense of the public sector; authoritarian populists who seek to defend the traditional family and religious orthodoxy; a technically-skilled fraction of the professional middle class that helps manage the prevailing accountability regime; and neoconservatives who seek to defend historically dominant cultural traditions and national cohesion (see also Buras, 1999b, Pedroni, 2007a). Each group is waging struggles on a number of fronts, whether economic, religious, political, or educational. Importantly, while their concerns and interests often intersect, they are sometimes contradictory. Moreover, the views and strategies adopted by such groups at times differ not only across but also within the various camps—something that this work attempts to understand in relation to neoconservatives.

In education, the market orientation and consumptive focus of neoliberals has led to the increasing commercialization and privatization of schools (Buras & Apple, 2005; Molnar, 1996, 2005; Plank & Sykes, 2003). Perhaps no place else in the nation has this trend been more apparent than in post-Katrina New Orleans, which has become an experimental ground zero for brutal attacks on the public sector and radical reconstructions of public schooling, including proposals for and efforts to lay the foundation of an all-charter school district premised on decentralization, managerial networks, and choice (Bring New Orleans Back Commission, 2005; Buras, 2005, 2007a, forthcoming).

Concerned with the maintenance of moral order, authoritarian populists have likewise influenced educational policy (Deckman, 2004; Delfattore, 1992; Reed, 1996). Take, for example, interventions in Texas to "restore" traditional definitions of marriage to high school health textbooks. Groups associated with the Christian Right called for textbook publishers to make clear in textbooks that marriage is a union between a man and a woman. This definition, they believed, was undermined by the use of words, such as "couple," which might be read by students as endorsements of same-sex couples rather than as references to a man and a woman (Buras & Apple, 2006). Beyond this, attacks on the "secular humanism" of the public schools and the related growth of home schooling, accompanied by initiatives to gain charter school status for technologically networked home schools or tax credits and vouchers for private religious education, speak to the ongoing efforts and power of this political segment (Apple, 2006b).

Members of the new professional middle class, armed with valued forms of technical and managerial expertise, seek positions within state social and educational bureaucracies as well as administrative positions in the economic sector, including newly created roles opening as schools rapidly align with the imperatives of efficiency, standardization, and industry's need for human capital (Apple, 1995). There is little doubt, moreover, that the No Child Left Behind Act has created an apparatus of its own, including state technicians and corporate managers who assess and monitor the educational "progress" of schools and administer the series of disciplinary measures that accompany this accountability regime (Meier & Wood, 2004; Smith et al., 2004).

Finally, neoconservatives have contributed to public efforts and educational initiatives that address a very specifically defined crisis in declining standards, lost tradition, decaying national culture, and a tense, fractured, and degenerating community life (Hirsch, 1987; Huntington, 2005; Schlesinger, 1992). Their most forceful battles are being fought on the terrain of culture, especially with regard to school curriculum, pedagogy, and reform. A variety of educational reforms have been advocated by neoconservatives, including curricula centered on "traditional" knowledge (Bennett, Finn, & Cribb, 1999; Hirsch, 1996), "high" standards (Ravitch, 1995; Stern, 2003), and "patriotic" national and Western histories untainted by divisive forms of multiculturalism and critiques of Eurocentrism (Finn, 2003; Kramer & Kimball, 1997; Leming, Ellington, & Porter, 2003). This book focuses on a key exemplar of such initiatives: What began in the late 1980s as a list of items assumed to define the "culturally literate" person (Hirsch, 1987) has since grown into an educational reform movement focused on the highly specified and sequenced Core Knowledge curriculum—one that has already been adopted by hundreds of schools nationwide and even some internationally.

These initiatives reveal the aggressive cultural agenda currently pursued by neoconservatives occupying positions in government, the private sector, universities, think tanks, and foundations. The Free Congress Foundation, Heritage Foundation, Hoover Institution, John M. Olin Foundation, Thomas B. Fordham Foundation, and others have intervened in conflicts over culture with reports for policymakers and funding for programs intended to defend an allegedly beleaguered Western tradition (deMarrais, 2006; Kovacs & Boyles, 2005). Perhaps the most influential neoconservative voice over the last decade has been that of E. D. Hirsch, professor emeritus of education and humanities at the University of Virginia and founder of the Core Knowledge Foundation. Hirsch formed his ideas on culture in the late 1970s and began presenting them at conferences and publishing sketches in the early 1980s. Initially funded by the Exxon Education Foundation, he began drafting a preliminary list of cultural literacy items with the assistance of two colleagues, historian Joseph Kett and physicist James Trefil (Hirsch, 1987). Establishing the Core Knowledge Foundation in 1986 and subsequently publishing *Cultural Literacy: What Every American Needs to Know* in 1987 and *The Dictionary of Cultural Literacy* in 1988 (Hirsch, Kett, & Trefil, 1993), Hirsch laid the foundations for the Core Knowledge movement. This movement threatens to be the most powerful arm of the neoconservative educational project. Although much more will be said in upcoming chapters about the spread of this reform over past two decades, it is important to provide some initial remarks on the establishment of Core Knowledge and to point toward some of the central dynamics that account for its appeal. In the process, I will also begin to detail some of the contours, questions, and arguments of the book and explain why an understanding of Core provides insight into the cultural politics and power of neoconservatives more generally.

TWO DECADES AND GOING: CORE KNOWLEDGE AND RIGHTIST MULTICULTURALISM

Two decades ago, Hirsch (1987) authored *Cultural Literacy*. This bestseller generated a wave of debate as it declared not only the importance of common culture to national unity, but defined the relevant content of that culture and blamed multicultural education for undermining it. Deemed Eurocentric by critics (Aronowitz & Giroux, 1991), *Cultural Literacy* nonetheless metamorphosed into Core Knowledge—a pre-kindergarten through eighth grade curriculum that includes specific content guidelines in history, language arts, math, science, and the musical and visual arts (Core Knowledge Foundation, 1998), and resources such as literary collections and history textbooks aligned with those guidelines (Hirsch, 2002). Under the auspices of Hirsch's Core Knowledge Foundation, the first school to implement the curriculum began in 1990. Since that time, Hirsch's vision has shaped a nationwide movement focused on reforming education through Core Knowledge, which has been adopted by nearly 1,000 schools in a diverse array of communities (Core Knowledge Foundation, 2004b, 2006a, 2007a). Why is it, we might wonder, that an educational initiative developed to mediate against the "threat" of multiculturalism has garnered support from a range of communities—some constituted by traditionally oppressed groups?

I plan to consider that question by first charting in chapter 1 some of the history of neoconservatism, which illuminates the blending of concerns below and above, left and right, within the Core Knowledge movement. It is the case, in fact, that long before they were new rightists, some neoconservatives were actually old leftists; here, I refer to the New York intellectuals—many of them from working-class, Jewish backgrounds—who represent a key group within a much broader neoconservative bloc that includes African American neoconservatives and others. This history echoes in Core and provides the background necessary for understanding the incorporation and partial synthesis of competing concerns in Hirsch's educational vision and the peculiar alliances that characterize the movement. In chapter 2, I critically examine Hirsch's vision of education and the ways in which his guiding assumptions function as discourses that appeal to unequally empowered groups. Here we begin to see how Hirsch has woven together critiques of cultural deficiency and dissolution with historic concerns over civil rights and democracy. Next, in chapter 3, I trace the dynamics and growth of the Core Knowledge movement over the past two decades, analyze the allegiance of dominant and subaltern groups to Core Knowledge, and underscore the tensions generated by diverse actors and interests within the movement. This analysis entails a close look, in other words, at the processes and efforts—local and national—that have defined, built, and challenged this reform initiative. In chapter 4, I assess the conditional representation of various groups in history textbooks edited by Hirsch for Core Knowledge schools. More specifically, I explore the identities, storylines, images, and relations of power that are conveyed and masked in Core texts and reflect on how the "*new old history*" constructed in these narratives potentially appeals to different communities. I also think through the momentous debates relevant to understanding the troubling historical epistemology reflected in Core constructions of the national past, one that pits the "facts" of older and allegedly more legitimate histories against the "fictions" of newer accounts presumed to be polluted by "ideology." Importantly, in chapter 5, I refocus the lens, view Core Knowledge as part of an historic continuum of cultural and educational struggle, and reveal that Core is actually a window onto the dynamics and debates that characterize neoconservative efforts around schooling and democracy. I provide some concluding thoughts on how the foregoing examination of Core generates critical insights into the newer hegemonic processes underway and reveal possibilities for disruption and democratic redirection of neoconservative educational reforms.

What might be learned from these analyses, I ultimately argue, is that we are entering an era in which more progressive forms of multiculturalism focused on subaltern experience, elite power, and emancipatory struggle (Buras & Motter, 2006; Freire, 1993; Giroux, 1995) are being redefined by dominant groups along distinctly conservative lines and embraced as part of a decisive compromise. Through such compromise, select reforms partly speak to the concerns of marginalized communities and often win their consent while they simultaneously sustain relations of cultural domination. Core Knowledge is undoubtedly a key instantiation of the exercise of hegemony. As Antonio Gramsci emphasized:

Hegemony presupposes that account be taken of the interests and the tendencies of the groups over which hegemony is to be exercised, and that a certain compromise equilibrium should be

formed—in other words, that the leading group should make sacrifices. (Hoare & Nowell Smith, 1971, p. 161)

In this regard, Nathan Glazer's (1997) proclamation that "we are all
multiculturalists now" is more than a little relevant. By this he meant
that the multiculturalism advocated by oppressed groups had gained
enough strength that "simple denunciation...would no longer do" (p.
33). "Multiculturalism of some kind there is, and there will be," he con-
ceded. "The fight is over how much, what kind, for whom, at what ages,
under what standards" (p. 19). When considering what kind of multiculturalism Glazer envisioned, it helps to recall his clarification that
the declaration "we are all multiculturalists now" mirrors past resigna-
tions "pronounced wryly by persons who recognized that something
unpleasant was nevertheless unavoidable; it [does not] indicate a whole-
hearted embrace" (p. 160).

Glazer's pronouncement points toward the first "lesson" of this book
and offers a way to begin thinking about the advance of Core Knowledge. The 1960s and 1970s were indeed decades of spirited social activism during which many subaltern groups—African Americans and
women to name just two—struggled for a more equitable distribution
of resources as well as cultural respect and recognition. Issues related
to the production and legitimization of knowledge were central to these
groups as they demanded that their perspectives and histories contribute to reconstructing the nation. The demands expressed by movement
activists fueled the ongoing refashioning of rightist politics, including
neoconservative reform efforts aimed at curtailing the influence of progressive multiculturalism in schools and society (Apple, 1996; Cornbleth & Waugh, 1999). In short, this kind of multiculturalism—focused
on oppressed identities and ignored histories—was understood as divisive and threatening to cultural cohesion, shared national identity, and
the supremacy of Western civilization (Bennett, 1992; Leming, Ellington, & Porter, 2003; Podair, 2002).

Cultural conservatives, it is true, began working to "restore" the traditions under siege, but this is where the story gets more complicated
than generally recognized. To say that "we are all multiculturalists now,"
even if some are reluctant multiculturalists, actually masks the diverse
strategies employed by various neoconservative factions. It complicates
any attempt to critically assess these different strategies for their relative success or failure in helping neoconservatives build alliances with
subaltern groups and in either reinforcing or undermining hegemony.
If the power of the right only betrays more radically democratic conceptions of existence, and those dedicated to such conceptions hope to

wage a "war of position" (Buras & Apple, 2006; Hoare & Nowell Smith, 1971), then we need to understand the processes through which the right forwards its agenda and bolsters its influence. Close study of the Core Knowledge movement provides a good deal of insight, particularly when compared with kindred initiatives.

Allow me to briefly illustrate what I mean by "diverse strategies of neoconservative factions." First consider the Free Congress Foundation (2004b) that announces its purpose in this way: "Our main focus is on the Culture War. Will America return to the culture that made it great, our traditional, Judeo-Christian, Western culture? Or will we continue that long slide into the cultural and moral decay of political correctness?" In its proposed "Declaration of Cultural Independence," the foundation's (2004a) Center for Cultural Conservatism suggests the following:

> Until recently, the objective of cultural conservatives...was to retake existing cultural institutions—the public schools, the universities, the media, the entertainment industry, and the arts—from those hostile to our culture and make them once again forces for goodness, truth, and beauty....Unfortunately, we must acknowledge that this strategy has not been successful....We [therefore] seek nothing less than the creation of a complete, alternate structure of parallel cultural institutions.

Unwillingness to compromise with the assumed-to-be-dominant multicultural tradition represents one strategy that has been pursued. However, other neoconservative factions have aimed to foster alliances with grassroots, even traditionally marginalized, communities. In an effort to win the consent of Latino parents, for example, Hirsch's Core Knowledge Foundation began translating its encyclopedic *What Your Kindergartner–Sixth Grader Needs to Know Series* into Spanish and distributing the volumes free of charge. These translated readers are intended "to provide supplements to the original books for concerned Spanish-speaking parents, to enable them to help their children read and learn from the corresponding English-language volume" (Hirsch in Hirsch & Holdren, 2001, About Supplement). Unlike the Free Congress Foundation that advocates an intolerant and separatist doctrine as a means for rebuilding power, the Core Knowledge Foundation has instead engaged in the complex task of fostering alliances on the battlefield of culture. In fact, its effort to defend dominant cultural forms—in this case, to utilize Spanish as a bridge to both the inculcation of English and Core content—has been far more successful than the Free Congress Foundation would suggest.

The propensity toward particular forms of compromise—namely, those capable of appealing to the cultural sensibilities of marginalized groups while at the same time steering those sensibilities in dominant cultural directions—reveals the emergence of a new and potentially more "successful" hegemonic strategy; this strategy might be called *rightist multiculturalism*. In calling this a new strategy, I mean to underscore that it is more sophisticated and encompassing than the additive multiculturalism (McCarthy, 1998) or curricular mentioning of "limited and isolated elements of the history and culture of less powerful groups" (Apple, 2000, p. 53) that have often characterized conservative cultural work. This point will be further elaborated, for instance, when I analyze Core history textbooks.

For now, let us acknowledge that while such compromises and efforts may serve to strengthen the neoconservative project, the ongoing task of building alliances is undoubtedly characterized by tension as differentially empowered groups maneuver on the contemporary battlefield of culture. All of this will be thoroughly interrogated in relation to Core, with the goal of refining our sense of the complex exchanges, distinct strategies, and hegemonic processes that currently define so much neoconservative work.

In emphasizing the present, it is essential to remember that struggles over cultural recognition are nothing new, although surely the contours of struggles are shaped by prevailing conditions, the matrix of power, and the form and content of elite and subaltern agency at any given juncture. In 1845, Frederick Douglass published a narrative describing his life as an American slave and his effort to secure freedom. It opened with a letter from his friend, Wendell Phillips, dated April 22 that same year:

> My Dear Friend: You remember the old fable of "The Man and the Lion," where the lion complained that he should not be so misrepresented "when the lions wrote history." I am glad the time has come when the "lions write history." We have been left long enough to gather the character of slavery from the involuntary evidence of the masters. (p. xv)

As Douglass's narrative and Phillips's letter remind us, the struggle over knowledge—over who has the power to shape the way both the past and present are understood—is a long-standing one. We might begin, therefore, by asking: Just how "neo" is neoconservatism? What are the origins of the present-day cultural right? And how are specific neoconservative educational initiatives, particularly the Core Knowledge movement, situated within this history? In short, what shaped the growth of neoconservatism in the United States and how has it come to so powerfully influence curriculum and reform?

Multiple histories could be written in response to these questions. For example, the clock could be rewound to the colonial era during which imperial expansion was closely intertwined with religious and cultural mission. In this case, a partial and more recent history will be offered in an effort to shed light on contemporary conservatism and the battle over cultural tradition and power.

In the process of highlighting Frederick Douglass's intervention in historic struggles over representation and knowledge, it is instructive to note that the Core Knowledge Foundation, which has produced a number of educational resources to support the teaching of Core, recently issued the *Narrative of the Life of Frederick Douglass* as an extension of its *Core Classics*—a set of readers covering literary content. With the *Narrative* now sitting alongside *Robinson Crusoe*, the "classic" touted by the urban school principal earlier mentioned, we should find ourselves provoked to investigate not only the strategic compromise behind its ultimate incorporation into the canon of Core literature and history, but some of the history that has itself shaped Core and its cultural politics. Part of that history is charted in the next chapter.

1

HISTORICIZING CORE KNOWLEDGE
Neoconservatism, Cultural Deficiency, and the Civil Rights Frontier

Multiculturalism is a desperate—and surely self-defeating—strategy for coping with the educational deficiencies, and associated social pathologies, of young blacks.... [Other groups] are fully preoccupied with the process of "Americanization."...Most Hispanics are behaving very much like the Italians of yesteryear; most Orientals, like the Jews of yesteryear.... Their integration into American society proceeds at different rates—but it does proceed.... What these radicals blandly call multiculturalism is as much a "war against the West" as Nazism and Stalinism ever were.

Irving Kristol in *Neoconservatism:*
***The Autobiography of an Idea* (1995, pp. 50–52)**

Bad schools hold back disadvantaged children disproportionately because disadvantaged homes are typically less able than advantaged ones to compensate for the knowledge gaps left by the schools.... This new struggle is more subtle and complex than the earlier one of sit-ins and freedom rides.

E. D. Hirsch in *The Schools We Need and*
***Why We Don't Have Them* (1996, p. 43)**

THE LONG REVOLUTION

THE STORY OF NEOCONSERVATISM often begins with the 1960s. The new left inspires a new right, including a neoconservative faction focused on the restoration of a "common" cultural tradition and a disciplined, socially cohesive nation. But long before they were new rightists, many neoconservatives were actually old leftists, a fact that helps to explain the synthesis of concerns both left and right within neoconservatism. Inadequate recognition of this history has been partly facilitated by the circulation of a narrative that constructs neoconservatism as an oppositional reaction to the movements of the mid-twentieth century, whether civil rights or other subaltern struggles for cultural respect and economic redistribution (e.g., see Apple, 2000; Banks, 2004; Cornbleth & Waugh, 1999). In one of the earliest accounts of neoconservatism, Peter Steinfels (1979) stresses that even during that era:

> There was much talk of people being "radicalized," and in turn much talk of right-wing "backlashes." But "backlash," as the word implies, was an angry, reflexive action. There was no term for the slower evolution of a significant party of liberals. They were, we might say, "conservatized." (p. 44)

In order to appreciate the slower evolution of these new conservatives, the politics that distinguished them from traditional conservatives, and the concerns that they developed regarding cultural deficiency and decay, national identity, and the defense of Western tradition, it is necessary to rewind the clock earlier than the 1960s. The 1930s is the starting point for much of the historical trajectory examined here. It is utterly essential to emphasize, however, that a number of significant currents have contributed to the neoconservative project. While I will focus on the history of neoconservatism within parts of the Jewish American and African American communities—these pasts are particularly relevant to understanding Core Knowledge—neoconservative strains have surely traveled through various other groups.

Charting such history is complicated, as historiography in these domains is just beginning to take shape (e.g., see Apple, 1999; Dillard, 2001). In 1999, Murray Friedman—former director of the Myer and Rosaline Feinstein Center for American Jewish History—edited a special issue of *American Jewish History* in which he underscored: "The fact is the story of neoconservatism, like the story of American Jewish conservatism itself, remains to be written" (p. 110). These two stories are partially intertwined and involve the political journey from left to right of a group of New York intellectuals from working-class, Jewish backgrounds, and their Gentile associates, over the course of several decades. Acknowledging this coalition, Friedman asserts, "There is no mistaking, however, the 'Jewish' ambiance of the [neoconservative] movement with its origins in the Jewish Left of the 30s and 40s" (p. 110).

One reason this aspect of the past has been neglected is that the writing of American Jewish history has disproportionately focused on liberal and leftist traditions in the Jewish community, often overlooking politically conservative segments, albeit a minority, that "draw from a deep wellspring of Jewish political philosophy, law, and historical experience" (Sarna, 1999, p. 113). Yet refocusing the lens involves volatile debates in the Jewish community and legitimate concerns that reactionary forces may conceive newly emerging histories as invitations to anti-Semitic scapegoating or use them as ammunition for diatribes on political conspiracy. There are those on the right, for example, who believe that a "cabal" of neoconservatives—Paul Wolfowitz and other Jewish officials—have orchestrated the foreign policy of the United States for the sole benefit of Israel (e.g., see Buchanan, 2003). Even on the left, there are those who contend that the disciples of German-Jewish émigré and philosopher Leo Strauss are largely responsible for the "stealth campaigns" that define the "real" neoconservative agenda (Drury, 1999, 2003).

Telling the story of American Jewish neoconservatism thus requires care and sophistication; in light of the murderous history of anti-Semitism, there is a danger in highlighting this dimension of the neoconservative project. The story of the New York intellectuals, however, provides an important starting point in exploring neoconservatism, as does examining neoconservatives of color. The history of the latter, in fact, has been similarly underexamined (Dillard, 2001) and has also proven to be explosive, as evidenced by the disparate reactions to the remarks of Bill Cosby—a successful and very wealthy African American comedian and actor—about poor blacks during an NAACP event marking the fiftieth anniversary of Brown v. Board of Education (see Dyson, 2005). In much the same way, African American mayor of New Orleans, Ray C. Nagin (2006), inspired much debate when he called for the restoration of the "chocolate city" after Hurricane Katrina, but simultaneously warned that the catastrophe indicated God was "upset at black America" for not "taking care" of its own problems (i.e., remedying the culture of poverty that is assumed to explain black suffering) (see Buras, 2007a, forthcoming).

In light of these issues, writing a chapter on the development of neoconservatism presents a challenge. All I can do here is to provide a glimpse into some of this history and illuminate its relationship to present-day school reform, particularly Core Knowledge. I hope that others will join the effort of teasing out the various intellectual streams, complexities, and tensions within neoconservatism as well as their relationship to current initiatives in education. Most of this chapter sketches the two aforementioned histories, with particular attention paid to the lineage of debates over culture. The conclusion highlights the relevance of these pasts to understanding the politics of Core Knowledge (see also Buras, 1999b, 2006, 2007b).

THE LITTLE RED SCHOOLHOUSE

In the 1930s, City College of New York was largely attended by working-class, Jewish young men—some of whom would become the foremost neoconservative intellectuals of a later era. These were the sons of turn-of-the-century Eastern European immigrants who worked in the sweatshops of New York City. Admission to Columbia University was limited by anti-Semitic quotas, which ensured a predominantly Protestant student body in such institutions. While the students at City College were competitive in talent, they especially distinguished themselves from Ivy League cohorts when it came to radical leftist politics. When the president of City College invited Italian students representing Benito Mussolini's fascist regime to speak on campus in 1934, the head of the student council, a member of the Young Communist League, welcomed "the tricked and enslaved students of Fascist Italy," with demonstrations thereafter persisting for weeks. It was this kind of spirited left-wing activism that earned City College the designation of "little red schoolhouse" (Dorman, 2000, p. 42).

Although most City College students had grown up poor, the Great Depression only further exacerbated existing inequalities. Irving Howe, who attended the school and later coined the term *New York intellectuals*, recalled: "There was a sense of chaos, of disintegration. And so the socialist view, the radical view... seemed to suggest a conceptual frame by which one could... give meaning to these very difficult experiences" (in Dorman, 2000, p. 32). In fact, it was in the cafeteria of City College, where a number of alcoves existed, that sects of every "religious, ethnic, cultural, and political group" segregated, congregated, and debated. Irving Kristol, a former student now known as the "father of neoconservatism," described this political milieu:

> I would guess that, in all, there were more than a dozen alcoves.... But the only alcoves that mattered to me were No. 1

and No. 2, the alcoves of the anti-Stalinist and the pro-Stalinist Left, respectively. It was between these two alcoves that the war of the world was fought. (1995, p. 472)

Reflecting on the subtle ways that "Jewish" experience informed debates within Alcove One, Daniel Bell—another member of this group—explains:

Socialism gave us answers to this world reading Marx, reading the *Communist Manifesto*, reading *Das Kapital*. . . . And you were able to take the same kind of reasoning that you learned in *kheder* [a school where young boys study the Torah and Talmud] and now deal with real-world problems. So we'd read *Kapital* the same way we read *humash* [Torah], line by line. In *kheder* there was a great pressure to learn by a sort of contrary logic. . . . Learning how to read is learning how to question. . . . That kind of *pilpul* [debate] trains you, arms you. (in Dorman, 2000, p. 35)

At the very same time, the "universal" call of Marxism for class consciousness and collective struggle appealed to the less particularistic sensibilities of these secular Jews at a time when ethnic and religious identification served to bolster forms of discrimination. "The embrace of Marxism," in other words, "was part of the Jewish intellectuals' search for a community to replace the Jewish one they denied and the American one denied to them" (Abrams, 2005, p. 14). This effort to finesse the tension between diversity and unity was reflected in *Partisan Review*, a communist and soon independent Marxist journal established in the mid-1930s by New York elders Philip Rahv and William Philips, and read by many in Alcove One's younger generation. Nathan Glazer, a member of the latter group, noted that "Jewish topics entered [Partisan Review] only if they passed a test of universal significance" (in Dorman, 2000, p. 10).

The members of Alcove One, including Howe, Kristol, Bell, Glazer, and others, would shift to liberal, even hard, anticommunist positions in the years ahead. In Alcove Two were students such as Julius Rosenberg, whose own fate symbolized the battles that would characterize the cultural Cold War. As the unspeakable atrocities of Hitler and Nazism gained wider recognition and stories of Stalin's own abuses (e.g., Moscow Trials, 1939 Pact with Hitler) emerged from the Soviet Union, the issue that increasingly preoccupied these young intellectuals was whether or not Stalin had betrayed Marxist ideals or revealed some inherent weakness in the communist vision (Steinfels, 1979). Kristol pondered, "Was there something in Marxism . . . that led to Stalinism? To what degree was there a connection? This was the question that...was a prelude to our future politics" (in Dorman, 2000, p. 54). Indeed, the shattering of their faith in the promise of collectivism was a crucial turning point in a slow rightward journey.

THE GOD THAT FAILED

In 1950, *The God That Failed* (Crossman, 1949) featured the political reflections of several American and Western European intellectuals originally committed to the communist cause, but ultimately disillusioned by the Soviet experiment. The book was "the collective autobiography of a generation," at least those segments centrally involved in the anticommunist struggle (p. vii). In the years following World War II, most of the New York intellectuals—Howe was an exception—deserted Marxism as a viable political philosophy. Fascism under Hitler and communism under Stalin, they proclaimed, were morally indistinguishable. "Just as Hitler had terrorized the world with concentration camps, genocide, [and] suppression of freedoms," Stalin had "done the same" (Gerson, 1997, p. 37). Revolted by the far left, which they believed consisted of naive Marxists at best and Stalinists at worst, this fraction of old leftists embraced an anticommunist position. This position entailed distinguishing themselves from radical leftists whose anti-anticommunism they felt would only compromise the liberal cause as well as from conservative anticommunists who hailed the efforts of Senator Joseph McCarthy to destroy the communist threat, even if his disregard for civil liberties provided ammunition for far left critiques of anticommunism (Gerson, 1997; Steinfels, 1979). Some, however, embraced a hard anticommunist position—something that caused a split within the American Committee for Cultural Freedom (ACCF) in which many were involved in the 1950s (Friedman, 2005; Kristol, 1952).

The anticommunist efforts of the ACCF revealed serious tensions around the meaning of "cultural freedom" and what was required to protect it. While Cold War liberals such as Arthur Schlesinger expressed the need for a "vital center" capable of showing regard for civil liberties *and* fighting communism, hard anticommunists placed more emphasis on an uncompromising strategy that aggressively countered Soviet "propaganda" and expansionism. The ACCF joined forces with the international Congress for Cultural Freedom (CCF), which maintained offices in 35 nations and supported various publications, including *Encounter*—a magazine co-edited by Kristol and Stephen Spender, a London-based contributor to *The God That Failed*. Symbolic of the increasing commitment of hard anticommunists to an unfettered defense of the United States and the West was their disregard for rumors—later confirmed—that the CIA was funding both the CCF and *Encounter* (Friedman, 1999, 2005b; Steinfels, 1979). It was then that the culture war for the West first began, rather than in later decades as has sometimes been assumed.

The central venue through which the New York intellectuals came to express themselves, however, was *Commentary*—a journal established by the American Jewish Committee in 1945 (Friedman, 2005a). When compared with other Jewish civic organizations in the United States, the American Jewish Committee was most accommodationist in its orientation. Long before and during much of the early post-World War II era, for example, it assumed a non-Zionist position and framed its concerns for displaced persons in Europe in "humanitarian" rather than "Jewish" terms. In comparison, the more left-leaning, confrontational American Jewish Congress embraced cultural pluralism as an ideal and pressed the nation to respond to the needs of European Jews as a persecuted minority. Significantly, it likewise learned that linking its project to "American" interests was often necessary for gaining wider support (Dollinger, 2000).

This tradition of accommodation—one undoubtedly facilitated by historic experiences of oppression—would shape *Commentary* in powerful ways. As a cultural project, *Commentary* evidenced a delicate balance (or perhaps, imbalance) between its Jewish and its American affiliations and "produced a discourse of a specifically Jewish American nature." Elliot Cohen, the journal's editor from 1945–1960, expressed in his first editorial statement: "As Jews, we are of an ancient tradition that...keeps a vigil with the past." At the same time, he stressed, "*Commentary* is an act of faith in our possibilities in America" (Abrams, 2005, p. 31). There was, of course, a complicated and deeply ironic politics at work—a kind that required "selective amnesia" to efface a history of anti-Semitism in the United States through the "memory" of an America more open to Jews than any nation in the Diaspora's history (p. 33). The process of constructing such a "memory" was assisted by very subtle checks on editorial independence. Abrams reveals that "the Jewish community's intellectuals had been screened through careful selection and then were co-opted by the American Jewish Committee" (p. 28).

Not only would *Commentary* aim to "bring the ideas of the New York intellectuals to a wider audience, especially upwardly mobile Jews," but it also aspired to "show that Jewish intellectuals, and by extension all American Jews, had turned away from their past political radicalism to embrace mainstream American culture and values" (Ehrman, 1999, pp. 160–161). Perhaps all of this was made easier—that is, the turn away from radicalism, especially for some intellectuals, toward liberal and conservative anticommunism and a romantic pro-American ideology—since an unprecedented opening of the society to Jews occurred in the late 1940s and 1950s. Growing up on the Lower East Side of Manhattan, Bell explained his early experience of "upward mobility" as moving from "a backyard tenement to a front yard tenement, to having a border so that you were able to afford to have some better places" (in Dorman, 2000, p. 29). Kristol likewise reports, "You must understand, no one I ever knew owned a car, or owned a home.... After ten years of Depression and four years of war, to be able to buy a house and have children and buy a car—that was fantastic" (in Dorman, 2000, pp. 83–84). During this period, moreover, many of the New York intellectuals moved into positions within the academy or functioned as public intellectuals within venues such as *Commentary* and other influential publications (Dorman, 2000; Friedman, 2005b).

Norman Podhoretz, editor of *Commentary* from 1960 to 1995, underscored the allure of the mainstream and centrality of upward mobility in his aptly-titled autobiography *Making It* (1967). It is extremely significant, then, that Irving Howe stopped writing for *Commentary* because it had "become an apologist for middle-class values, middle-class culture and the *status quo*" (quoted in Abrams, 2005, p. 35). Unlike many of his now liberal peers, Howe remained committed to democratic socialism and thus devoted his energies to co-founding *Dissent* in 1954 with still-radical colleagues (Mills & Walzer, 2004). Indeed, *Commentary* and *Dissent* reflected serious tensions within the New York intellectual community—something that prompted Woody Allen to humorously suggest that the two publications should unite under the title *Dysentery* (Friedman, 2005b, p. 136). In reality, though, the political fall out would be far less "entertaining" to those involved in this (un)civil war within the liberal camp and between liberals and leftists (Friedman, 2005b; Podhoretz, 1979). It would also have serious implications for groups later targeted by the arguments of those who ultimately made the neoconservative turn. Notably, some of these same groups would be targeted by Hirsch for redemption through Core Knowledge, the curricular embodiment of "mainstream American culture" and the key to "upward mobility."

THE TURN TO NEOCONSERVATISM

The communities represented by *Commentary* and *Dissent* came to express dramatically different views on civil rights, the welfare state, the counterculture, the new left, and other issues during the 1960s and 1970s. By the late 1970s, the transition of many old leftists from liberalism to neoconservatism would be complete. The crossing—it is essential to recognize—would not bring them into the camp of traditional conservatism defined by pre-modern political philosophy, religiosity, anti-Semitism, racism, anti-statism, and isolationism, or even into the traditional but modernized conservatism represented by William F. Buckley and his *National Review* (Judis, 1998; Shapiro, 1999). They were undeniably a *new* breed of conservatives; their roots, political trajectories, and ideological positions would distinguish them, often in ways that invited disdain from both the right and the left. Reflecting on such distinctions, Kristol writes:

> The conservatism of National Review interested us not at all. There were many points of repulsion, but it was National Review's primordial hostility to the New Deal that created a gulf between us and them. We were all children of the depression, most of us from lower-middle-class or working-class families, a significant number of us urban Jews for whom the 1930s had been years of desperation, and we felt a measure of loyalty to the spirit of the New Deal.... Nor did we see it as representing any kind of statist or socialist threat.... All of us had ideas on how to improve, even reconstruct, this welfare state.... It was when the Great Society programs were launched that we began to distance ourselves... from the newest version of official liberalism.... The prescribed cure for poverty was defined as militant political action...that would result in the redistribution of income and wealth.... Having known poverty first-hand—the authors of the War on Poverty were mainly upper-middle-class types—and witnessing the ways poverty was overcome in reality...we were utterly contemptuous of this idea. (n.d., pp. 3–4)

In a similar way, Nathan Glazer (2005) clarifies:

> All of us had voted for Lyndon Johnson in 1964.... Skepticism was only evoked by its [the Great Society's] more speculative...extensions into "social engineering," as in the community participation effort in the War on Poverty, or the movement from civil rights to affirmative action.... Had we not defended the major social programs, from Social Security to Medicare, there would have been no need for the "neo" before "conservatism." (p. 3)

Indeed, a fusion of concerns from across the political spectrum would define the neoconservative vision.

The rise of the Civil Rights movement in the 1950s and the legislative gains of the mid-1960s were supported by the New York intellectuals and their associates. They embraced the idea that individuals should be considered equal before the law, regardless of religion or race. Nonetheless, when it came to demands for recognition rooted in identity politics or more militant racial assertions—whether for multiculturalism, Black Power, or affirmative action—these elicited strong condemnation. Consider "My Negro Problem—and Ours" written by Podhoretz in 1963 for *Commentary*. After recounting episodes in which he—a working-class Jewish boy in Brooklyn—was victimized by African American youth in his neighborhood, Podhoretz asks:

> Will this madness in which we are all caught never find a resting-place? Is there never to be an end to it? In thinking about the Jews, I have often wondered whether or not their survival as a distinct group was worth one hair on the head of a single infant. Did the Jews have to survive so that six million innocent people should one day be burned in the ovens of Auschwitz?... And when I think... about the image of integration as a state in which the Negroes would take their rightful place as another of the protected minorities in a pluralistic society, I wonder... *why* they should wish to survive as a distinct group.

What was required, he argued, was "not integration" but "assimilation" and "miscegenation," as "the Negro problem can be solved...in no other way" (1996, p. 17). In stark terms, Podhoretz reveals an aversion to identity politics and a faith in cultural assimilation as the answer to racial difficulties. In a postscript, he calls affirmative action "a diseased mutation of integrationism," laments "the damage done to the precious American principle...of treating individuals as individuals" and criticizes the "destructive balkanization of our culture" (pp. 20–21). Echoed here are central tenets of neoconservative ideology—that liberalism has been deformed, meritocracy compromised, and culture fragmented. Undoubtedly problematic, this way of thinking is at least partially "understandable" when one considers how an oppressive history has schooled parts of the Jewish community to support accommodation for the purpose of advancement, or to criticize quotas, which were earlier used to limit rather than to increase Jewish representation. What is most noteworthy is how this set of positions simultaneously embraces the ideal of racial inclusion, while it inscribes hegemonic notions of culture through its delineation of how the "Negro problem" will be resolved. Moreover, a parallel is drawn between the historic experiences of Jewish Americans and African Americans with little recognition of significant differences, including the disparate subject positions available to "ethnic" and "racial" groups. Put another way: Was "whiteness," for instance, an identity that every group could plausibly assume—or would want to assume (see Delgado & Stefancic, 1997; Goldstein, 2006; Podair, 2002; Roediger, 1991)?

Equally significant, although these chastened intellectuals defended the New Deal and retained some confidence in state activism, they increasingly advocated a more limited welfare state and expressed concerns that Great Society programs and the War on Poverty were creating a culturally deficient underclass dependent on government intervention (Kristol, 1996; Steinfels, 1979; Wildavsky, 1996). An early and by now iconic example of this position is a government report issued in 1965 by Daniel Patrick Moynihan—an associate of the New York intellectuals—entitled "The Negro Family" (1996). According to him, the damage wrought on the African American family by past mistreatment remained the primary barrier to black progress. Illegitimacy, single parenthood, and welfare created a dire situation in which "the present tangle of pathology is capable of perpetuating itself without assistance from the white world" (p. 36).

This line of argument was most thoroughly developed and advanced by *The Public Interest*—a journal founded that same year by Kristol and Bell that exclusively examined new government programs and their "unintended consequences," including the perpetuation of "social pathologies" in America's underclass. Reflecting the direction such work would take over the coming decades was James Q. Wilson's "The Rediscovery of Character: Private Virtue and Public Policy" (1996). He lauded the "growing awareness that a variety of public problems can only be understood—and perhaps addressed—if they are seen as arising out of a defect in character formation" (p. 291). Referring to the leading advocate of interventionist government spending, Wilson continues, "John Maynard Keynes was not simply an important economist, he was a moral revolutionary.... Deficit financing should be judged, he argued, by its practical effect, not by its moral quality" (p. 298). Put another way, Keynes had presumably failed to grasp the wider implications of his financial doctrine. State spending on public programs is not solely an economic endeavor, it is a cultural one—and the resulting gains and losses are not monetary alone; the deficit of greatest concern, Wilson says, is one of discipline and virtue.

The rightward drift of these intellectuals was also evident in their response to the counterculture and the new left. It was not simply poor communities of color that needed cultural reformation. Those pushing the boundaries of gender and sexuality, those demonstrating on campuses for free speech, those protesting the Vietnam War—all were seen as contributing to the degradation of tradition and authority, cultural relativism, and ultimately a kind of moral void or nihilism that would undermine cherished institutions and national stability (Dorman, 2000; Gerson, 1997). Glazer (1996) explained his position on student radicalism in this way:

> I have made some commitments: that an orderly democracy is better than government by the expressive and violent outbursts of the most committed; that the university embodies values that transcend the given characteristics of a society...; that the faults of our society, grave as they are, do not require...the destruction of those fragile institutions which have been developed over centuries to transmit and expand knowledge....My first reaction to student disruption...is to consider how the disrupters can be isolated...and how they can be finally removed from a community they wish to destroy. (pp. 54–55)

Not without significance, Glazer deeply regretted the "failure" of liberal intellectuals to challenge these attacks and of neoconservatives to "answer effectively" when leftists in the academy, such as Noam Chomsky, "explained [to students] how the world operated" (p. 63). Todd Gitlin, a founding member of Students for a Democratic Society, reflects on the conflict between many once old leftists and new leftists and suggests that in the minds of the former, Stalinism had been "a conclusive refutation of revolutionary possibilities" (in Dorman, 2000, p. 143). Perhaps it is even more complicated, as the university itself represented for many of these intellectuals a domain that ultimately offered to them long-denied privileges and power.

In 1973, Michael Harrington referred in the pages of *Dissent* to an emergent group of conservatives—former liberals and leftists who drifted right—whom he called "neoconservatives." Most, however, vehemently denied the shift and eschewed the "neoconservative" label. "What was now called liberalism, they insisted, was a countercultural perversion of traditional Democratic politics. They had not changed, they claimed, but were reminders of what American liberalism stood for before it was radicalized by the Movement [activism of the 1960s]" (Dorrien, 1993, p. 1).

NEO/CONSERVATIVES IN THE 1980s

The election of Ronald Reagan as president in 1980 represented a turning point; many neoconservatives cast Republican votes for the first time. As they saw it, the Democratic Party had been captured by the radical left, so there was little choice in the matter. Yet it was still unclear to many traditional conservatives—and many neoconservatives—whether or not neoconservatives were *actually* conservatives. Traditionalists (sometimes called *paleoconservatives*) believed that neoconservatives were a "schism of the left," "rightwing liberals," and "social democrats who posed as conservatives." Even neoconservatives suggested that they might be better described as "paleoliberals" since the liberalism of recent decades had moved, in their view, so far to the left (Shapiro, 1999). In 1986, one paleoconservative warned:

> The offensives of radicalism have driven vast herds of liberals across the border into our territories. These refugees now speak in our name.... [But their language] contains no words for the things that we value. Our estate has been taken over by an impostor, just as we were about to inherit. (in Shapiro, p. 205)

Another traditionalist expressed his concerns in this fashion:

> It has always struck me as odd, even perverse, that former Marxists have been permitted, yes invited, to play such a leading role in the Conservative movement.... It is splendid when the town whore gets religion and joins the church. Now and then she makes a good choir director, but when she begins to tell the minister what he ought to say in his Sunday sermons, matters have been carried too far. (in Nash, 2005, p. 163)

Much was at stake in the struggle over what constituted genuine conservatism, including positions in Reagan's administration and grants from conservative foundations. In one contest over who would be appointed as chair of the National Endowment for the Humanities, traditionalists supported M. E. Bradford while neoconservatives wanted William Bennett. When Brooklyn-born Bennett was chosen over pro-Confederate Bradford, tensions only worsened (Dorrien, 1993; Nash, 2005). Neoconservatives of later generations—Kristol's son, William Kristol, Podhoretz's son-in-law, Elliot Abrams, Chester Finn, Diane Ravitch, and others—would indeed assume positions alongside traditionalists under Reagan and become key players in right-wing foundations and think tanks (Friedman, 2005b; Kovacs & Boyles, 2005; Selden, 2004).

Despite existing tensions, paleoconservatives and neoconservatives mutually influenced one another throughout the 1980s. More traditional conservatives reconciled themselves to the fact that particular civil rights and welfare state provisions had gained wider legitimacy, while neoconservatives became more critical of the welfare state and began to incorporate moral and religious concerns into their cultural agenda (Judis, 1988; Nash, 2005). In the end, however, neoconservatives exercised greater influence on conservatism—that is, they "wrought a profound change in the scope and the character and the ethos of American conservatism" (Podhoretz in Shapiro, 1999, p. 213). The ability to appeal to a wide array of groups has probably been their most noteworthy contribution, something that we will see undeniably accounts for the growth of the Core Knowledge movement. Starting out on the left and migrating to the right (at least the first generation) meant that neoconservatives could often connect with groups beyond the reach of traditionalists, even if these relations were strained and contradictory. This "double set of relationships" was evident at a dinner in the mid-1970s for Senator Henry Jackson, whose campaign for the Democratic presidential nomination was supported by many neoconservatives before their move to the Republican Party. Among those present were Moynihan, civil rights and labor activist A. Philip Randolph, teachers' union leader Albert Shanker, and Podhoretz (Steinfels, 1979).

The work of the New York Jewish intellectuals and their Gentile associates has been carried forward by subsequent generations—"*Commentary's* children," as Ehrman (1999) has referred to the lineal heirs of neoconservatism. Despite the central role of the New York intellectuals in forging neoconservatism, neoconservatism has not won over the broader American Jewish community, which remains liberal in its politics, particularly at the national level (Friedman, 1999; Heilman, 1995). Kristol (2005) has himself acknowledged his "renegade" status in the Jewish community, stating that his embrace of the Republican Party was:

> ...the equivalent of a Jew ostentatiously eating pork on Yom Kippur. It was an act of self-excommunication. In fact, some of my critics regarded it as especially heinous for a Jew to abandon the creed of liberalism. For them, neoconservatism was seen as a religious as well as a political heresy. (p. 3)

However, the discourses and political vision of this bloc of former leftists and their descendents have resonated with a spectrum of other groups. As such, a far more extensive neoconservative network—one consisting of segments characterized by backgrounds and historical trajectories quite different from the New York intellectuals—has developed. Roman Catholics such as Michael Novak, conservatives of color such as Thomas Sowell, Linda Chavez, Dinesh D'Souza, and Francis Fukuyama, and middle-class constituencies of various ethnic and regional affiliations have joined the neoconservative effort (Dorrien, 1993; Friedman, 2005b; Haggard-Gilson, 1998; Podair, 2002).

As an example, consider the progression of neoconservatism in parts of the African American community. Drawing selectively upon preexisting traditions of black thought, including the philosophy of Booker T. Washington and more elitist understandings of racial uplift, "Negro-cons" (Kelley, 1998) have more recently called for greater personal responsibility, an enhanced work ethic, and improved character to remediate the "pathologies" they perceive in poor communities of color (Dillard, 2001; Dyson, 2005). According to a number of African American neoconservatives, the "heroic" phase of the Civil Rights movement from *Brown* to the legislative victories of the mid-1960s was eventually deformed by radical identity politics aimed at securing group preferences. It would be wiser, some contend, to deemphasize racial identity in the broader public sphere and to instead define oneself as "American," thereby opening the way to assimilation and even the integration experienced by other ethnic groups. Part and parcel of the unfortunate and damaging shift toward group politics was the expansion of the welfare state, or "Little White Father," which paternalistically looked after the black poor, established a cycle of dependency, and facilitated a culture of poverty. Building on Cold War sentiments, moreover, such neoconservatives have articulated an anti-welfare state, pro-market ideology that centers black economic independence and rejects government intervention as a means to upward mobility (see Dillard, 2001).

Clearly, a number of intersections exist between the neoconservative vision articulated by the New York intellectuals and the ideological underpinnings of African American neoconservatism. Indeed, some African American neoconservatives followed a comparable political trajectory, with George Schuyler, for instance, moving:

> from the socialist-oriented and anticolonial Left in the 1930s to the anticommunist Right in the 1960s.... Schuyler worked with many of these intellectuals in the American Committee for Cultural Freedom.... [And he] was highly critical of the "civil rights industry" of his day. For Schuyler, the category "civil rights activist" became, in the 1950s and 1960s, nearly synonymous with a dangerous and subversive collectivism. (Dillard, 2001, pp. 46–47)

Although frequently allied with the New York intellectuals and their descendants, black neoconservatives have built not only complementary but distinct, relatively autonomous, politically conservative traditions rooted in historic debates in the African American community. Much as the New York intellectuals established journals such as *Commentary* and *The Public Interest* to disseminate their views, print venues such as the *Lincoln Review* make public the perspectives of Negrocons with the intent of influencing social and educational policymaking. It would be wrong to conclude that Kristol and Moynihan, for example, are the lone figureheads of neoconservatism. Black neoconservatives such as Stanley Crouch, Glenn Loury, Thomas Sowell, Shelby Steele, Clarence Thomas, Elizabeth Wright, and others have taken center stage as an embattled minority delivering an unpopular but, as they see it, necessary message about the redemption of dysfunctional urban blacks and their middle-class counterparts in the civil rights establishment (Dillard, 2001; see also Haggard-Gilson, 1998; Kelley, 1998; Sowell, 1984; Steele, 1998).

Aside from coalitions built between various camps *within* neoconservatism, neoconservatives have affiliated with other major groups of the new right, including economic and religious conservatives. While neo-liberals valorize the free market based on economic arguments related to efficiency and competition, neoconservatives have contributed to its defense on *cultural* grounds by emphasizing the creative and communal aspects of capitalism (e.g., "innovatively" responding to "community needs")—grounds that they believe resonate more strongly with the American people and therefore function as the most reliable safeguard against communist appeals. Shared concerns over social decay and moral decadence and a common commitment to protecting the Judeo-Christian tradition from feminist, gay, and lesbian assaults have also led neoconservatives to establish ties with religious conservatives (Dorrien, 1993; Gerson, 1997). Understanding the commonalities and differences within the neoconservative bloc and its complex relationship both to the new right as a whole and to traditionally marginalized groups is work that is still underway (Apple, 2006a; Apple & Buras, 2006; Apple & Pedroni, 2005; Buras & Apple, 2005; Dillard, 2001; Pedroni, 2007b). Such work is crucial if the left is to adequately assess the spaces for interrupting rightist efforts, which are characterized, in actuality, by an often fragile balance of interests.

1990s—FROM THE COLD WAR TO THE CULTURE WAR?

With the so-called collapse of communism in 1989, what would hold together neoconservatism, heavily defined by its activism against the "Soviet threat?" "Like their conservative allies," writes Dorrien (1993), "the neoconservatives were united mostly by their anticommunism" (p. 323). Under Podhoretz, *Commentary* had reinvigorated the fight against communism in the 1970s and a number of neoconservative figures even formed the Committee on the Present Danger—an effort that aimed to educate an unduly lax public and government about the (allegedly) escalating threat of Soviet domination (Friedman, 2005b; Powers, 2005). To a notable degree, then, neoconservatism had wedded itself to the anticommunist struggle.

That said, accounts of neoconservatism have too frequently emphasized foreign policy and defense issues, thereby framing the "culture war" as a post-Cold War development in the chronology of neoconservatism. Not long after the collapse, for example, Christopher Hitchens "argued that neoconservatism had lost the enemy on which it was dependent and therefore had outlived its usefulness to the conservative movement" (Dorrien, 1993, p. 350). In short, the struggle for cultural order was perceived as relatively new or at least as too peripheral to be a driving concern. It may be that neoconservatives *escalated* their battle on the cultural front in the 1990s, but such analyses overlook the significant cultural dimension of neoconservative work all along. My intent is to render visible the long-standing cultural agenda of neoconservatives and to demonstrate that these cold warriors were Western cultural warriors early on. Core Knowledge, as such, must be understood as an educational reform that reinterprets and further advances an already established cultural initiative.

Writing an entire decade before the collapse of communism, Steinfels (1979) questions:

> To what extent do neoconservative concerns for national order and stability spring from a perception of international threat? To what extent does the insistence on international threat spring from a desire to shock society into national order and stability? ... Neoconservatives are undoubtedly sincere in their anxiety over international affairs, at the same time as the essential source of that anxiety is not military or geopolitical or to be found overseas at all; it is domestic and cultural and ideological. ... The existence of an ideologically armed and intact elite is the crucial ingredient, and its role in resisting external pressure is only the reverse side of its role in resisting internal disintegration. (pp. 68–69)

This is a crucial insight: The Cold War was as much about "enemies" within as without. We need only to consider Kristol's attack on multiculturalism in the early 1990s in which he declared, "What these radicals blandly call multiculturalism is as much a 'war against the West' as Nazism and Stalinism ever were" (1995, p. 52). In this way, the "present danger" was never an external one only. Let us recall that the American

Committee for Cultural Freedom operated on the home front. So did *The Public Interest*, which Moynihan wanted to name *Consensus* to signify that the making of public policy required technical knowledge rather than divisive, ideological debate (Steinfels, 1979, pp. 43–44). Indisputably, the Cold War against the diversification of knowledge began long before 1989, and long before a "backlash" emerged against the radicalism of the 1960s. Acknowledging this enables us to consider contemporary neoconservative school reform as the product of a more extensive and complex history and to better discern the spaces for dissent and for more democratic educational mobilizations.

NEOCONSERVATISM PAST AND PRESENT: CORE KNOWLEDGE AND THE CIVIL RIGHTS FRONTIER

The marks of this history are apparent in Core Knowledge, the curriculum reform effort under the guidance of neoconservative visionary E. D. Hirsch and his Core Knowledge Foundation (2006c). It is important to think in lineal terms. Whereas the New York intellectuals represent an earlier neoconservative generation, Hirsch is part of a later one. He maintains close ties with various intersecting neoconservative circles, but especially associates with those who followed in the footsteps of predecessors. Through various think tanks and foundations, Hirsch joins neoconservatives who publish in common venues, grant awards and offer recognition to one another, extend speaking invitations to each other, and collectively engage in policy work and educational reform efforts. Allow me to provide just a few illustrations.

At the Hoover Institution, Hirsch stands with fellows such as Seymour Martin Lipset (another New York intellectual), Chester Finn, and Diane Ravitch (who held posts in one or another administration under Nixon, Reagan, and Bush, and alongside neoconservatives such as Daniel Patrick Moynihan, William Bennett, and Irving Kristol's son, William), and Thomas Sowell and Shelby Steele (well-known African American neoconservatives). Hirsch also sits on Hoover's Koret Task Force on K-12 Education and on the editorial board of *Education Next*, a journal produced by the foundation, with a few of the figures above as well as other established cultural and economic conservatives, such as John Chubb and Terry Moe. He has likewise authored a number of weekly essays for Hoover, with such pieces simultaneously appearing in *National Review*, *Commentary*, and *The Weekly Standard* (Hoover Institution, 2006; see also *Education Next*, 2006; Hirsch, 1999a, 2001b; Koret Task Force, 2006). Aside from his contributions to Hoover, Hirsch has on select occasions written for the American Enterprise Institute, where Kristol, Michael Novak, Lynne Cheney, and others are fellows, and for the Thomas B. Fordham Foundation headed by Finn (e.g., Hirsch, 1997a, 2003). The Fordham Foundation, in fact, gave Hirsch an award for "Excellence in Education" in 2003 along with $25,000 dollars (Thomas B. Fordham Foundation, 2003b). Meanwhile, the National Association of Scholars (2006), which includes among its members Finn, Kristol, Steele, James Q. Wilson, and others, and concerns itself with the "absence of core curricula," "dogmatic hostility to Western civilization," and "politicization of scholarship and teaching," highlights the Core Knowledge Foundation as a kindred initiative; perhaps not surprisingly, Hirsch participated in 2004 on an education panel at the association's annual conference (National Association of Scholars, 2004). Financial links also exist between the Core Knowledge Foundation and other conservative funding sources, including the John M. Olin Foundation and the Walton Family Foundation, which have contributed over $6,000,000 dollars in grants to Core (Media Transparency, 2006). Expertise is similarly exchanged, such as when Ravitch invited Hirsch to speak at Brookings's annual policy forum (Hirsch, 2005), while Hirsch invited Ravitch to speak at the Core Knowledge national conference and to sit on the Core Knowledge Foundation's board of trustees (Core Knowledge Foundation, 2006b; Ravitch, 1996). Such examples reveal an intricate network of relationships and underscore the company that Hirsch chooses to keep with neoconservatives, although associations like these do not preclude other strategic affiliations (see also deMarrais, 2006; Kovacs & Boyles, 2005).

The traces of this history will indeed be more evident, but I would like here to point out just a few more specific connections to be kept in mind. This will provide a foundation for thinking more critically about the dynamics underlying Core as an educational initiative—one that can be understood as a descendent of some of the history charted in this chapter.

Of utmost significance are the ideological resonances between early neoconservative intellectuals, Hirsch, and Core. Indeed, a distinct combination of elements left and right, concerns over the appropriate balance between diversity and unity, the perception that the left now exercises inordinate power over policy, an aversion to radical forms of identity politics and a desire to bolster national stability, faith in the merits of accommodation, the call to remedy cultural deficiencies and pathologies that presumably plague poor communities and communities of color, and even a tempered commitment to civil rights—all of this is reflected and perhaps most importantly *reinvented* within Core Knowledge.

Remember, for instance, how Hirsch's *Cultural Literacy* (1987) underscored the necessity of a common culture for national cohesion and warned of the dangers of multiculturalism, particularly those strains that emphasize a "narrow tribal culture." "The acculturative responsibility of the schools is primary and fundamental," he emphasized (p. 18). It might, then, seem curious that Core Knowledge—an educational initiative partly developed to mediate against the balkanizing effects of identity politics—ultimately gained support from a wide range of communities, including those groups one might presume would be alienated by the assimilative dimensions of Hirsch's agenda. Let us recall, however, the history just traced: Neoconservatism is an "in-between" politics, a politics of strategic compromise, a politics suffused with the residue of the left but also permeated by the compositions of the right. This gives it a certain power to respond to disparate interests, though not without tension.

Consider Hirsch's educational vision, which I detail in the next chapter. It has all the imprints of neoconservative thought. According to him, progressivism has overtaken schools and rendered the curriculum incoherent. This incoherence not only threatens the common culture of the nation—something Hirsch assumes should be shared by all groups to maintain political stability—but likewise puts "culturally deficient" groups at risk since a fragmented curriculum cannot remedy impoverished dispositions and knowledge. He emphasizes that "bad schools hold back disadvantaged children disproportionately because disadvantaged homes are typically less able than advantaged ones to compensate for the knowledge gaps left by the schools.... This new struggle is more subtle and complex than the earlier one of sit-ins and freedom rides" (1996, p. 43). In a spirit both optimistic and foreboding, he warns: "Young children who arrive at school with a...limited knowledge base can fortunately be [helped]...[but] when this language and knowledge deficit is not compensated for early, it is nearly impossible...in later grades" (p. 146). Hirsch thus skillfully and, as I will show, problematically blends criticisms of cultural illiteracy with concerns for equality, social mobility, and civil rights. Indeed, he contends that Core Knowledge is part of the "new civil rights frontier" (see also Buras, 1999b). In this way, Hirsch manages to transport us from more abrasive discourses focused on deficiency and social pathology to the more liberatory terrain of civil rights and racial justice, even if framed in ways that are questionable in their definition of that terrain.

According to Hirsch, multiculturalism is partly responsible for the cultural crisis that he perceives. Interestingly, we will see that this leads him not to reject multiculturalism, but to redefine it along more conservative lines. "Multiculturalism comes in different guises," Hirsch asserts. "There's a progressive form that will be helpful to all students, and a retrogressive kind that...tends to set group against group" (p. 1). Rather than the retrogressive and "particularistic" tradition of "ethnic loyalty" which he says promotes social divisions, he advocates a "universalistic" tradition of "cosmopolitanism" which stresses being "a member of humanity as a whole" (1992b, p. 3). Unlike some neoconservatives who have urged a less hospitable response to issues of diversity, Hirsch clearly agrees with Glazer's (1997) declaration that "simple denunciation... [will] no longer do" (p. 33).

This vision and the strategic compromises that accompany it have enabled Hirsch to bring multiple groups into an alliance around Core Knowledge—much like the aforementioned dinner in the 1970s honoring Senator Jackson. As forthcoming chapters will reveal, many suburban schools have adopted Core in an effort to "reclaim" the classics and "restore" traditional knowledge. At the same time, there are urban schools in communities of color that embrace Core as a way of advancing the interests of marginalized children—all the while renovating the curriculum to "include the traditions" of African American, Latino/a, and Native American children (see also Buras, 2006b). The composite nature of the Core alliance does not escape Hirsch, who notes: "To be liked by the Bushies and the American Federation of Teachers [AFT]— there's something peculiar going on" (in Lindsay, 2001, p. W24). Indeed, the AFT gave Hirsch an award in 1997 and its former president, Sandra Feldman, sat on the board of the Core Knowledge Foundation. But Hirsch also associates with neoconservatives through numerous right-wing foundations, as previously noted.

As I will discuss later, the curriculum also negotiates the tensions between old and new histories by adopting in Core textbooks (Hirsch, 2002) what I have called "*new* old history." Whereas old histories centered on dominant groups through a narrative of consensus and new histories on subaltern groups through a narrative of conflict, Core's *new* old history recognizes both elite and subaltern groups. This occurs, however, through a major storyline that largely ignores unequal power and conflict. When oppressive experiences are detailed, this occurs through a minor storyline in which *relations* with dominant groups are discursively masked. Such narratives, moreover, are strategically packaged. Despite Hirsch's fear of identity politics, upper-grade textbook

covers feature a president, a Native American, and other group representatives, rather than a "unifying" image such as the American flag
(see also Buras, 2006b).

Not surprisingly, Hirsch evidences the political identity crisis of so
many neoconservatives who denied their shift rightward and claimed
that they were the defenders of true liberal ideals. He deems himself
"a political liberal and an educational conservative" and insists that
"political liberals really ought to oppose progressive educational ideas
because they have led to...greater social inequality. The only practical way to achieve liberalism's aim of greater social justice is to pursue
conservative educational policies" (1996, p. 6). This formulation leads
Hirsch (1996) to dedicate one of his books—*The Schools We Need and
Why We Don't Have Them*—not to some Western cultural restoration-
ist, but to Antonio Gramsci, the late Italian leftist revolutionary whom
Hirsch and his associates at the Core Knowledge Foundation (Spencer, 1999) argue was actually an educational conservative. Although I
have shown that this is clearly not the case (Buras, 1999a), such a move
still sutures together a left-wing agenda with right-wing activism (see
appendix B, this volume, for correspondence on the politics of Antonio
Gramsci).

Taken together, Hirsch's elitist educational vision expressed through
concerns for democracy, his alarm over cultural deficiency combined
with his reformulation of the civil rights agenda, the alliance of differently situated groups around Core Knowledge, and the *new* old history contained in Core textbooks constitute a neoconservative strategy
that I am calling *rightist multiculturalism*. It may seem as contradictory
as Kristol's advocacy of a "conservative welfare state," but it has given
Hirsch and the Core Knowledge Foundation wider legitimacy and the
power to advance the neoconservative agenda in schools. Importantly,
this has required efforts to discipline curricular deviation and diversity
within the Core Knowledge movement, reminding us that subaltern
groups may appropriate dominant forms in unanticipated ways (Buras,
2006b).

In the sixth grade, Core Knowledge students read about turn of the
twentieth century immigrants. The last of several chapters is entitled
"Becoming American" and it opens with an excerpt from Israel Zang-
will's 1908 play, *Melting Pot*:

> America is...the great Melting Pot where all the races of Europe
> are melting....Here you stand...when I see you at Ellis Island...in
> your fifty groups, with your fifty languages and histories....But
> you won't be long like that....Into the Crucible with you all! God
> is making the American. (Hirsch, 2002, p. 260)

The chapter concludes in a celebratory tone, indicating that the ways of the old country had disappeared by the third generation. In seeking to reconcile diversity and unity, Core participates in the arguments that divided the New York intellectuals. During a *New York Times* interview in 1990, Hirsch mused: "Do you know the mural at City College in New York, which shows the immigrants being blessed by the Goddess of Education? Well, that's my ideal. Assimilation. That's how everyone else did it, and we know it works" (in Hitchens, A32). This uncomplicated rendering of the workings of assimilation clearly requires more substantial examination.

In *World of Our Fathers*, Irving Howe (1976) affirmed the culture of Eastern European Jewish immigrants in New York and mourned its disappearance, thereby revealing the costs of accommodation to Jews (Michels, 2000), and by extension, to other groups struggling against cultural domination. Perhaps the "great Jewish-American synthesis" is not all that Jewish neoconservatives thought it to be (Goldstein, 2006; Wolfe, 2005).[1] This issue—the merits, possibilities, and costs of cultural accommodation and its relationship to equality and democracy—is one that will be critically considered throughout this book and revisited in the concluding chapter through an historic episode: the Ocean Hill-Brownsville struggle over racial identity, cultural recognition, school curriculum and educational governance in the late 1960s. By moving from past to present and back again, we stand to learn a number of Core lessons about neoconservative school reform.

2

QUESTIONING CORE ASSUMPTIONS
A Critical Reading of E. D. Hirsch's Educational Vision

It is naive to think of the school curriculum as neutral knowledge. Rather, what counts as legitimate knowledge is the result of complex power relations and struggles among identifiable class, race, gender, and religious groups.

Michael Apple in *Official Knowledge* (2000, p. 44)

Even those experts who hold strongly to the principle of local control of curriculum might well concede the need for a voluntary agreement about a common sequence in the curriculum—at least in those areas like math and science and the basic facts of history and geography, which, unlike sex education, are not and should not be subjects of controversy.

E. D. Hirsch in *The Schools We Need and Why We Don't Have Them* (1996, p. 37)

WHAT NEOCONSERVATIVES BELIEVE

LONG BEFORE E. D. HIRSCH presented his views on culture and curriculum, the foundations of a neoconservative vision were being laid. Writing in 1979, Peter Steinfels examined the major tenets of neoconservative thought in *The Neoconservatives: The Men Who Are Changing America's Politics*. These included the presumption that "a crisis of

37

authority" had "overtaken America and the West generally," that the crisis was "primarily a cultural crisis, a matter of values, morals, and manners," that government was the "victim of overload," and that such dissolution could be confronted through an insistence that "authority be reasserted" and "government protected" (pp. 53–69).

Indeed, the assumed hegemony of the left in major social institutions, the threat posed by countercultures to American and Western civilization, and the fragility of national unity in light of identity politics were frames that had given shape to neoconservative work in an array of areas—domestic policy, foreign affairs, the arts, and ultimately education. The traces of this history are quite apparent in the educational vision laid out by Hirsch. There is tremendous resonance, in fact, between my own critique of Hirsch's educational vision and its underlying assumptions (see also Buras, 1999b) and Steinfels' (1979) discussion of what neoconservatives believe. The degree of continuity between these analyses is important, particularly at a time when neoconservatism is undoubtedly influential and its effects widely debated, while its character too often remains unclear and much of our understanding dehistoricized. I therefore want to be very specific in my examination of the Core assumptions underlying Hirsch's views on schooling.

Hirsch has presented his analysis of education in the United States and his vision of how schools need to change in a variety of published works and speeches. *The Schools We Need and Why We Don't Have Them* (Hirsch, 1996) is his most comprehensive treatment of schooling and may actually be read as a manifesto for the Core Knowledge movement. In this chapter, I focus most heavily (though not solely) on that text, offer a critical reading of its guiding assumptions, and suggest how those assumptions resonate with groups above and below. After all, it is imperative to understand the role these assumptions play in building political alliances between a diverse array of groups, particularly within the Core Knowledge movement. *The Schools We Need* is not a solitary work produced in a vacuum; it represents a set of discourses that undoubtedly contribute to Core as a growing school reform effort and that characterize an increasingly conservative political landscape.

THE SCHOOLS WE NEED

Opening with the foreboding words, "Failed Theories, Famished Minds," Hirsch explains, "What chiefly prompts the writing of this book is our national slowness...to cast aside [the] faulty theories that have led to the total absence of a coherent, knowledge-based curriculum, but are nonetheless presented...as remedies for the diseases they themselves have caused" (1996, p. 2). According to Hirsch, the progressive educational theories that took shape at Teachers College during the first quarter of this century have held an intellectual and institutional monopoly on schools, especially since the 1950s. They are, he claims, responsible for the deteriorated condition of education. Hirsch aligns American progressive education with European Romanticism's view of the child as a being whose development "should be encouraged to take its natural course." Referring to this body of theory and practice as "Thoughtworld," he contrasts this perspective with Enlightenment thinking that viewed a child as "a still-to-be-formed creature whose instinctual impulses need less to be encouraged than to be molded to the ways of the society" (pp. 72–74).

Tracing the writings of canonized literary icons such as Friedrich Schelling and William Blake, as well as historic education scholars such as John Dewey, Hirsch outlines what he perceives as Romantic fallacies. These include, among others, naturalism, formalism, localism, professional separatism, and the repudiation of standardized tests. According to Hirsch, these have contributed to the emergence of a curriculum that lacks well-defined content and focuses instead upon the abstract tools and metacognitive strategies needed for future learning. As a result, he argues, social inequities have deepened as children who come to school lacking intellectual capital find an incoherent curriculum and process-oriented teaching unable to remedy their "deficits." The new civil rights frontier, Hirsch proclaims, consists of assuring that the knowledge gaps of disadvantaged children are filled.

To guarantee what he perceives as educational justice, Hirsch makes a case for a core curriculum. Based on international comparisons of student test scores, Hirsch contends that systems with a national curriculum contribute to greater fairness, as evidenced by a normal distribution of test scores within such nations, and excellence, as demonstrated by their scores in comparison to other nations. To further support his position that a core curriculum is essential to fairness and excellence, Hirsch turns to "mainstream consensus research" in cognitive psychology and neurophysiology. Discussing the role of short- and long-term memory in learning, the function of schemas in prohibiting mental overload, and the importance of automation in facilitating effective thinking, Hirsch calls for a system to deliver predetermined, concrete, sequential, and relevant background knowledge to students and thereby infuse a form of capital that will have later trade value in the common culture and national marketplace. The ultimate promise of such an education, Hirsch claims, is not only the realization of an upwardly mobile underclass and greater social equality, but also the promotion of a shared public culture essential to stable and genuine democracy.

Hirsch bases his analysis on a series of assumptions that warrant close scrutiny. Having sketched his vision broadly, I will now turn to a more thorough examination of the premises underlying it.

ASSUMPTION I: PROGRESSIVISM HAS A MONOPOLY ON SCHOOLS

"Critics have long complained that public education in the United States is an institutional and intellectual monopoly," writes Hirsch (1996, p. 63). He describes this monopoly as a romantic-progressivist body of guiding educational beliefs and practices that value student-centered, naturalistic, hands-on, process-driven, and thinking-skills-oriented schooling. The sovereignty of progressivism, says Hirsch, has supplanted verbal instruction (lecture) focused upon transmission of a body of coherent, discipline-based, and factual content (dominant knowledge) reinforced by distributed practice (drill, repetition, and memorization). If progressive thought enjoys the transcendence that Hirsch claims, and if it has shaped the educational practices responsible for the decline of American schools, one would expect a wealth of evidence to support this contention. Instead, Hirsch provides no support for his claim—at least none that withstands critical analysis.

To document the emergence and subsequent ascendancy of the progressive monopoly, Hirsch traces its history through the writings of various literary figures and educational scholars. After quoting Romantic poets about the divine nature and inherent goodness of the child and citing academic passages on child-centered schooling authored by early progressive curriculum scholars, Hirsch infers:

> Education schools...converted to progressivism in the 1920s and '30s. From these cells, the doctrine emerged victorious in the public schools in the 1950s.... Thereafter, it took a full generation of progressive students, extending from preschool to high school, before the full effects of Romantic progressivism manifested themselves in the graduating seniors of the 1960s. (1996, pp. 78–79)

Seeking to demonstrate the continuing dominance of progressivism, Hirsch writes, "There is, in short, little in the current literature of school reform that does not yield a powerful sense of déjà vu to anyone who has read the Romantic, progressive literature of the teens, twenties, and thirties of this century" (p. 53).

In his attempt to provide evidence of the favored status of progressivism, Hirsch oversimplifies educational history by denying the existence of competing educational discourses. Referring to the field of education as a fortress, Hirsch contends that progressive dominance was an inevitable result of an educational thoughtworld that promoted only progressive ideas. Bemoaning this alleged conformity, Hirsch quotes Arthur Bestor's observation that "one of the most shocking facts about the field of education is the almost complete absence of rigorous criticism from within" (Hirsch, 1996, p. 65). Citing the preeminence of Teachers College in the field of education, Hirsch points out that William Heard Kilpatrick, a well-known progressive educator who taught there in the first half of this century, "trained some thirty-five thousand students during his career," a statistic Hirsch believes "helps explain the relative uniformity of current American educational doctrine" (p. 118).

While it is naive to deny that particular discourses maintain hegemony within disciplines, it is also erroneous to view any field as completely devoid of ideological conflict. Herbert Kliebard (1995), for example, traces four varied ideologies active in the struggle to define the American curriculum from 1893 to 1958. In that period, humanists advocated the development of student intellect through the study of subjects pertinent to Western civilization. In contrast, developmentalists emphasized the need for a curriculum geared toward the nature of the child. Articulating another perspective, social meliorists stressed that schools should be organized around issues of social justice and transformation. Social efficiency educators, posing a different viewpoint, called for a curriculum tied to the functional needs of society. Over the course of more than half a century, representatives of each group advanced competing and sometimes intersecting arguments over what should be taught in schools. Significantly, this history reveals the varying impacts these different educational discourses had on actual school practice. Contrary to Hirsch's descriptions of an ideological monopoly, great disparities existed between the theories espoused and the curriculum studied in the majority of schools. Instead of grappling with these ideological struggles and discussing the way in which social context shaped the relative impact of these ideologies on curriculum, Hirsch characterizes the field of education as one mired in progressive doctrine only and ignores the schism between theory and practice.

In a sense, Hirsch confuses intellectual history with material historical conditions. In their review of *Cultural Literacy*, Stanley Aronowitz and Henry Giroux (1991) critique Hirsch's reductionist approach:

It assumes that ideas are the determining factor in shaping history.... Hirsch's history lacks any concrete political and social referents, its causal relations are construed through a string of ideas, and it is presented without the benefit of substantive argument of historical context. While ideas are important in shaping history, they cannot be considered to be so powerful as to alter history beyond the density of its material and social contexts. (p. 232)

Hirsch repeats this error in *The Schools We Need*, this time mistaking the expression of progressive ideas with their material existence. Yet as James Shaver, O. L. Davis, and Suzanne Helburn (1978), John Goodlad (1984), and Larry Cuban (1993) have documented, schools overall remain traditional institutions that offer teacher-centered, whole-class, textbook-focused instruction. These findings suggest that Hirsch's claims are not merely historically inaccurate, but empirically false.

Hirsch goes on to explain the mechanism through which he believes schools of education currently ensure the continued proliferation of progressivism in public schools nationwide:

This monopoly is sustained by its power to certify teachers. Education schools and their allies in state departments of education perpetuate themselves by requiring prospective teachers to take a specified number of courses...in order to be credentialed.... When ... intellectual conformity is combined with administrative control over employment...it is not surprising that the citadel should become an institutional monopoly. (1996, pp. 63–65)

Had Hirsch apprised himself of certification requirements in even a few states or investigated any number of teacher education programs, he would quickly have realized the errors in his position. The courses required for professional teacher certification are not predominantly grounded in progressive philosophy (e.g., see Irvine, 2003). Rather, the work required is largely focused upon the psychology of learning, classroom management, educational standards, assessment, and subject matter (Andrews, 1996; Goodman, 1986; Tryneski, 1997)—the domains of educational thought Hirsch claims have all but disappeared due to this progressive monopoly.

In deconstructing Hirsch's assumption that progressivism monopolizes schools, it is important to avoid making the opposite claim that traditional philosophies and practices have absolute control over schools. Progressive struggles have had an impact on schools. Such gains, however, have not significantly transformed curricular content and pedagogical practice overall. For example, many multicultural reform efforts have concentrated on changing individual attitudes or the superficial insertion of cultural and historical information about oppressed groups into the already dominant organization of school knowledge. At the same time, critical forms of multiculturalism that critique the privileging of particular perspectives, engage in a more nuanced discussion of cultural relations and identities, and question the nature of power have yet to enter many schools (McCarthy, 1993; Dixson & Rousseau, 2006). These partial efforts to accommodate progressive demands may be explained by what Apple (2000) has called "the politics of cultural incorporation"—a politics in which the curriculum is "the product of often intense conflict, negotiations, and attempts at rebuilding hegemonic control by actually incorporating the knowledge and perspectives of the less powerful under the umbrella of the discourse of dominant groups" (p. 53). While schools have been responsive in particular ways to appeals for greater representation of marginalized knowledge, such inclusion has not significantly altered the status of canonized school knowledge. On the whole, traditional curricular and pedagogical forms remain intact, and progressive practices are more often the exception rather than the rule. This is increasingly becoming the case under the No Child Left Behind Act of 2001 (Meier & Wood, 2004).

In the end, Hirsch provides no concrete evidence to support the claim that a progressive monopoly exists. Perhaps what is most important, though, is not the presence or absence of evidence, but why Hirsch and others on the right perceive a progressive monopoly and how this shapes their agenda. Why has the impact of demands for representation tended to be exaggerated in the minds of neoconservatives? One possibility is that fear of subverted power and undermined cultural authority distorts neoconservative interpretations of schooling.

ASSUMPTION II: THE EXISTING CURRICULUM IS INCOHERENT

"The idea that there exists a coherent plan for teaching content," writes Hirsch, "is a gravely misleading myth" (1996, p. 26). According to him, the progressive monopoly has rendered the existing curriculum incoherent—that is, schools lack an agreed upon scheme for the transmission of specific content to students. Hirsch maintains that various aspects of progressive education, including formalism, naturalism, and localism, have contributed to this incoherence.

Hirsch claims that the curriculum is incoherent as a result of the formalism, or anti-intellectualism, of the progressive monopoly. Formalism, or "the belief that the particular content which is learned in school...is far less important than acquiring the formal [intellectual] tools which will enable [the learning of] future content" (1996, p. 218), has left the curriculum in shambles. In Hirsch's view, the curriculum, over the past seventy years or so, has become an exercise in metacognition at the expense of solid, specifically defined content. He writes that "American educational theory has held that the child needs to be given the all-purpose tools that are needed for him or her to continue learning and adapting. The particular content used to develop those tools need not be specified" (p. 21).

Hirsch contends that naturalism, or "the belief that education is a natural process" that should be "connected with natural, real-life goals and settings" (1996, p. 218), has also contributed to the vagueness of the curriculum. In short, he argues that naturalism has resulted in the proliferation of process-oriented, child-centered pedagogies throughout the school system. Hirsch writes that although the doctrine of natural pedagogy "assumes that the proper way of learning involves lifelike, holistic projects which...teach [children] how to work together and use knowledge," it nonetheless "turns out to be a very insecure way of learning" (p. 86). Such teaching methodologies, broadly applied and prescriptively weak, are thus responsible for the curriculum's indistinct state.

Hirsch asserts that another cause of curriculum incoherence is localism, or the tradition of determining locally what children should learn. He maintains that other nations have recognized the need for "translocal commonality in the content of early schooling." "Nonetheless," he continues, "it is quixotic to resist educational localism in the United States, where there is no plausible mechanism for replacing this sanctified arrangement.... Granting the inevitability of localism,...a chief aim of educational policy ought to be to compensate for its most egregious shortcomings" (1996, p. 97). In Hirsch's opinion, the curriculum is decentralized, highly unregulated, and vulnerable to the whims of localism.

Yet Hirsch underestimates the centralizing and regulatory role of textbook adoptions, patterns of textual representation, function of standardized testing, and use of predetermined curricular packages in the coherence of curriculum—all of which held sway even before the era of No Child Left Behind. While none of these guarantees the unmediated transmission of dominant culture, each shapes a cohesive and patterned body of knowledge accorded status through institutionalized channels.

In the case of textbooks, it is essential to recognize that "while there is no official federal government sponsorship of specific curriculum content in the United States...the structures of a national curriculum are produced by the marketplace and by state intervention in other ways" (Apple & Christian-Smith, 1991, p. 32). State textbook adoption processes, for example, have a tremendous influence on the regulation of school knowledge. Although not all states have statewide adoption policies, almost half do, and the portion of the market controlled by this sector largely determines which texts are available for sale across the entire nation. Therefore, the composition of state textbook committees, access to resources for mobilizing around content issues, and even the way that labor is structured within the publishing industry have an impact on the official knowledge embodied in the text (Apple, 2000; Apple & Christian-Smith, 1991).

Since the late 1970s, rightist groups have organized campaigns to influence textbook content. These battles over textbook knowledge continue and their outcomes suggest that conservative interests have been well served (Cornbleth & Waugh, 1999; Delfattore, 1992; Gabler & Gabler, 1985). In light of such struggles, it is important to recall Hirsch's claim that localism renders the curriculum fragmented and that formalism and naturalism make content a peripheral concern. Instead, it appears that textbooks form a national network regulating the distribution of knowledge and that content is a central preoccupation on the minds of publishers, members of the state educational apparatus, professional associations, and community groups, with each attempting to make certain the curriculum coheres in a way that serves particular interests (Deckman, 2004; Ravitch, 2004; Symcox, 2002).

Also relevant in deconstructing the assumption of curricular incoherence are studies that address the issue of symbolic representation in school textbooks. For example, in examining texts utilized across a number of grade levels and subject areas, many have discovered relatively coherent patterns of representation of race, class, gender, and disability (chapter 4, this volume; see also Anyon, 1983; Banks, 1969; Cobble & Kessler-Harris, 1993; Commeyras & Alvermann, 1996; Cruz, 1994; Hahn & Blankenship, 1983; Potter & Rosser, 1992; Sleeter & Grant, 1991). Findings clearly show the extent to which content focuses on dominant groups while according the experiences of women, labor, and other such groups marginal status. Despite Hirsch's claim, patterns of textual representation reveal that the curriculum does have coherence and is far from neutral regarding content. Discussing the implications of historical texts, Howard Zinn (1995) stresses that while "selection, simplification, [and] emphasis...are inevitable," textual representations are "released into a world of contending interests, where any chosen emphasis supports...some kind of interest, whether economic or political or racial or national or sexual" (p. 8). Undoubtedly, the impact that such representations (or lack of) have on student knowledge is of great consequence, and the terms under which particular groups are either included in or negated from texts render claims of content incoherence illegitimate.[1]

Standardized testing also challenges Hirsch's assessment of curriculum incoherence. Testing represents a multimillion-dollar national industry in this country (Educational Testing Service, 1998). The widespread uses of testing in American culture, the role of tests as gatekeepers to social resources, and the centrality of assessment as an accountability mechanism of state educational policy underscore the regulatory functions of tests. Significantly, Geoff Whitty (1985) researched the politics surrounding the transformation of Britain's public examination system where a number of interest groups sought to influence the process. Teacher control over examinations was opposed by rightist groups who believed it "permitted teachers to use their professional mandate in the interests of [leftist] political goals" (p. 123). Conservative humanists, concerned with preserving tradition and setting parameters on what was taught and measured in classrooms, advocated control of course syllabi and assessments by external boards. Although the United States does not have an official system of comprehensive national testing as does Britain, it is evident that tests nonetheless serve to ensure that specific content is given priority in American classrooms. Just think of the No Child Left Behind Act and the differential status and classroom attention given to "tested" versus "untested" subjects. Even Hirsch (1996) acknowledges that tests set boundaries on what constitutes relevant knowledge when he acknowledges the widespread practice "of teaching narrowly to high-stakes" tests and using them "as tool[s] of accountability" for teachers (pp. 192–193). In the end, then, systems of testing do lend coherence to the curriculum by way of their regulatory power. We need only to recall the findings of Linda McNeil (2000a) that the Texas Assessment of Academic Skills (now the Texas Assessment of Knowledge and Skills) means that:

> Substantial class time is spent practicing bubbling in answers and learning to recognize "distractor" (obviously wrong) answers. Students are drilled on such strategies as the pep rally cheer "Three in a row? No, No, No!" [This is because]...the maker of a test would not be likely to construct three questions in a row with the same answer indicator. (p. 730)

More often than not, such interventions are most aggressively pursued in those schools attended by poor students and students of color, who presumably need such discipline to raise faltering test scores (see also McNeil, 2000b; Valenzuela, 2004).

Finally, Hirsch fails to recognize the increasing regulation of content through prepackaged curricula. One trend has been for school systems to purchase "a total set of standardized material, one that includes statements of objectives, all of the curricular content and material needed, prespecified teacher actions and appropriate student responses, and diagnostic and achievement tests" (Apple, 1995, p. 131). Such developments seem to indicate that the inverse of Hirsch's position is true: the curriculum, rather than being incoherent and local, is tacitly micromanaged and centralized.

Though Hirsch is partially insightful in recognizing the absence of an explicit curricular logic, he fails to note those mechanisms that indirectly combine to lend coherence. As mentioned earlier, Hirsch's perception is likely associated with the threat posed by demands for the integration of diverse cultural and historical perspectives into the curriculum. For Hirsch, then, incoherence is not the absence of content; instead, it is the inclusion of content that has traditionally been excluded. Gerald Graff (1992) suggests that conservatives tend to confuse curricular coherence with consensus over what constitutes legitimate school knowledge. He argues that challenges to canonical knowledge need not lead to a curriculum consisting of disconnected components. Rather, the lack of consensus itself has the potential to constitute a common educational experience around which students and teachers discover "what is at stake in one way of knowing against another" (p. 186). From this perspective, coherence is not compromised by cultural struggle. It is cultural struggle that unites the educational experience.

ASSUMPTION III: EDUCATION IS A COGNITIVE-TECHNICAL PROCESS THROUGH WHICH FACTUAL CONTENT IS TRANSMITTED

Hirsch (1996) complains that a major barrier to improving education has been "the politicization of educational issues that are at bottom technical rather than political" (p. 66). He sees education as a cognitive-technical process through which factual content is transmitted to students for storage in memory. Using cognitive psychology and neurophysiology, or what Hirsch terms "consensus research," as a basis for his educational theory, he asserts that excellence in schooling necessitates an appreciation of the centrality of short- and long-term memory, repetition and automation, development of mental schemas consisting of vocabulary and specific facts, and the continuous acquisition, chunking, assimilation, and stocking of new information in an accurate fashion. Using the words of John Dewey, Hirsch warns that the result of failing to effect "genuine and thorough transmission" will be the relapse of "the most civilized group...into barbarism and then into savagery" (Hirsch, 1996, p. 121). His view of schooling thus seems more descriptive of an inculcative rather than an educational process.

Learning, for Hirsch, is the consumption of what he variously calls core content, relevant background knowledge, intellectual capital, traditional subject matter, book knowledge, shared national culture, vocabulary, and solid facts. These referents shelter Hirsch from having to discuss the political nature of knowledge and schooling. He never questions the role of power in determining what is considered relevant, whose knowledge is worthy of knowing, or why particular accounts pass as "fact" in classrooms. Indeed, he consciously chooses not to explore such issues, reasoning that "once you start down that road, where will you stop?" (1996, p. 31). Instead of exploring this political slippery slope, Hirsch emphasizes the need to reach an agreement on a common sequence in the curriculum, "at least in those areas like math and science and the basic facts of history and geography, which, unlike sex education, are not and should not be subjects of controversy" (p. 37). Discounting the validity of conflict over knowledge, Hirsch chides, "The educational community's identification of knowledge with 'elitism'—a theme that long antedated the recent addition of 'Eurocentrism' to the antiknowledge armory—is a strategy born more of hostility than of rational principle" (p. 116). Hirsch's world is free of cultural struggle; it is a world in which one needs only to disarm, reclaim abandoned sensibilities, and soberly internalize unproblematic content. Considering which and whose knowledge constitutes school curriculum is, much to Hirsch's dismay, an ongoing "road" we need to continuously travel. The danger resides not in the inability to "stop" questioning, but in the suggestion that we should ever cease asking these questions.

Hirsch urges, "One of the fundamental aims of an adequate education is to gain a large vocabulary—to become what [is] disparagingly call[ed] 'a dictionary.'" He continues:

> Whether a word is learned by targeted practice or by the contextual method of enriched language use, its actual meaning is, for the most part, just a brute fact.... There is rarely a comprehensible connection between a word and a thing, only a cultural connection that has to be memorized, not "understood." (1996, p. 111)

Emphasizing transmission rather than critical reflection, Hirsch argues that memory is an active and constructive process. "Unless one believes in thought transference or mental telepathy...the only way a student can understand what a teacher is saying...is through a complex, sometimes strenuous activity of constructing meaning from words" (p. 134). In essence, Hirsch is claiming that because it takes effort to memorize something or grasp its "intended" meaning, this process of mental gymnastics constitutes engaged learning. He does not recognize the important difference between having students participate in continuous dialogue and reflection to construct knowledge and meaning, and simply expecting them to acquire a static and mandated perspective and commit it to memory through repetitive practice. While Hirsch fleetingly acknowledges the need for children to "ask questions like 'How does he know that?' about a wide range of claims," he insists that "absent a great deal of solid knowledge," critical thinking is impossible (pp. 142–143). His idea that students should passively accept "solid knowledge," only later to think critically about it, is particularly misguided. It seems that "solid knowledge" is what students should question from the start.

Hirsch, however, rejects such descriptions of his position as inaccurate, arguing that his educational stance has been caricatured. Regarding his earlier work, Hirsch complains, "Among the several criticisms of *Cultural Literacy*, the most dull-minded was that it advised educators to teach disconnected, rote-memorized words and facts" (1996, p. 145). And yet, while Hirsch insists he does not advocate such pedagogy, the ideas he articulates, along with the evidence leveraged in support, reveal the opposite. For example, Hirsch references what he calls "consensus research" on effective teaching, explaining that findings have indicated "almost anything connected with the classical recitation pattern of teacher questioning (particularly direct factual questions rather than more open questions) followed by student response, followed by teacher feedback, correlates positively with achievement" (Brophy & Good, quoted in Hirsch, 1996, p. 161). Ideally, Hirsch clarifies, students will be able "to supply the right answer or to follow the right procedure very fast, without hesitation" (p. 164). To acquire such intellectual efficiency, Hirsch reminds us that memory studies have shown that "the best approach to achieving retention in long-term memory is 'distributed practice'" (p. 223). Thus, Hirsch concludes, although progressives may abhor "traditional schooling indoors—at desks, in rows, and largely by means of words and drill and practice," research tells us that "wherever there is an absence of 'traditional' schooling—there is also an absence of secure and universal learning" (pp. 217–218). For Hirsch,

education is a cognitive act of memory facilitated through a "scientifically" validated pedagogy; learning and teaching are technical matters,
not ideological or political ones.

His denial of the role of politics in education extends as well to
standardized testing. Discussing testing in a highly technical manner, Hirsch argues that standardized testing is not political. Instead,
he maintains, it is the fairest form of assessment. Unlike authentic
assessments[2] that often yield different scores depending on who does
the grading, Hirsch stresses that the same score is always awarded for
the same performance on standardized tests. Scoring thus becomes the
only criterion of fairness; the nature of the questions and the knowledge being privileged and tested are not, for Hirsch, issues that warrant
serious consideration. He dismisses the claim that standardized tests
are culturally biased (what he refers to as the racial-social objection).
"Americans, to their credit, have been pioneers in developing objective
tests," he says (1996, p. 177). This assumption of objectivity not only
reveals a naiveté regarding the politics of knowledge, but is also historically inaccurate. Stephen Jay Gould (1996) examines the nativistic,
racist, sexist, and classist origins of testing in the United States in great
depth. When standardized testing is examined in historical context—
something that Hirsch typically overlooks—the claim of cultural bias
is not so easily dismissed.

Clearly, Hirsch's theories of knowledge, pedagogy, and testing are
plagued by his denial of cultural politics and his insistence that education is apolitical. *Cultural Literacy* (1987) provides an important insight
into his denial of the importance and role of politics in education.
Hirsch discusses the drafting of the preliminary list of cultural literacy
items:

> Early in our project, my colleagues and I decided that our list
> should aim to represent but not to alter current literate American
> culture.... We have tried to avoid any of the prescriptiveness that
> is inherent in cultural politics.... We are aware that the suspicion
> may be entertained that our list is merely academic or male or
> white.... But a similarity of shared knowledge... controverts the
> ad hominem assumption that, because a list was made by so and
> so, it merely reflects so and so's view of American literate culture.
> (pp. 136–137)

Hirsch's belief that he can represent American literate culture unprob-
lematically reveals an unwillingness to avow his own politics.

Perhaps even more revealing is the story behind the naming of
Hirsch's Core Knowledge Foundation. Initially called the Cultural

Literacy Foundation, Hirsch explains his decision to change its name: "Teachers pointed out that the term 'Cultural' raised too many extraneous questions, whereas the term 'Core Knowledge' better described the chief aim of the reform...to introduce solid knowledge in a coherent way into the elementary curriculum" (1996, p. 13). Replacing Cultural Literacy, a designation that raised "extraneous" questions (such as whose culture), with Core Knowledge, a term conveying a certain universality, was an interesting tactical maneuver for one who disassociates himself from cultural politics. This highly symbolic shift illustrates Hirsch's ongoing attempt to depict that which is political and cultural as an unprejudiced educational project in the general interest of all.

In the end, Hirsch fails to acknowledge that schooling is a cultural undertaking rather than a cognitive-technical matter. The questions of what and whose knowledge defines an educated and literate person and the implications of these questions are at the heart of critical examinations of schooling. That the construction of knowledge is a political process and that the privileging and obliteration of culture have been central to the history of this nation (Adams, 1995; Woodson, 1933) are sticky issues Hirsch knowingly or unknowingly evades. For him, the inherent worth of education lies in its stabilizing potential, its ability to reinforce tradition and transmit "literate" culture and "core" knowledge. In challenging the meaning of education Hirsch embraces, it is perhaps appropriate to pose the question as Paulo Freire (1993) might: Is education about the depositing of information into the minds of people, or is it about engaging in a process of reflection and action, naming the world in order to transform it?

ASSUMPTION IV: SCHOOLS MUST COMPENSATE FOR THE KNOWLEDGE DEFICITS OF CHILDREN FROM CULTURALLY IMPOVERISHED BACKGROUNDS

Embracing the findings of the Coleman Report (1981) that correlated particular home backgrounds with academic failure, Hirsch emphasizes that "this pattern of social determinism...still persists in the schools" (1996, p. 21). He advocates compensating for the deficits of disadvantaged children so they may "secure the knowledge and skills that will enable them to improve their condition" (p. 7). In fact, Hirsch's enthusiastic support of a national curriculum is based largely on his understanding of it as a compensatory measure. Hirsch views schooling as an assimilative and civilizing process that ensures the proper maintenance of "tradition" and protects against the dangers of incoherence, social disintegration, and savagery lurking on the cultural periphery. Though the racial and class overtones of this discourse are apparent, the position is articulated with a certain benevolence, an air of good will, a concern that democratic ideals be upheld.

Hirsch's position on schooling is founded on a sort of cultural supremacy that fails to recognize itself as such. In talking about lower levels of educational achievement of children from disadvantaged backgrounds, Hirsch explains that it is "overwhelmingly clear that the chief explanation must be cultural rather than individual or genetic" (p. 103). To support his argument that particular cultural backgrounds hinder proper schooling, Hirsch cites Orlando Patterson—a fellow traveler of neoconservatism (Dillard, 2001) and scholar of color who compares the achievements of blacks in Jamaica with those of African Americans in the United States:

> A comparison of the two school systems suggests that attitudes are much more critical than the material resources of the schools or the homes of students....School success ... is more profoundly related to attitudes towards the dominant culture....If we [Patterson/other black students in Jamaica] wanted to succeed, *we had to acquire this thing*; if we didn't, well, it was up to us. (Patterson quoted in Hirsch, 1996, p. 103; italics added)

For Hirsch, the true source of disadvantage lies in deficient cultural traditions that differ from and resist replacement by that "thing" called dominant culture. For children from culturally impoverished backgrounds to advance, he argues, they need to acquire some genuine cultural capital. Hirsch reasons that "students from good-home schools will always have an educational advantage over students from less-good-home schools" (p. 43). He does not address why the cultural traditions, linguistic practices, or social mores of one home are considered good, while others are viewed as symptomatic of illiteracy, ignorance, and cultural deficit. His propensity to dismiss nondominant forms of knowledge is epitomized in the explication: "Just as it takes money to make money, it takes knowledge to make knowledge.... Those children who arrive at school lacking the relevant experience and vocabulary— they see not, neither do they understand" (p. 20). Yet, Hirsch expresses guarded optimism:

> Young children who arrive at school with a very small vocabulary, and a correspondingly limited knowledge base, can fortunately be brought to an age-adequate vocabulary by intelligent, focused help...[but] when this language and knowledge deficit is not

compensated for early, it is nearly impossible...in later grades. (p. 146)

Drawing startling parallels between knowing and unknowing students, Hirsch praises the benefits of core knowledge and traditional pedagogy for "the palace-tutored prince as well as the neglected pauper" (p. 226).

His perspective prevents him from recognizing that children—whether of color, working class, or Spanish-speaking—bring to the classroom lived experiences, cultural traditions, and languages that are diverse and rich sources of knowledge that have the potential to serve as a powerful critique of dominant ways of knowing.[3] Based on her ethnographic research in schools, Gloria Ladson-Billings (1994) suggests that successful teaching occurs not when students are required to abandon their cultural identities in order to learn, but when educators view student culture as an asset rather than an impediment. Ladson-Billings discovered that successful teachers of African American students saw "teaching as 'digging knowledge out' of students" and had "an overriding belief that students come to school with knowledge and that that knowledge must be explored and utilized" (p. 52). Such teachers viewed "knowledge as something that is continuously re-created, recycled, and shared" (p. 81), rather than something static and passively acquired from an external, objective source. These findings imply a vision of schooling, a promise, that Hirsch denies. In contrast to his argument, it appears "the schools we really need" are those that relentlessly seek to embrace students as knowers.

Hirsch's perception of particular cultural forms as normative, if not superior, results in the derogation and non-recognition of student knowledge, especially the knowledge possessed by those viewed as deficient. Some educators, however, have uncovered the potential of a pedagogical perspective very different from Hirsch's. For example, Rosa Hernandez Sheets (1995) and Maisha Fisher (2007) illustrate that students' first language and neighborhood dialect can be powerful means for developing literacy. In a related vein, others have revealed that counterstories and oral histories within Chicano/a and Native American communities—stories usually not included in the traditional curriculum—can enrich schooling for all students (Delgado Bernal, 2002; Klug & Whitfield, 2003; Michie, 1999). Moreover, William Tate (1995) and Eric Gutstein (2006) document approaches to teaching math based on African American and Latino/a community experiences. Indeed, entire school communities have affirmed the educational and social impact of democratic efforts aimed at recognizing student knowledge. At the Rindge School of Technical Arts in Cambridge, Massachusetts, for example, teachers, students, and community members participated in an ongoing collaboration that entailed the application of student knowledge to the assessment and resolution of community needs (Apple & Beane, 2007). These examples illustrate the promise of an education that is culturally relevant to students.

Hirsch contends that one of the major reasons students fail is "boredom compounded with humiliation—emotions that are induced and exacerbated by lack of shared knowledge in the classroom" (1996, p. 25). Hirsch has articulated a partial insight; many children do understand their education to be irrelevant and degrading, but not for the reasons Hirsch advances. He could perhaps find a fuller explanation in Paul Willis's (1977) argument that children increasingly resist schooling as their own knowledge is deemed insignificant in the educational process. Forced into a system that denies their experience and renders their identities meaningless, they resist—or in Hirsch's language, they fail.

Minimizing the importance of representation in the school curriculum, Hirsch insists: "Wherever public schools have offered the choice of truly effective mainstream academic training...minority families have signed up in disproportionate numbers.... These parents clearly recognize the direct connection between economic advancement for their children and the mastery of...mainstream culture" (1996, p. 208). Hirsch fails to note the predicament in which many "minorities" find themselves—they must submit to cultural dominance or risk even greater economic hardship. Rather than having a profound respect for the "mainstream," it is more likely that marginalized groups seek to maximize chances of security (e.g., see Harris, 1995). The coercive nature of this situation seems to escape Hirsch's critique. The question that needs to be posed is: What are the costs of citizenship and economic survival in this society? Undoubtedly, the costs to identity, culture, and language are great indeed.

Contradicting the picture Hirsch paints of an empowering "mainstream" culture, many have discussed the personal struggle entailed in trying to succeed academically while at the same time maintaining cultural identity (Deyhle, 1995; hooks, 1994; Kissen, 1993; Kumashiro, 2001; Ladson-Billings, 2005; Villanueva, 1993; Willis, 1995). Glenabah Martinez (2006), for example, has revealed the dilemma faced by Native American students in an urban high school, who must constantly balance the need to command "white" required knowledge against a desire to deepen "red" elective knowledge. Also important here is the work of Cornel West (1993), who has argued that the most significant problem confronting the African American community is the "nihilistic threat" that he describes as "the lived experience of coping with a life of hor-

rifying meaninglessness, hopelessness, and (most important) loveless-
ness" (p. 23). He maintains that self-loathing and lack of meaning result
from the "white supremacist beliefs and images permeating U.S. society
and culture" (p. 27). Although West does not mention schools specifically, one of the major institutions contributing to nihilism is most certainly the school, for on a daily basis, children of color are subjected to
a curriculum that reflects little of them. The compensatory impulse that
Hirsch regards as constructive is, from this vantage point, destructive.

From Hirsch's perspective, however, a bit of "destruction" is necessary; it is the cost of maintaining a cohesive society. In an article written several years prior to *The Schools We Need*, he explains that while
"the theme of lost ethnicity is as old as antiquity, [the] benefits con-
ferred by...civilization entail the pain of some cultural loss" (1992b, p.
2). For Hirsch, the social good requires conformity to dominant culture
and a compensatory measure capable of securing its continual hegemony, guaranteeing the suppression of disparate voices, and protecting
against the corruption of the grand tradition. Subsumed beneath a discourse of deficit and compensation, one discovers highly undemocratic
cultural presumptions.

ASSUMPTION V: A COMMON CULTURE IS SHARED BY ALL MEMBERS OF SOCIETY AND SHOULD BE PROMOTED THROUGH A NATIONAL CURRICULUM IN SUPPORT OF DEMOCRACY

Hirsch's nonrecognition of culture as a site of struggle is sustained by his
belief in the historical existence of a common culture. Praising Thomas
Jefferson's conception of a "common grade-school," he describes Jefferson's aspiration to "create a literate and independent citizenry as
well as a nesting ground for future leaders" (1996, p. 17). Hirsch claims
that America's founders "desired that the laws and customs of the public sphere should favor no single sect but should promote the general
welfare" (p. 234). Hirsch, however, remembers his history selectively,
omitting evidence that would disrupt his fantasy of an inclusive public space. For example, though Jefferson's advocacy of public schooling
was unique for his time, Hirsch overlooks the fact that the educational
system proposed by Jefferson was gradational and intended to function
as a filtering mechanism through which "the best geniusses [sic] will be
raked from the rubbish" (Peden, 1982, p. 146). Guided by a republican
ideology that emphasized the maintenance of a virtuous citizenry—a
group narrowly constituted along lines such as gender and race—

Jefferson hoped schools would foster a more informed, independent, incorruptible populace and an aristocracy of talent capable of leading the new nation.

Hirsch repeats this limited reading of history in his analysis of the common schools, claiming that they had "the goal of giving all children the shared intellectual and social capital" necessary for participation in "the economy and policy of the nation" (1996, p. 233). His uncomplicated rendering of history enables him to forget that the intellectual capital transmitted by the common school was not "shared." As Carl Kaestle (1983) has shown, common schools were founded upon a native, Anglo-American, Protestant, republican, capitalist ideology that left many groups alienated. Furthermore, the underlying purpose of the common school was to promote moral, social, and cultural stability rather than genuine educational and political development.

Hirsch's social and educational vision is built on the notion that a utopian public sphere—a mythic one that has never existed—is being undermined by the educational initiatives and politically divisive perspectives of progressives. His politicized reconstruction of the past allows him to evade the complexities and contradictions of a history shaped by struggles against unequal power. Within the parameters he sets, Hirsch chooses not to acknowledge that common culture is a particular rather than a shared tradition, a specific and highly exclusive construction of class, race, gender, sexuality, language, and history.

Hirsch's obsession with the maintenance of a common culture and the need to protect it against potential dissolution is best encapsulated in his ongoing discussion of cosmopolitanism. Hirsch articulates his position in an article entitled "Toward a Centrist Curriculum: Two Kinds of Multiculturalism in Elementary School" (1992b). Focusing on multiculturalism, Hirsch explains:

> There's a progressive form that will be helpful to all students, and a retrogressive kind that...tends to set group against group.... The universalistic view...might be called cosmopolitanism.... The other is a particularistic vision that stresses loyalty to one's local culture. It could be called... "ethnic loyalism."

The central question, Hirsch asserts, is "do we define ourselves as belonging to a particular 'ethnos' or...a broad 'cosmopolis'?" (pp. 1–2). Hirsch's distinct understanding of multiculturalism and the posing of this question reveal his fear of difference, the need for its appropriation or subversion, and its close association with the disintegration of tradition and social cohesion. For the cosmopolis to thrive, challenges to cultural dominance must be silenced and demands for representation, rooted in "ethnic loyalism," must be strategically mediated and fended off. Critiques of power are impossible because, in the cosmopolis, we are all the same. The cosmopolis is thus an ahistorical place where a mythical consensus overshadows the ugly reality of racial, cultural, and economic oppression.

One cannot underestimate the importance of consensus to Hirsch's theory of schooling and society. Democracy, for Hirsch, depends on consensus and falters without a commonly embraced culture. This conception of democracy, however, is highly questionable and raises some crucial concerns. Does diversity compromise the democratic ideal or does it protect it? Further, how can a democracy be sustained without an ethic of criticism? When dialogue ceases, might democracy gravitate toward fascism? Perhaps most importantly, in a society in which class, race, and gender have played a central and historical role in the formation of present-day realities, can democracy come into being without recognizing the ways differences have functioned in shaping relations of power and exploitation?

Hirsch is preoccupied with how to uphold the Jeffersonian ideal amid contemporary threats to cosmopolitanism. If the schools are currently controlled by the progressive monopoly, as Hirsch claims, and cultural disintegration is imminent, then the United States must act to stabilize incoherence by creating a mechanism through which consensus will be enforced, differences quarantined, and the cosmopolis maintained. For Hirsch, that tool is the public school system. "In a large, diverse nation," Hirsch asserts, "the common school is the only institution available for creating a school-based culture that, like a common language, enables everyone to communicate in the public sphere" (1996, p. 233). To break the progressive stronghold and reclaim the common school, the adoption of an official national curriculum is thus needed. This core curriculum would promote a common culture and protect against the leftist multicultural threat. As a compensatory measure, Hirsch promises that it will remedy deficiencies and protect the culturally impoverished from themselves. Most importantly, it will fulfill Hirsch's vision of the ultimate democratic ideal—entrance into the marketplace.

The adoption of an official national curriculum is not the apolitical matter Hirsch claims. In considering any curriculum, one must ask: What and whose knowledge will be included or excluded? Who will decide? And what does the finality of deciding imply? Regarding the issue of what and whose knowledge will be granted official status, Hirsch states:

In the United States, the process of reaching agreement about a
sequence of common learnings in the early grades is likely to be
lengthy, conflict-ridden, and, at the start, unofficial.... Gradually,
however, general agreement on such a core might be developed
if the public and the educational community became fully per-
suaded that some degree of grade-by-grade commonality is necessary. (1996, p. 235)

Hirsch's preoccupation with reaching an agreement overshadows questions related to why particular forms of knowledge would constitute
the core curriculum while others would not. Further, Hirsch assumes
that a consensus over knowledge should exist. His emphasis on moving beyond conflict to consensus reveals the degree to which he views
knowledge as the common possession of agreed upon, grade-by-grade
distributed facts. "The strongest resistance to commonality in schooling may come from a widespread fear of uniformity," says Hirsch (p.
237). The opposite, of course, could be concluded. The need for commonality, in other words, may be the result of a fear of diversity. And it
is precisely this fear of diversity that raises serious concerns about what
and whose knowledge would comprise the core curriculum.

The second question relevant to the adoption of an official national
curriculum is who decides—no minor consideration since democracy
relies on involved and collective participation. Yet, except to note that
such a process would be conflictive, Hirsch does not address this issue.
The answers to key questions such as who has access to channels of
decision-making power, whose voice is valued within those channels,
and what exactly are the channels and processes of negotiation are by
no means inconsequential and must be relentlessly and unromantically
interrogated in relation to how power is distributed (Apple & Buras,
2006; Fraser, 1997). Although clearly parents of middle-income status
more often have the financial and cultural resources necessary for inter-
vening in educational decision making (Ball, 2003; Benveniste, Carnoy,
& Rothstein, 2003; Buras & Apple, 2005), negotiations surrounding
the current public school curriculum have taken little account of these
issues. In much the same way, the politics surrounding the production of the Core Knowledge Sequence, the curriculum affiliated with
Hirsch's Core Knowledge Foundation and adopted by Core Knowledge
schools across the nation, have not been explicitly discussed. Hirsch
simply describes the curriculum as one that was "reviewed and revised
by panels of teachers [and] further revised by almost 100 people of
diverse backgrounds" (Hirsch, 1993, p. 2). Who decided and the pro-

cesses by which decisions were made remain unclear (see Buras, 2006, and chapter 3 of this volume).

The third issue pertains to the implications of reaching a final consensus on the contents of an official national curriculum. For Hirsch, consensus and commonality are part and parcel of not only national culture, but school culture as well. Reaching a final consensus over school curriculum, however, implies that knowledge is static and unchanging, a problematic tenet. Hirsch's conception of knowledge as a relatively settled and fixed entity is revealed quite clearly when he states:

> For most problems that require critical thought by the ordinary person...the most needed knowledge is usually rather basic, long-lived, and slow to change. True, just as physics is under revision at the frontier, so American history...is constantly under revision in certain details....But behind the ever-changing front lines, there is a body of reliable knowledge which has not changed, and will not change very much. (1996, p. 155)

Knowledge, for Hirsch, is a stable body of fact occasionally altered by the addition of newly discovered details. But clearly, this conception of knowledge should be eschewed. Knowledge results from ongoing cultural struggle and is constructed and reconstructed through complex social processes. It is produced through conflict on the front lines, efforts to reclaim forgotten and suppressed histories, and demands for curricular representation (e.g., see Delgado Bernal, 2006), all of which Hirsch trivializes in the midst of praising the uncompromised status of the canon.

In sum, the curriculum that currently dominates public schooling and the official national curriculum Hirsch advocates are undemocratic. Ultimately, one must ponder a more just and viable alternative. Such reflection may provide an avenue for imagining possibilities as well as a direction for counterhegemonic work. As I and others have argued, any democratic curriculum will pay particular attention to what and whose knowledge constitutes the curriculum (Apple & Buras, 2006). R. W. Connell (1993) lays out the specifications of a model of curricular justice and gives significant consideration to the knowledge valued in schools. Primary to any socially just curriculum, Connell believes, is the widespread adoption of the perspective of "the least advantaged." Making the knowledge of the least advantaged the center of curriculum requires that "we think through economic issues from the standpoint of the poor....gender arrangements from the standpoint of women....race relations and land questions from the standpoint of

[I]ndigenous people.... questions of sexuality from the standpoint of gay people" (p. 43). The suggestion that the cultural and historical experiences of oppressed groups be privileged within schools seems democratic, for it is difficult to fathom how advantaging the knowledge of the elite and powerful could promote a more just society. In some respects, such a curriculum might resemble that of Central Park East, a high school in East Harlem that maintained as one of its guiding curricular questions: From whose viewpoint am I knowing (Meier & Schwartz, 2007)?

The idea that multiple voices shape the curriculum through an ongoing process of negotiation over knowledge, and that conflict, rather than consensus, constitutes the curricular foundation must also be considered in any discussion of democratic educational initiatives. It is conceivable that Hirsch would question the degree to which schools could operate, students learn, and society remain intact without a consensus about what specifically constitutes knowledge in the educational sphere. Yet, Graff (1992) articulates a curriculum theory that responds to political struggles over school knowledge, appreciates the changing nature of knowledge, addresses the difference between consensus and coherence, and concerns itself with the social implications of knowing. He stresses the tendency to "speak as if the content of [common] culture were already settled—as if there were no question about what the common culture will include and who will have a voice in defining it" (p. 45). Instead, Graff recommends that ongoing struggle and conflict over knowledge constitute the school curriculum. We need to imagine, Graff stresses, "how conflict, disagreement, and difference might themselves become a source of educational and cultural coherence—indeed, the appropriate source of coherence for a democratic society" (p. 143). It should be underscored, however, that Graff does not envision his proposal as a means for defusing tension through the promotion of a relativistic pluralism. Rather, such a curriculum would enable students to understand the social implications of different ways of knowing and increase their awareness regarding "how knowledge is produced... thus [making] them capable of playing an active role in their society, enabling them to intervene in the dominant discourses of their culture" (p. 186).

Graff's emphasis on heightened consciousness and social action brings into focus the final point to be considered with regard to any democratic curriculum. As Freire acknowledges, critical dialogue, reflection, and social action are important in any transformative educational project aimed at the realization of the collective good. He notes that "as [teachers and students] attain... knowledge of reality through

common reflection and action, they discover themselves as its perma-
nent re-creators" (1993, p. 51). Hence, any democratic form of schooling will endow students, through processes of engagement, with the
knowledge needed to re-create self and society.

HIRSCH'S EDUCATIONAL VISION AND
THE CORE KNOWLEDGE MOVEMENT

Having called into question some of Hirsch's Core assumptions, one
inquiry still remains: Why, despite the problematic nature of the educational and social foundations of the neoconservative vision, does it
nonetheless appeal to a range of different groups? Part of the answer
lies in the ability of neoconservatives, and the right more generally, to
"work on popular sentiments, to reorganize genuine feelings, and in the
process to win adherents" (Apple, 2000, p. 20). Using what Apple (2000)
calls "the politics of common sense," the right has tapped into the real
concerns of many people, subsequently rechanneling and rearticulat-
ing them in ways that support more conservative agendas. This insight
into the dynamics of rightist politics provides a framework for discussing how neoconservative assumptions—particularly those expressed in
The Schools We Need—function as discourses that appeal to individuals' understandings of the world, thus spurring them to join the Core
Knowledge movement and often the broader conservative alliance. At
the same time, it must be added that neoconservatives, particularly the
more populist fractions within this segment of the right, have especially
recognized the power of compromise to secure the consent of traditionally marginalized groups. A good deal of this—namely, the disposition
to embrace elements left and right and the capacity to reconfigure them
into nothing less than a highly resonant, if contradictory, rightist multicultural strategy—may likewise be explained by some of the history
from which neoconservatism emerged.

For example, Hirsch's call for a return to tradition—in the guise
of reinstating curricular coherence—appeals to prevalent fears about
race, gender, and sexuality. In the midst of demands for the recognition of diverse cultural perspectives, cultural and religious conservatives tired of Latinos, gays and lesbians, women, and others politicizing
everything conceivably find themselves attracted to the position that
the school curriculum need not generate political struggles, but should
rather be recognized as an avenue for transmitting "factual" content.
Indeed, those who feel anxious about losing privileges afforded by traditional social arrangements believe that Core Knowledge can partly
mediate the threat. Some may even hope that a commonly shared

culture nurtured by the schools will diminish racial divisions and engender greater social cohesion, albeit without having to address the cultural domination and unequal distribution of resources and power at the center of these tensions. On multiple levels, then, Hirsch's educational vision synthesizes and redirects a plethora of racial and other difference-related feelings and convictions.

In another vein, Hirsch claims that by acquiring needed intellectual capital through the Core curriculum, students traditionally condemned to economic marginalization will gain entry into a marketplace that promises financial stability and greater access to material resources. He writes: "Improving the effectiveness and fairness of education through enhancing both its content and its commonality has more than educational significance. The improvement would...diminish the economic inequalities within the nation" (1996, p. 238). The curricular initiative proposed by Hirsch thus becomes associated with a broader distribution of economic goods.

Although it is difficult to understand how groups denied cultural recognition will, at the same time, obtain greater equality within the economic sphere—especially since struggles for recognition and redistribution are often closely interrelated (Fraser, 1997)—this is precisely Hirsch's argument. Despite the flaws of its logic, particularly in relation to market realities under capitalism, the assurance of upward mobility is something no parents would wish to deny their children. As families endure a persisting economic crisis marked by aggressive attacks on the public sector, increased poverty, unaffordable housing, inaccessible health care, and corporate layoffs, combined with a job market principally offering low-paying work in the service sector, many parents understandably want security for their children and fear withholding from them anything that may enhance their future chances of financial survival. It is not difficult to appreciate, then, why many poor or even anxious middle-class parents would mobilize around a curriculum that provides the background knowledge needed for their children to "succeed economically."

Hirsch's *What Your Kindergartner–Sixth Grader Needs to Know Series* (1991, 1998a) is certainly meant to appeal to this sense of urgency. Like many parents, school administrators and teachers are also joining the effort around Core Knowledge. Under tremendous public pressure to do something to alleviate problems in schools, many turn to adopting Core with the hope that such a curricular reform will make a difference.

It is equally significant that Hirsch frames his initiative in terms of civil rights and compensation. Building on this argumentation, Hirsch

(1999b) has inveighed, "In the wake of the *Brown* decision, at the very moment of our highest hopes for social justice, the victory of progressivism over academic content had already foreclosed the chance that school integration would equalize achievement and enhance social justice" (para. 2). Forging an even closer relationship between Core Knowledge and racial equality, he highlights: "The late James Farmer, the great civil rights activist, once honored our annual Core Knowledge conference by giving a keynote address in the tradition of Du Bois which said, in effect, that strong common content in the early grades is the new frontier of the civil rights movement" (para. 9). Interestingly, this is not what Farmer said—as I will show in the next chapter—yet such a bold statement powerfully connects Core to histories of struggle from below and to civil rights, a long-standing concern for communities of color and for many other subaltern groups, too.

In quite another way, Hirsch's educational position fuses with citizens' beliefs in the "best" of U.S. traditions—the pursuit of fairness, meritocracy and the provision of equal opportunity, and the desire to strengthen democracy. Moving beyond domestic concerns, the discourse on educational excellence, with its nationalistic flair, is alluring because of its focus on international competition and U.S. dominance within the global economy, a market ideology embraced by many. Although this brief discussion only begins to consider the ways neoconservative discourses are being mobilized to build alliances—much more will be said in the next chapter—it does illuminate some of the reasons why the Core Knowledge movement is growing and why neoconservatives (and the right) are prevailing more generally.

Hirsch's neoconservative imaginary rests on a host of problematic assumptions. Still, the discourses adopted by him have resonated with the experiences, anxieties, and hopes of differently situated groups. It took more than a vision, however, to build the movement around Core. It also took a specific curriculum, the Core Knowledge Foundation, the work of school communities in a range of contexts, and more. Let us now take a closer look at the nationwide movement that has developed around Core over the past two decades. Only by gaining insight into the dynamics of this movement may the power of neoconservatives be potentially disrupted and the fears and desires of people reoriented in more emancipatory directions.

3

TRACING THE CORE
KNOWLEDGE MOVEMENT

You, as teachers and leaders of Core Knowledge schools, must foment a revolution.... America needs *more* Core Knowledge schools.

Diane Ravitch at the National Core Knowledge Conference
(1996, p. 11)

[For Core Knowledge] to be liked by the Bushies [Bush allies] and by the American Federation of Teachers—there's something peculiar going on.

E. D. Hirsch in the *Washington Post*
(Lindsay, 2001, p. W24)

BEYOND CORE ASSUMPTIONS

E. D. HIRSCH HAS CLEARLY ARTICULATED the assumptions made by neoconservatives in relation to education (Buras, 1999b, 2006). These assumptions have shaped a national movement focused on reforming preschools as well as elementary and middle schools through the adoption of Core Knowledge. In short, Hirsch's vision has moved far beyond guiding assumptions to become a Core curriculum and an educational crusade.

At the 5th National Core Knowledge Conference sponsored by the Core Knowledge Foundation, Diane Ravitch—a well-known cultural conservative, education historian, Brookings Institution fellow, and present member of the foundation's board of trustees—called upon educators to "foment a revolution" by expanding the presence of Core schools nationally. Three years later, William Bennett, former Secretary of Education under President Reagan and fellow at the Heritage Foundation, along with Chester Finn and John Cribb (1999), published *The Educated Child: A Parent's Guide from Preschool Through Eighth Grade*. This national bestseller deemed the Core Knowledge curriculum the cornerstone of a good education and its content guidelines the appropriate measure for assessing the quality of classroom teaching generally. In 2003, the Thomas B. Fordham Foundation, headed by Finn, awarded Hirsch a "Prize for Excellence in Education" for his contributions to school reform, while it concurrently issued reports (Leming, Ellington, & Porter, 2003; Stotsky, 2004) that multiculturalism is responsible for the demise of American and Western historical traditions. Since the first Core Knowledge school opened in 1990, the number of schools has continuously increased, with hundreds of preschools, elementary schools, and middle schools across the nation now using the Core curriculum (Core Knowledge Foundation [CKF], 2003e, 2004b; Hirsch, 2006).

Arguably, Core Knowledge constitutes the most "successful" neoconservative initiative in education. As such, tracing the growth and character of this reform movement and considering its implications are important—particularly for those of us concerned about unequal power, cultural representation, and the democratization of curriculum and schooling. A number of questions come to mind. How did *Cultural Literacy* transform into the Core Knowledge curriculum? What role has the Core Knowledge Foundation played in relation to Core schools? Where are the hundreds of schools that have adopted the curriculum, and what have been the mechanisms and channels through which Core has spread? Which communities have embraced this reform, and why? If there are tensions within the Core Knowledge movement, what are they and why are they significant? Examining these questions will provide more than a timeline charting the growth of the movement. Such an inquiry will illuminate the complex network of alliances that has formed around Core Knowledge and help point toward the diverse interests and tensions embedded within the movement.

When Hirsch first authored *Cultural Literacy: What Every American Needs to Know* (1987), it provoked a great deal of criticism (e.g., see Aronowitz & Giroux, 1991). He recollects:

> It was an enormously controversial book.... Coming at the height of fierce debates over multiculturalism and gender politics, it was

damned with great hostility by cultural reformers and education professors as a reactionary tract aimed at preserving the intellectual domination of white Anglo-Saxon males, and as a means of boring children with mindless drills and stuffing them with "mere facts." (Hirsch, 2006, p. 6)

Deemed Eurocentric by critics, *Cultural Literacy* nonetheless metamorphosed into Core Knowledge—a content-specific, sequenced prekindergarten through eighth grade curriculum (CKF, 1998) that has become increasingly popular. Why is it, we might ask, that an educational reform initially "damned" as elitist has since acquired support from a range of communities—some constituted by traditionally oppressed groups? In the previous chapter, I analyzed Hirsch's educational vision and suggested how that vision speaks to a variety of concerns from above and below. Let us now take a critical look at the history and dynamics of the Core Knowledge movement itself.

FROM *CULTURAL LITERACY* TO CORE KNOWLEDGE

In the late 1970s, Hirsch, a professor of English at the University of Virginia, began formulating his ideas on cultural literacy and circulating them at professional meetings. In 1983 he published an essay titled "Cultural Literacy" in *The American Scholar,* a well-known neoconservative journal. He declared English and history "central to culture making," then charged:

> In English courses, diversity and pluralism now reign without challenge.... If we want to achieve a more literate culture than we now have, we shall need to restore the balance between [the] two equally American traditions of unity and diversity. We shall need to restore certain common contents to the humanistic side of the school curriculum. (pp. 160–161)

Professing his emergent philosophy, Hirsch captured the attention of the Exxon Education Foundation, which supported his production of a tentative list of cultural literacy items (Hirsch, 1987). Meanwhile, he established the Cultural Literacy Foundation, which initially received grants from Exxon and the National Endowment for the Humanities, with the intent of "developing a core curriculum and pilot programs for teaching it" (Hitchens, 1990). In a maneuver to depict his educational initiative as detached from politics, Hirsch (1996) explained the decision to change the organization's name to the Core Knowledge Foundation: "The term 'Cultural' raised too many extraneous questions, whereas the term 'Core Knowledge' better described the chief aim…to introduce solid knowledge in a coherent way into the elementary curriculum" (p. 13). Since 1986, the foundation has provided a good part of the organizational structure and resources needed to transform his vision into a national reform effort. With the publication of Hirsch's *Cultural Literacy* in 1987 and *The Dictionary of Cultural Literacy* the next year (Hirsch, Kett, & Trefil, 1988), the *Core Knowledge Sequence*—content guidelines for the various subject areas—soon followed (CKF, 1998).

According to the Core Knowledge Foundation, the content guidelines were "the result of a long process of research and consensus-building." Reports issued by state departments of education and professional associations were examined for recommended educational outcomes. Additionally, the organization "tabulated the knowledge and skills specified in the successful educational systems of several other countries, including France, Japan, Sweden, and West Germany." An advisory board on multiculturalism was invited to suggest "diverse cultural traditions that American children should all share." "Three independent groups of teachers, scholars, and scientists around the country" were provided with the materials and asked to generate master lists. Those lists were used to create a "draft master plan," which was then finalized by "some 100 educators and specialists" who formed "twenty-four working groups" at a gathering in March 1990. The *Sequence* was then piloted and refined during its first year of implementation at Three Oaks Elementary School, the first Core Knowledge school, in Florida. The foundation clarifies, however, that there has been "more stability than change in the *Sequence*," particularly considering the "inherent stability of the content of literate culture" (CKF, 1998, pp. 1–2).

The foundation's description may appear to render transparent the process by which Core was produced, but the issues associated with its production are more complex than acknowledged. The politics that shaped the standards advocated in state reports, for example, were not considered. These standards, along with those assumed to guide successful educational systems in other nations, were apparently embraced without criticism. The process is described in highly technical terms— content recommendations were tabulated and a list was developed. The commissioning of an advisory board on multiculturalism raises a host of issues that remain unarticulated, including the issue of how its members and participants at the 1990 meeting were chosen. Reflecting several years later on the convocation that met in 1990, Hirsch explained, "I mean, we didn't have Lithuanians, but we did have 24 working groups" (Goldberg, 1997, p. 84). Such a statement hardly addresses the most fundamental questions. Who determined what should count as Core Knowledge? Did particular conflicts emerge during the process? If so, how were they resolved? If the politics of knowledge were not explicitly engaged, as suggested by the foundation's technical approach, then what implicit interests might have determined the content? Questions about *whose* knowledge is valued in schools are worthy of continuous and collective reflection, and the answers reveal a good deal about the quality of democratic life within the nation (e.g., see Buras & Apple, 2006). Yet, the politics surrounding the production of Core Knowledge have been rendered to a significant degree invisible and beyond the pale of inquiry.

That the process for determining state standards and texts is often comparably opaque does not exempt Core from such critiques. The scope of the foundation's agenda and the ever-increasing popularity of Core warrant the posing of scrutinizing questions. Hirsch advocates a national curriculum; an effort is even underway to align Core with educational standards in all 50 states, meaning that a plan for schools would exist in each state that charts how to blend Core with state-specific content requirements (CKF, 2003e). Unlike state standards and testing, Core Knowledge has been pursued with missionary zeal and has evidenced a grassroots appeal not associated with state educational mandates. Core has indeed generated an educational movement—one that has, in part, been facilitated by the foundation.

THE ROLE OF THE CORE KNOWLEDGE FOUNDATION

The development of local, regional, and national networks around Core Knowledge has been assisted by the Core Knowledge Foundation. The foundation's work has progressed from piloting Core in a single school in 1990, to working with some 300 schools by mid-1996 (CKF, 1996c), to coordinating a network of nearly 1,000 Core Knowledge schools in 46 states by 2007 (CKF, 2004b, 2006a, 2007a). Moreover, the number of educators using Core is even greater if more loosely affiliated supporters are counted, including home schoolers and non-Core schools that utilize Core Knowledge content guidelines and teaching materials without formal recognition by the foundation as Core schools (CKF, 2003e, 2004b, 2006d). Although Core initially covered grades K–6, the curriculum for pre-kindergarten and grades 7–8 was subsequently developed (Marshall, 1997d, 1997e; CKF, 2007d). Approximately half of Core Knowledge schools are public, one-third are charter schools, and the remaining fraction are private or religious schools. In urban, suburban, and rural areas, Core has likewise captured attention; a quarter of the schools are rural, with the remaining percentage divided almost evenly between urban and suburban areas (CKF, 2004b, 2004c, 2007a).

With such an array of communities on board, the foundation has mandated that schools comply with increasingly rigorous implementation and reporting standards in order to gain recognition. A school can qualify as either a "friend of Core Knowledge," an "official Core Knowledge school," or a "visitation site" deemed "model." Depending on its status, the school may need to complete an annual profile, but may also be required to participate in professional development offered by the foundation, fully implement the curriculum, host site visits by foundation representatives, and accommodate a strong push to utilize Core resources, such as Core Knowledge history textbooks, and provide achievement data through standardized, Core Knowledge-referenced tests (CKF, 2003b, 2003c, 2003d, 2004b). This heightened monitoring, I will later argue, may be driven by a desire to discipline the very diversity that has enabled the movement's growth. But we should first consider the role the foundation has played in facilitating this growth and why differently situated communities have embraced Core.

The foundation has organized a National Core Knowledge Conference annually since 1992. The 1st National Conference was attended by 50 people (Goldberg, 1997). In comparison, the 15th gathering in San Antonio in 2006 was attended by 2,175 administrators, teachers, and parents (CKF, 2006a). At the conference, participants attend formal addresses by invited speakers, receive awards for their school's progress in implementing Core, and even tour local Core Knowledge schools. An entire day is dedicated to teachers presenting lesson plans based on the *Sequence*. Actually, it is difficult to overstate the role such activities have played in mobilizing teachers around Core. Under conditions where teachers are generally blamed for the failures of the educational system, Core Knowledge teachers are viewed as professionals whose curricular ideas contribute to enhancing the quality of education in Core schools. At the 2004 National Conference in Atlanta, Hirsch called teachers "the heart and soul of the movement." He continued:

> Our potential is being realized because of you great people in this room. I feel that every time I come to one of these conferences.... Even though it's hard work to do Core Knowledge and it's hard to get up and teach the knowledge that's in the *Sequence* and it's hard to convey it well to students, it's work that dedicated teachers are engaging in because they realize that it

is best for children.... And it's also very rewarding for teachers. Many of you have told me that. (Buras, 2004)

The populist tenor of the movement is apparent in Hirsch's words and throughout the conference, where names are put to faces and hugs are exchanged between foundation staff and their grassroots allies. Foundation staff carefully listens to teachers, as revealed in one session during which draft teacher handbooks for Core were shared with teachers for their feedback (Buras, 2004). Though the balance between teachers' professional autonomy and the foundation's production of resources has generated tensions, the national conference is clearly a time for building community among a national network of Core Knowledge advocates.

The foundation also distributes a newsletter called *Common Knowledge*. Browsing its pages reveals a great deal about the philosophy of the foundation, and partly illuminates the character of the movement. Skimming *Common Knowledge*, the reader will often find essays by Hirsch that elaborate the guiding vision behind Core, such as "Why General Knowledge Should Be a Goal of Education in a Democracy" (1998b). Typically, feature articles such as "The Bad News about Discovery Learning" (Marshall, 1998b) or "What do Scientists Know About How We Learn?" (Willingham, 1999) convey the foundation's endorsement of direct instruction techniques. Other pieces announce important developments and communicate a sense of progress. One headline reads "Coast to Coast, Trainers Spread Core Knowledge with Enthusiasm" (Siler, 1999), while another declares "Core Knowledge Offers Blueprint for Content-Rich Teacher Education" (Davis, 2002). It is also not uncommon to discover an odd convergence of "traditional" and "multicultural" elements on the page, albeit with no regard for how those elements might be critically connected. Newsletter highlights of one national conference illustrate this point:

> From the school visits...to the closing comments by Foundation President E. D. Hirsch...the theme of "Content Counts" was underscored by speakers, presenters, and teachers. They talked of math and land bridges, of women's rights and classical music. Teachers shared slides of Antarctica and Japanese snacks.

One picture from the meeting shows two older, white, female teachers with huge eyeglasses performing "a ceremonial dance of the Aztecs" with an olive-complexioned, long-haired man dressed in Native American garb. Another reveals elementary students wearing bonnets and performing "songs from the Civil War" for conference attendees. Other photos portray students at a local Core Knowledge school marching "a Chinese dragon through the halls" and a charter school board member reading *Cultural Literacy* during the conference (Siler, 1998, pp. 10–11).

While the conference and newsletter attempt to define the movement's vision and foster a collective sense of mission, other foundation resources provide more tangible home and classroom support. The *What Your K-6 Grader Needs to Know Series* (e.g., Hirsch, 1998a) is a wildly popular, encyclopedic set of volumes sequenced in accordance with the Core curriculum. By title, these books summon parents based on myriad anxieties about the knowledge required for upward mobility. The literary *Core Classics* (Marshall & Hirsch, 1997) are child-friendly versions of works covered by Core, including *Robinson Crusoe, Treasure Island, Pollyanna*, and *Don Quixote*. The historical *Rats, Bulls, and Flying Machines: A History of the Renaissance and Reformation* is a text meant to introduce students to early European history (Prum, 1999). Such resources exist alongside the recently published *Pearson Learning-Core Knowledge History and Geography Textbooks* on U.S. and world history (Hirsch, 2002). To pull it all together, *Teacher Handbooks* detail "what teachers need to know" to teach the curriculum (CKF, 2004d), while the *Core Knowledge Monthly Organizer* (CFK, 2000) and *Day-by-Day Planner* (CKF, 2007c) help classroom teachers plot the presentation of content throughout the school year.

Curriculum resources have multiplied in recent years, but support services have also been enhanced. The foundation sponsors Core adoption seminars and professional development workshops (CKF, 1997, 2003a). It offers guidance to low-income schools that want to adopt Core but need help applying for funds under the federal Comprehensive School Reform Program (Shields, 2003b). The foundation likewise maintains a Web site (CKF, 2004e) that serves as an avenue of communication, and continuously produces informational literature and books that help sustain the organization financially, assist teachers and parents pedagogically, and support the movement ideologically (e.g., see CKF, 1996b, 2004f; Hirsch, 1992a, 1996, 2006).[1] When the Core Knowledge Foundation first opened its doors, Hirsch and two part-time workers distributed information on the initiative (Hitchens, 1990). Now, twenty years later, approximately thirty staff members work for the foundation (CKF, 2007e); the Total Net Assets at the end of 2006 were $5.8 million, with money coming from a foundation endowment, other conservative foundations, donor contributions, and proceeds from the educational resources and books produced by Hirsch and the foundation (CKF, 2006a).

THE MAKING OF A MOVEMENT

The foundation's work has been pivotal in advancing Core Knowledge as a reform, but it is important to look more broadly at the movement. Core has flourished due to the motivations and efforts of a variety of actors, communities, and foundations. It is essential to provide just a few highlights.

In several areas, Core has been adopted districtwide in the public school system. In the small district of Hobbs, New Mexico, Core is taught in every K–8 school (Rounds, 2004). Larger districts have likewise implemented Core, including Polk County, Florida, and Nashville, Tennessee (Jones, 1997a). In Polk County, 63 elementary schools with 37,000 children adopted Core, and several middle schools joined later. Recalling his election campaign, District Superintendent Glenn Reynolds explained the decision to adopt the program districtwide. "I kept hearing that the public schools were not competitive....Our public schools were losing credibility and trust. The public was ready for major change" (in Marshall, 1997c, p. 1). Major change was likewise introduced when 42,300 elementary students in 73 different schools began studying Core during its first year of districtwide implementation in Nashville, with middle schools subsequently adopting Core (Jones, 1997a).

Though not part of a districtwide effort, there are notable concentrations of Core Knowledge schools elsewhere. Baltimore, where approximately 15 Core Knowledge schools have developed, is home to the Baltimore Curriculum Project. Funded by the Abell Foundation which aimed to support a "promising education reform model," the project is dedicated to generating lesson plans that correspond with Core content guidelines. Several Baltimore schools are directly affiliated with the project and have piloted the lessons, combining them with direct instruction programs in reading, language arts, and math (Baltimore Curriculum Project 2004a, 2007a, 2007b; Buras, 2004; CKF, 2007a; Marshall, 1997a). Another effort in Baltimore has revolved around the implementation of Core in three elementary schools in the Sandtown-Winchester neighborhood. In this low-income, predominantly African American community, educator Sylvia Peters (a founding member of Chris Whittle's Edison Project) collaborated with the Enterprise Foundation to facilitate the initiative—one supported by an annual budget of more than $500,000 (Enterprise Foundation, 2000; Morris, 1992; Scherer, 1996). Attending the National Core Knowledge Conference, Peters addressed teachers and called them the "most important links in recivilizing our society" (in Siler, 1997, p. 1). "Core Knowledge is about the soul of our country," she declared (p. 8). Words used by Peters like "recivilizing" and "soul" capture the missionary spirit of the Core Knowledge movement, which partly seeks to effectuate the cultural conversion of poor communities, particularly those of color.

In Atlanta, there are eight Core schools, though the state of Georgia has about 25 (CKF, 2004b, 2007a). The city of Atlanta was the site for the 2004 annual meeting, where attendees watched students from a local Core Knowledge school perform songs from the curriculum. With Hirsch sitting in the front row of a packed ballroom, a student choir from Morningside Elementary put on a well-polished show. The rapid-fire performance of a selection of songs that included the patriotic "America," country western "The Yellow Rose of Texas" (which in popular myth refers to an indentured mulatto woman), and African American spiritual "Swing Low, Sweet Chariot" revealed the awkward and uncritical relationship between the traditions of knowledge embodied in Core. Nonetheless, this parade of songs assured that there was something for everyone, which is one of the reasons for Core's popular appeal (Buras, 2004).

In Colorado there are over 70 Core Knowledge schools (CKF, 2004b, 2007a). William Moloney, the former school superintendent of Calvert County, Maryland (the first system to adopt Core districtwide) was appointed commissioner of education in Colorado in 1997 (Siler, 1997; Jones 1997b). He became a member of the Core Knowledge Foundation's board of trustees that same year, and gave a keynote address at the national conference in Atlanta the next year. Moloney's (1998) speech resounded with concerns about the stability of tradition and nationhood:

> The odyssey of Core Knowledge is a remarkable story of the American journey in search of better schools....I would first take us back to 1983 and the landmark report, "A Nation at Risk," which served as a springboard for the current school reform movement in general and for the Core Knowledge movement in particular....Americans wanted answers to questions and concerns that had been building for many years.... Why did every survey of public opinion reveal our people's concern that the schools were failing to uphold the values, the discipline, and the work ethic that have been the foundations of our national heritage?

The reason for this decline, Moloney pronounced, was that "serious mission confusion began when schools were declared the ideal forum to resolve explosive issues of class, language, race, religion, and sexuality." Dismissing multiculturalism as mission confusion, he next invoked a racially coded discourse to explain the erosion of national order, emphasizing, "In more stable settings, it would be possible to paper over the cracks in the edifice, but in less stable settings, notably our large urban systems, it was impossible to mask the descent into educational chaos" (p. 5). For Moloney, the descent into educational chaos called for ongoing advocacy of Core, and he was not alone in this crusade. Holly Hensey, originally a Core Knowledge teacher in Texas where some 50 Core schools exist (CKF 2003e, 2007a; Hitchcock, 2002), was recruited by the Core Knowledge Foundation to organize in the Colorado region. She has raised nearly $900,000 in grant money and has instituted many initiatives in the state, including a Web site, an annual Summer Writing Institute for Core teachers to develop lesson plans, an annual Colorado Core Knowledge Conference, and a project that aligned Core with educational standards in Colorado (Colorado Schools, 2003; National Core Knowledge Coordinator of Colorado, 2004).

In Texas, where Hensey originally worked, Trinity University and the Core Knowledge Foundation co-sponsored a seminar in 1996 on leadership in Core Knowledge schools (Jones, 1996). Trinity University has also partnered with Hawthorne Elementary, a Core Knowledge school in San Antonio, where students of education gain experience teaching the curriculum during their practicum. Bruce Frazee, the Trinity professor who coordinates the partnership, has been actively involved with 17 other Core schools in the San Antonio area and works with the foundation as a national coordinator.[1] Sam Ayers, another national coordinator, assists 20 Core Knowledge schools in Lubbock, Texas (CKF, 2003e, pp. 11–12; Frazee, 1996; Hitchcock, 2002).

Eighteen schools participated in the Arkansas Core Knowledge Initiative, a three-year project which began in 1997 and encompassed the gradual implementation of Core (Jones, 1997b, 1997c). Two new projects are underway in the state since that time. Beginning in 2003, the Walton Foundation granted three years of funding to expand Core to preschools serving low-income families in the Arkansas Delta, an undertaking that builds on prior grants and about 80 preschool sites already in existence. In addition, the Core Knowledge Foundation is piloting a K–8 initiative in the Delta, one that includes a full-time director, intensive training for teachers, an extended period for phasing in Core, and use of the new *Day-by-Day Planner* as a resource (CKF, 2003e, pp. 12, 18–19; New, 2003).

A seminar intended to introduce interested groups statewide to Core Knowledge was arranged by the Minnesota Humanities Commission in 1997 (Jones, 1997b, 1997c). Mae Schunk, a gifted and talented teacher at a Core Knowledge school in St. Paul, assisted in aligning Core with

Minnesota standards and became Minnesota's Lieutenant Governor in 1999. In this position, Schunk introduced Core to parents and school officials across the state, explaining that "Core is just common sense" (in Marshall, 1999a, p. 3). St. Paul is home to the Midwest Core Knowledge Center sponsored by the Minnesota Humanities Commission. The state has 31 Core Knowledge schools, and another 25 exist in nearby Michigan (CKF, 2004b, 2007a).

In California, few Core Knowledge schools existed in the late 1990s. Perhaps most significant to increasing interest in the state was Hirsch's invitation to address the California State Board of Education. "If I were a member of your Board," Hirsch admonished, "I would begin to shift rather large resources into academically effective, very-early education" (1997b, p. 7). Concluding, he stressed, "If reliable research does become your guide...it may come to be said that this was the Board that put an end to the era of educational fad and failure" (p. 8). The exhortation to adopt an educational reform based on "reliable research," a reference that often invokes rather narrow conceptions of scientific method, evidence, and educational performance, is an approach frequently taken by Hirsch and the foundation—and it has some allure. There are presently 32 Core Knowledge schools in California (CKF, 2004b, 2007a).

During the early years of the movement, the foundation supported three Regional Core Knowledge Centers—one in Colorado, another in Minnesota, and a third in Texas. Since then, national Core Knowledge coordinators in those states and Tennessee have replaced most centers. These coordinators offer a range of support services to Core schools and organize various initiatives regionally (Siler, 2001c). With the diffusion of Core in regions across the United States, it is not surprising that media attention has followed. Widely circulated publications such as *The Wall Street Journal* (Putka, 1991), *Life* (Meyer, 1991), *Newsweek* (Kantrowitz, Chideya, & Wingert, 1992), *Reader's Digest* (Perry, 1994), and *Forbes* (Summers, 1999) have positively highlighted the movement. Core has also been featured on televised programs, such as *ABC World News* (CKF, 1996a) and *60 Minutes* (Hawthorne Elementary School, 1998).

The growth of the Core Knowledge movement and the limelight it has enjoyed are indicative of the appeal this reform has secured in diverse kinds of communities. Having an even closer look at specific schools and particular associates of Core may illuminate further why certain groups are drawn to the reform, how those groups are differently positioned, and what interests are at play when alliances are formed.

PECULIAR ALLIANCES

At the predominantly European American, middle-class Washington Core Knowledge School (now Traut Core Knowledge School) in suburban Fort Collins, Colorado, parents' descriptions of the curriculum in non-Core public schools are "often filled with images of erosion. Many describe how the curriculum they knew as children, the one rooted in the granite truths of Western civilization, has disappeared from most schools." Concerned about cultural disintegration and loss of tradition, these parents petitioned the school district for the solution—a Core Knowledge school that would "emphasize a content-rich curriculum that would leave nothing to chance... [and] be teacher-directed from beginning to end" (Ruenzel, 1996–97, p. 8). In this community, it appears that Core made possible a return to "better" days before the multicultural assault on truth and the dominant order.

At Classical Charter School in the town of Appleton, Wisconsin, a comparably white and middling community, a parent touts Core as the embodiment of the "Great Books" tradition, something reflected in the very name of the school. This particular school has also attracted students who were formerly home schooled by parents using Core Knowledge curriculum materials, likely appreciated for their depoliticized "just the facts" packaging, classical and biblical content, and sequenced, parent-friendly nature (Buras, 2004).

In contrast, Nathaniel Hawthorne Elementary School is a mostly Latino/a, low-income, urban Core Knowledge school in San Antonio, Texas. Two teachers (Mentzer & Shaughnessy, 1996) at Hawthorne reflect on the school before its adoption of Core:

> We, as teachers, were frustrated. Things were not working well. We did not know what to do.... We were all scared about what was going to happen to our children if we couldn't find an intervention.... We could see that if we did not do something to stop the cycle of failure our children would end up on the streets or dead. (pp. 14–16)

Bruce Frazee (1996)—the faculty member from Trinity University who collaborates with Hawthorne—recalls the reform exploration process, indicating, "Many small groups formed to experiment with change; however, no particular focus emerged to create a systemic whole-school reform agreement" (p. 27). After a careful look at Core by teachers and parents, the teachers report, "We found our missing piece.... What we had not had was a common content." Expressing a similar view, another teacher put it this way: "To be given a two hundred- to three hundred-page textbook and let loose... is really a lot more difficult than being given a very specific body of knowledge... to teach.... With Core Knowledge, we have come together" (McPike, 1996–97, p. 15). For this school, Core was understood as contributing to renewal by providing a unifying educational vision and plan conducive to the advancement of struggling children. Though the specificity of content was deemed important, teachers underscored their partial renovation of the curriculum, stating "We then added items we thought were important for our students to learn such as Hispanic culture and traditions" (p. 20).

At the Courtland School in the Bronx, New York, a low-income Latino/a and African American Core Knowledge school, administrators similarly emphasize Core's coherent vision and sequenced content, which they say eases the socialization of new teachers under conditions of high turnover. Reporting that Core also fosters a home-school partnership, this school provides parents with the grade-appropriate book for their child from the *What Your K-6 Grader Needs to Know Series* (Buras, 2004). In both of these cases, then, Core was appreciated for the new and promising horizon it seemed to offer to urban schools facing an array of challenges.

Finally, administrators at Caney Creek Elementary, a rural school in Pippa Passes, Kentucky, say that many of the school's students—economically poor and European American—have never left their geographically isolated community. With Core, they believe the "concepts are so diverse that it allow[s] students to learn things normally not taught." For instance, Core's resources have allowed the school to integrate the arts into the curriculum (Buras, 2004).

In the rural town of Crooksville, Ohio, the adoption of Core by Crooksville Elementary—a largely low-income, European American school—has similarly meant that "students will get to see and understand the world beyond the mountains." For example, students will "learn the stories of Zeus and Hades and Persephone," "attend Renaissance Fairs, read *Don Quixote*, listen to Shakespearean actors, research and re-enact Civil War events," and "eat with chopsticks, and pantomime treaty agreements with Native Americans" (Vail, 1997, p. 14). Timm Mackley, the Superintendent of Crooksville, emphasizes, "We are dealing with kids who are narrowly confined to their small world. We are trying to share the wealth of human knowledge with them" (in Vail, p. 15; see also Mackley, 1999). These particular rural schools thus view Core as connecting isolated students to a wider multicultural world.

Aside from Core's appeal in regions throughout the United States, the curriculum has also been used internationally by select schools in

Canada, Honduras, Nicaragua, Switzerland, Taiwan, Thailand, United Kingdom, and elsewhere (CKF, 2007a). At the Saipan International School in Saipan, a Mariana Island and U.S. territory in the Pacific, the world history portion of Core is utilized in classrooms. Saint Augustine Preparatory School, a private, bilingual, Catholic school located in Managua, Nicaragua, has also adopted Core. The school has found its English-language materials to be particularly helpful in teaching a bilingual curriculum in a predominantly Spanish-speaking country (Locke, 2002). Regarding why a school in Nicaragua would rely on a curriculum largely centered on U.S. content, one school leader stressed that "the United States is the dominant culture." "If our students are lucky, many will attend American universities, where this information will be key." Core was also perceived as a "liberal arts curriculum," which countered the degradation of the humanities in a Nicaraguan school system driven by a "careerist orientation" that most prioritized the skills needed to secure employment in a struggling domestic economy (Buras, 2004). Partly reflecting these sentiments, the Cofradia Bilingual School in Honduras, where the majority of teaching is conducted in English, has embraced the *What Your K-6 Grader Needs to Know Series* for the purposes of lesson planning and student research (Locke, 2002). Meanwhile, the American School in Switzerland (TASIS)—a college-preparatory boarding school where a majority are English as Second Language students—has opened an Elementary Day School that implements Core, a curriculum that teachers say "complements the TASIS Middle and Upper School curriculum with its emphasis on the milestones of Western civilization" (TASIS Staff, 2007). It should come as little surprise that the *Dictionary of Cultural Literacy* has been translated into Chinese, Dutch, German, Japanese, and Swedish (Hoover, 2002). In these ways, Core has been exported and imported as the curricular embodiment of "American" culture, allowing its civilizing mission to extend beyond U.S. borders. Core's adoption internationally, a testimony to the naked hegemony of the United States, is likely viewed by Hirsch as indicative of the cosmopolitan character of its content and the importance of English as a shared language.

That schools in such different contexts could embrace Core Knowledge reveals the complex alliances that have been forming in the movement. Hirsch is quite aware of this situation, stating, "To be liked by the Bushies [Bush allies] and by the AFT [American Federation of Teachers]—there's something peculiar going on" (in Lindsay, 2001, p. W24). The reality is that Hirsch and the foundation have worked to build such affiliations. Hirsch's relationship with former AFT president Albert Shanker goes back to the mid-1980s. It was then that Shanker began praising Hirsch's newly articulated theory of cultural literacy as the means to greater educational equity, with the union later arguing that Core was a more promising reform for school improvement than vouchers (AFT, 2003; Lindsay, 2001). The AFT granted Hirsch the QuEST (quality educational standards) Award in 1997, and Sandra Feldman, past president of the AFT, accepted a seat on the Core Knowledge Foundation's board of trustees in 1998 (Marshall, 1997b, 1998a). Since that time, the AFT has become an upper-tier donor to the Core Knowledge Foundation (CKF, 2006a).

Moreover, scholars and members of historically marginalized groups were courted by the foundation, particularly after *Cultural Literacy* had been attacked for its Eurocentric content. For instance, Henry Louis Gates, professor of Humanities and Afro-American studies at Harvard and a "liberal pluralist" who is not fully at home with the cultural "hard left" or cultural "conservatives" on the right (see Gates, 1992), was invited to be on the Core Knowledge multicultural advisory committee (Hirsch, 1992b). In addition, the editorial assistance of Sterling Stuckey (1987), a leftist scholar of African American history, and the late Elizabeth Fox-Genovese, a scholar of women's history whose turn to neoconservatism made her "a pariah in feminist circles" (American Enterprise, 1996), was also solicited for the *What Your K-6 Grader Needs to Know Series* (Hirsch, 1991, Acknowledgments, Advisors on Multiculturalism). Yet the formation of such alliances has not been without rifts. James Farmer, the well-known founder and civil rights activist of a different CORE—the Congress of Racial Equality—was invited to speak at the 1996 National Conference. He underscored in his speech the idea that "we are bound together," then prompted Core Knowledge teachers and the foundation:

> What I'm asking for is something that maybe you have as a part of your curriculum. And that is a pluralistic culture. It's not difficult for a people in a society like ours to love themselves and at the same time join with others in loving their history and traditions. I . . . *urge you* to come together with me and us in *celebrating ourselves* as well as *you celebrate yourselves*. It's not difficult at all if people are taught that way. *Perhaps the teaching of that should also be part of the core curriculum* [italics added]. (1996, p. 2)

While Farmer's presence at the conference might be read as an endorsement of Core Knowledge—as suggested by Hirsch (1999b)—it may also be read as a challenge to more significantly incorporate the knowledge, culture, and history of oppressed groups into the curriculum rather than teaching children about the culture of more powerful groups only.

Equally telling, Richard Rodriguez, a noted Chicano author and lecturer, was welcomed to the conference the following year. In comparison to Farmer's talk, his speech emphasized that "assimilation happens." He declared to Core Knowledge advocates:

> This is not the voice I talked with in the first grade. It is not the way I sounded. This is *your* voice. This is the voice *you* shoved down my throat.... There was a time in my life I would describe myself as a minority and because of you I am not a minority in the cultural sense. (1997, p. 12)

Relegating his own language and culture to the "private" sphere, Rodriguez stressed the necessity of minority children embracing "public" culture, meaning dominant ways of speaking, acting, and knowing. He went on:

> There are lots of teachers in this bilingual, ebonics age that simply do not get the point that the point is not mere self-expression. The point is trying to get children to be able to speak in a way that other people can understand them. That is what we mean by "public school." (p. 13)

To a much more significant degree than Farmer, Rodriguez supported accommodating dominant culture rather than demanding cross-cultural literacy. The fact that both have given addresses at the conference highlights the varying ideological commitments that inform the movement and the tensions that characterize existing alliances. The foundation's desire to build such relationships is even more interesting when one recalls the aforementioned effort to translate the *What Your K-6 Grader Needs to Know Series* into Spanish for use alongside the English version (Hirsch & Holdren, 2001). Clearly, the force behind this intervention is more aligned with the views of Rodriguez than Farmer, though both have been welcomed under the canopy of Core Knowledge.

As Hirsch has noted, the canopy stretches far and wide. Efforts have been made by Hirsch and his supporters to invite not only parents and children into the Core coalition, but even those at the highest levels of government. In 1996, a cadre of individuals associated with Mathematically Correct issued a letter to President Bill Clinton, asserting, "There is every reason to believe that standards based on content and academics will be subverted before they ever reach the classrooms of America" (para. 2). Opposed to "whole math," a method that emphasizes conceptual understanding and exploratory problem-solving, this organization has called for ongoing drill and memorization of formulas—approaches that they believe have disappeared from schools. With such educational conditions in mind, the group implored Clinton:

> All we ask is that you, personally, read *The Schools We Need & Why We Don't Have Them*....It is our belief that in reading this book you will gain important insight into the gravity of the problem....We even believe that you will come to feel, as we do, that it is imperative that you bring E. D. Hirsch into your service to advise you directly. (para. 3–4)

A year later, Wayne Bishop, one of the undersigned and a math professor, analyzed at the Core Knowledge Foundation's request various math textbooks for their usefulness in teaching Core; those emphasizing heavy review and scripted teacher guides came out on top (Marshall, 1997f). These approaches are the same as those advocated by the "Bushies," who have been supporters of the educational forms endorsed by Hirsch and Mathematically Correct (Hoff, 2002).

Not surprisingly, Hirsch has spent some time building alliances in Washington, D.C., where in April 2003 he addressed the White House Forum on Civic Literacy and was honored at a dinner by Vice President Dick Cheney and his wife, Lynne Cheney. A few months later Hirsch returned, only this time for a celebration sponsored by the Center for Education Reform that was attended by then Secretary of Education Rod Paige, Florida Governor Jeb Bush, and John Walton of the Walton Family Foundation, a financial backer of Core Knowledge. Regarding these networking efforts, the Core Knowledge Foundation observes, "Hirsch continues to be our roving ambassador, promoting educational reform and seeking like-minded allies" (CKF, 2003e, p. 20).

Yet Hirsch himself has acknowledged that not all his allies are exactly like-minded. Careful attention to various streams within the movement reveals the uneasy fit often existing between diverse associates of Core. Henry Louis Gates and Lynne Cheney have both, at different points, associated themselves with Hirsch's educational campaign. Yet their positions on culture are by no means identical. Consider the following exchange during an interview of Gates by Cheney (1991):

Cheney: It seems to me that in fact the Western tradition is the opposite of narrow. I can't think of a culture in the whole history of mankind that has been more open to new ideas.

Gates: That's not true. This is where we disagree. Think of all that we've lost because of the pressure that immigrant groups felt to conform when they came to this country....We [African Americans, Italian immigrants, and Irish immigrants] had to conform to an imagined notion of unitary culture that was Anglo American.

Cheney: That's a paranoid view that there was some force out there making people conform.

Gates: There was.

Cheney: People wanted to conform.... Richard Rodriguez is the most eloquent person on this subject I know.... He writes about becoming a part of mainstream culture, and what he lost by that. The pain is enormous, but he doesn't doubt that he made the right choice. (p. 6)

On the theme of Western civilization, Cheney continues:

Cheney: I'm perfectly willing to talk about all of the flaws of Western culture, but in many ways I do view America, the international nation, as the ultimate flowering of Western culture because it has taken this idea of openness and brought it to a fruition that it's never experienced anywhere else in the world. It strikes me as such a noble and mighty thing that we've accomplished.

Gates: I think it's a noble and mighty ideal.... But the vision that you just described, I don't think we have yet realized.

Cheney: Of course not. But we have moved closer than any other society on the face of the earth.... (p. 7)

Gates: You come across as using a concern about what's good about Western culture to keep out heretofore excluded groups. (p. 8)

Cheney, Gates, Rodriguez, Farmer, Fox-Genovese, and Stuckey—all have associated with Core Knowledge despite their disagreements on the nature of American and Western culture and history. In much the same way, school communities in diverse contexts have opted for Core as the educational reform of choice.

How is it, then, that privileged suburbanites and low-income urban and rural communities, assimilationists and cultural pluralists, subaltern parents and state officials, the American Federation of Teachers and conservative foundations, and scholars and activists of various political stripes are brought together around Core Knowledge? Why is it, to use the words of Minnesota's Lieutenant Governor, that Core is "just common sense?" As we have seen, Core Knowledge is officially framed in terms of social mobility and civil rights, concerns central to subaltern groups. Beyond this, its curricular "coherence" offers a promising horizon for urban schools facing various challenges. The association of well-known people of color with Core—some of whom have quite moderate positions on culture and schooling—also gives the reform an air of respectability in marginalized communities. Moreover, poor communities and communities of color that have adopted Core are strategically highlighted by the foundation. The message is that Core has the interests of these groups at its center. All of this serves to shield the reform from criticisms of elitism and Eurocentrism and helps to further the foundation's agenda on this front.

Additionally, cultural restorationists in the government, with rightwing foundations, or on the ground in suburban school districts may also securely advocate Core—a reform partly premised on a defense of tradition and order. Those who believe the national heritage is "at risk" and even those who forward a rightist cultural agenda under the banner of "reliable research" and science find Core Knowledge a comfortable home. In these cases, however, the Foundation generally eschews directly propounding the classed and raced demands of such groups and uses instead democratically appealing language about common culture and national unity that masks the more coercive aspects of the reform.

AUTONOMY AND DISCIPLINE: CORE KNOWLEDGE IS THE "WHAT" AS WE LEAVE THE "HOW" TO YOU

The disparate social positioning of Core Knowledge advocates and the various interests being folded into movement are indeed "peculiar," as Hirsch points out. The tensions generated by this balance of forces within the movement should not be overlooked. After all, these diverse investments have led the foundation to redefine its relationship with Core Knowledge schools.

With the movement nearly a decade in the making, Hirsch (1998b) assured teachers that they were its vanguard rather than the foundation: "Core Knowledge has been from the start a *bottom-up not a top-down movement.... You've done it without coercion* and with dedication, and with ever-increasing numbers [italics added]" (pp. 1, 14). Guided by Core content guidelines, teachers across the nation have spent countless hours searching for relevant materials and developing original lesson plans, often sharing them with colleagues down the hall or at the annual meeting. Many of those plans have been placed on the foundation website (CKF, 2004e), and even compiled on "Share the Knowledge" CDs (CKF, 2004g). In the beginning, this work was essential because the content guidelines were virtually all that existed.

In a report (Datnow, Borman, & Stringfield, 2000) based on a three-year longitudinal study from 1995 to 1998 of the implementation of Core Knowledge in a national sample of schools (Stringfield, Datnow, Borman, & Rachuba, 1999)—a study solicited by the Core Knowledge Foundation—researchers indicated that implementing Core "promoted collegiality" as it "forced many teachers to work together, because they found that doing the necessary research, finding materials, and planning lessons were overwhelming if done alone" (p. 184). While teachers clearly experienced a heightened sense of professionalism and community due to collaboration, the intensification of labor was often exhausting. Interestingly, the liberty to plan lessons and choose teaching methods without foundation interference meant that many teachers did not view Core as prescriptive. In addition, many "uncritically accepted the content of the Core curriculum," so *Sequence* guidelines were not seen as restrictive (p. 185). In short, a delicate balance existed between the freedom to creatively collaborate and the immense labor that such an arrangement necessitated.

Although teachers reported that Core Knowledge enhanced levels of curricular coordination within the school, "this did not mean that all schools taught the content in exactly the same way." Rather, this relative autonomy, in diverse hands, led to interpretations of Core that fell outside the ambit of the official vision. One such example emerged during interviews with Core Knowledge students:

> All Core Knowledge schools are to teach fifth graders about Thomas Jefferson....At a school serving a majority African-American population, the students recalled that Jefferson fathered children with one of his slaves. However, students at a majority white school in a suburban area [said] that Jefferson was a hero. (Datnow et al., 2000, p. 183)

It is well-known that teachers mediate educational initiatives in their classrooms (Grant, 2001; Schweber, 2004), and the lesson plans independently developed by Core Knowledge teachers indicate that a degree of diversity has historically prevailed when Core content is taught. Teaching in Marlinton Middle School, a rural school in West Virginia, an educator concerned about her students' relative cultural isolation and the presence of a nearby neo-Nazi compound concentrated heavily on the content guidelines pertaining to the Civil Rights movement—a curricular intervention intended to counter the influence of white supremacists on her students. In another case, a teacher at Platte River Academy in suburban Colorado created a unit on the United States Constitution for second graders, one that celebrated the nation's founders and downplayed the exclusions and inequities that shaped the Constitution and characterized the period (Buras, 2004).

In a similar way, Core schools differ in the constitution of their programs, with some schools solely teaching Core Knowledge and others blending it with alternative curricular initiatives. At the American Horse School (Hammock, 2004) on the Pine Ridge Indian Reservation in South Dakota, for instance, Core is taught alongside a Lakota studies and language program. Moreover, Coral Way Elementary School in Miami has adopted Core as part of a broader two-way bilingual, bicultural program, offering "a welcoming gesture to the cultural and linguistic diversity that has become the trademark of South Florida" (Pellerano, Fradd, & Rovira, 1998, p. 3). By comparison, Hobbs Municipal Schools in New Mexico have adopted Core districtwide with Accelerated English and Saxon Phonics programs as area schools are increasingly populated by low-income, Latino/a students. And although Core's world history content on Mexico receives some appreciation in Hobbs, classical music by Mozart and the ancient Greeks and Romans appear to be the more important curricular themes, at least officially (Rounds, 2004). In these ways, Core has been recontextualized at the local level with the framing of and emphasis on particular content often varying across sites.

An array of teaching methods have also been discovered in Core Knowledge schools despite Hirsch's insistence on the dangers of progressive education, the foundation's corresponding advocacy of direct instruction in its newsletter, and the proliferation of vendors selling direct instruction programs at the national conference (Hirsch, 1996; Buras, 1999b, 2004). The schools reported on by Datnow et al. (2000) utilized not only direct instruction, but also "project teaching, more hands-on, build-it, create-it types of teaching, and less dependence on textbooks than ever," as one teacher put it (p. 183). Though many Core Knowledge schools have adopted Core and direct instruction, this is not the case universally. The foundation has been willing to compromise on this point, strategically emphasizing to teachers: "Core Knowledge is the 'what.' We leave the 'how' to you" (Buras, 2004). The more serious concern has been deviation from and particular interpretations of Core content—all of which was encouraged by the historic lack of standardized resources to accompany content guidelines.

Disparate implementation *levels* across sites were also discovered, meaning that Core Knowledge schools often failed to teach all of the specified content (Datnow et al., 2000). This finding was used by researchers to explain differences in student achievement across Core Knowledge schools. Scores on standardized tests and researcher-developed Core Knowledge tests, they stressed, were lower at schools where implementation was less consistent and complete. Most important, the researchers concluded that failure to fully implement Core Knowledge at least partially resulted from "limited supportive structures, with respect to implementation guidelines, lesson plans and materials, and staff development" (p. 188). None of this went unheeded by the Core Knowledge Foundation.

THE REMAKING OF A MOVEMENT

Prior to 1998, Core Knowledge schools by no means existed independent of the foundation, but they did have a *measure of relative autonomy*. There was indeed something to Hirsch's acknowledgment, "You've done it without coercion," but it was becoming increasingly apparent that some schools were not doing it fully or appropriately. In recent years, various disciplinary mechanisms—Core Knowledge history textbooks and teacher guides, teacher handbooks, refined foundation requirements for Core schools, Core curriculum-referenced tests (CKF, 2004a, n.d.), achievement data collection (Telling, 2003), and a nascent elementary teacher education reform initiative (CKF, 2002)—have begun to take shape as the foundation seeks to redefine its relationship to Core teachers and schools.

By early 1999, the foundation had announced its intent to develop a K–6 history and geography textbook series (Marshall, 1999b). Edited by Hirsch (2002), the series, which will be analyzed in the next chapter, covers the history and geography of the United States and various parts of the world, and includes teacher guides with objectives, activity recommendations, review questions, handouts, and unit assessments. Regarding the decision to produce the textbooks, the foundation explains:

> Since teachers first examined the *Core Knowledge Sequence* in 1990, almost invariably they asked, "Where are the books and other materials to help me teach all these topics?" Over the years, an informal body of materials has accumulated.... Hundreds of schools across the nation have implemented Core Knowledge programs with little more than an intrepid spirit, the willingness to create their own lesson plans, and the tenacity to acquire what they can from existing materials. Other schools, however, have hesitated... without a more familiarly packaged set of materials. Primarily in response to the growing demand from these schools, the foundation has enlisted Pearson Learning to produce a comprehensive program supporting Core Knowledge. (Marshall, 1999b, p. 2)

Through such textbooks, both new and veteran Core Knowledge teachers might be supported and disciplined at the very same time.

In addition to history textbooks, the Core Knowledge Foundation—using a grant from the Walton Family Foundation—created "a six-volume set of Core Knowledge Teacher Handbooks, providing solid, accurate content for every subject taught according to the *Sequence*, plus advice on how to teach that content" (Hitchcock, 2002, p. 6). The handbooks, the first of which made its debut in 2004 (e.g., CKF, 2004d), contain introductory essays on Core content written for teachers, indicate what students need to learn, specify relevant vocabulary for both teachers and students, suggest the amount of time that should be spent on various topics, and provide teaching suggestions, review questions, and activities. The foundation has also produced a *Day-by-Day Planner* for teachers (Buras, 2004). These more definitive resources exist alongside the aforementioned Baltimore Curriculum Project, which drafted lesson plans for all Core content. Many of these plans include specific directions for what teachers should do and say when teaching a given lesson and Core schools are encouraged to use them (CKF, 2003d, see Obtain and Document the Provision of Necessary Materials; Baltimore Curriculum Project, 2004a, 2004b).

It is noteworthy that after the first Core Knowledge school opened in 1990, its principal Connie Jones (1991) emphasized:

> Our teachers were pleased with the *amount of independence and autonomy* that the *Core Knowledge Sequence* afforded them. . . . Selection and use of resources and materials were *completely at the discretion of the teachers*. . . . [We] decided to "take the plunge" and implement the program with no guides or materials in hand. . . . Our faculty *would not look favorably on publication of a strict Core Knowledge textbook with teacher's guides*; we found that one of the *most exciting and rewarding aspects of this program was the creativity* that the teachers brought to it [italics added]. (p. 10)

Clearly, autonomy, creativity, and associated (even burdensome) labor were factors that these teachers balanced against the ease and regimentation that highly standardized curricula often bring. Whatever the case, one thing is certain—Jones's words foreshadowed the tension between autonomy and discipline that currently haunts the movement. Core Knowledge textbooks with teacher's guides *have* been published, along with other standardized resources. The question becomes the degree to which these materials will exercise disciplinary influence.

In 2004, these tensions surfaced at the national conference. On one hand, many teachers were quite vocal about their desire for more Core

Knowledge resources, including subject area textbooks and teacher handbooks. The fact that the majority of existing Core resources address the elementary grades caused a near uprising of middle school teachers who begged the foundation at one session to end their ongoing "scramble" for materials by producing more texts for the seventh and eighth grades. One teacher challenged, "Why doesn't the *Grader Series* include the middle grades?" On the other hand, concerns were expressed about the ways that standardized Core resources might erode teacher autonomy and creativity. "With all these resources," a teacher asked during a session on teacher handbooks, "will our unit writing and conference presentations be negated?" In response, teachers were directed by the foundation to view such texts as "resources" and to retain their own lesson plans and "professional judgment." During another session on the Pearson Learning-Core Knowledge history and geography textbooks, some teachers uttered aloud "thank you" as the books were discussed; others expressed anxieties regarding the implications of the project. One foundation representative pointed out that two factions existed within the movement, explaining, "Old timers who had few resources in the beginning have been opposed to the texts; some have been won over. Another group, largely consisting of newcomers, wants this support." To complicate matters, proclamations by the foundation about respect for teacher autonomy are not the whole picture. The same representative commented that although use of Core texts is not required— except in Core Knowledge schools participating in the Comprehensive School Reform program—the foundation believes teachers "should use them if they are serious about Core Knowledge." Another representative offered further clarification on the status of these texts in Core Knowledge schools: "We don't want to use the word *required* with a capital *R*. But we would like to say that they are *strongly* recommended, with a capital *S*" (Buras, 2004).

Indeed, the foundation has mandated that schools comply with increasingly rigorous implementation and reporting standards in order to gain recognition. Previous to August 2003, a school could be either a "friend of Core Knowledge" or an "official Core Knowledge school." Status as a friend, which required an initial and annually updated two-page profile, allowed the foundation to welcome interested schools into the network. Official schools, by comparison, documented at least an 80% implementation level through self-report and submitted a year-long plan that outlined the coverage of Core content and its integration with state standards (CKF, 2003c).

Since August 2003, the process for acquiring recognition by the foundation has changed. A school may now qualify as either a friend or an official school, but the criteria are more elaborate. To become a "visitation site"—a new designation—a school *must* participate in three years of professional development through the foundation, *fully* implement the curriculum, and agree to *site visits* by foundation representatives. This kind of school is strongly encouraged to utilize Core Knowledge history and geography textbooks, Baltimore Curriculum Project lesson plans, and other Core resources and is considered a "model" by the foundation. Official schools still abide by earlier requirements, but *must* now participate in foundation-sponsored professional development (with waivers sometimes available for preexisting official schools after an implementation analysis and follow-up visit by the foundation). Schools are still welcomed to continue or establish themselves as friends of Core, but their status is less highly regarded as implementation standards have been raised (CKF 2003b, 2003c, 2004b).

Regarding these changes, the foundation (CKF, 2003b) stresses:

> Regretfully, *some* schools may be referring to themselves as Core Knowledge schools without adhering to the *Sequence* and our standards. It is important for us (and you!) to have in-person verification of the great work that goes into implementing the Core Knowledge curriculum effectively. By personally visiting your site and working closely with you, we can enhance your prestige. (see Why Are We Asking)

By instituting new standards, the foundation has attempted to acquire greater control over how and the degree to which Core is taught and has sought to distinguish those schools most aligned with its vision of Core from other, less disciplined schools. And while the mantra that Core is only supposed to constitute 50% of the curriculum is an oft-repeated one, the reality is that Core, when fully implemented, consumes more time than teachers and students have available. Those schools hoping to incorporate what Hirsch calls "local" interests (e.g., content on subaltern groups) will have to sacrifice something from Core—a choice that is bound to dissatisfy the foundation. As it stands, the foundation has even begun providing additional training for existing and new Core Knowledge principals, particularly since "studies of Core Knowledge implementation have provided useful information about the common characteristics of high-performing Core Knowledge schools," including "the presence of a strong instructional leader who supports his or her teachers in their efforts to fully implement the *Sequence*" (Siler, 2001b, p. 14).

A Core Knowledge testing program is yet another innovation in the foundation's monitoring process, one tied not only to discipline but efforts to enhance the legitimacy of Core as an educational reform. The foundation explains that it "accepts the need for accountability... and believes that Core Knowledge schools need some objective way of measuring how effectively they are teaching the *Sequence*" (CKF, n.d., para. 1). The Core Knowledge-TASA curriculum-referenced tests are one such measure; they cover grades 1–5 and assess Core content in history and geography, language arts, math, and science. They are untimed tests administered at the end of the school year and are graded by TASA Scoring Services (CKF, 2004a). Should test results be unsatisfactory, the foundation "stands ready" with assistance, as "no school will ever be criticized or embarrassed... because of its test results" (CKF, n.d., para. 5). Quite naturally, the foundation would not wish to advertise Core Knowledge schools with low scores. At the same time, the foundation's helpful stance starkly contrasts with high-stakes state accountability regimes—another point for Core Knowledge on the school reform scoreboard. Though the tests are presently required only for Core Knowledge schools funded through Comprehensive School Reform, the importance of raising and documenting performance on these tests is important to the foundation and it is likely that their administration will be a requirement for obtaining visitation and official school status in the future (CKF, 2003d, see Establish Program Evaluation Plan).

One perplexing issue related to the tests is part of the foundation's explanation for creating them. The foundation clarifies, "Most state or district mandated assessments are tests of general knowledge or achievement. Useful, but not directly related to the subject matter outlined in the *Core Knowledge Sequence*" (CKF, 2004a, para. 3). In light of Hirsch's (1996, 1998b) claim that Core Knowledge represents "general knowledge," one wonders why state or district assessments which test "general knowledge" would *not* be directly related to Core. This inconsistency should lead us to reflect more deeply on the foundation's motivations for generating and collecting this specific test data. It appears that while administration of the Core Knowledge exams may at some point exert pressure on Core Knowledge teachers, they may serve the more immediate need of securing and maintaining legitimacy for the reform.

A few studies (Davis, 2003), some of questionable empirical validity, have been done to examine student achievement in Core Knowledge schools, but they have generally relied on state and national tests. The foundation does encourage Core schools to collect and submit these kinds of test data and has even developed forms on which standardized state and national test results can be recorded. A school might pursue any number of options, the foundation suggests, such as the collection of data that compares the Core Knowledge school to schools with similar demographics or with other district or state schools. A "matched pair design" study is even encouraged (Telling, 2003). Advocacy of this kind of data collection and educational "research" is fully aligned with definitions of "scientifically-based research" embedded in the No Child Left Behind Act and the Institute of Educational Sciences (Education Department, n.d.; Shavelson & Towne, 2002). This certainly helps to substantiate the foundation's process. At the same time, if standardized test scores are not to the foundation's liking, then perhaps the Core Knowledge-TASA test scores will provide the data needed to boost Core's prestige on the national education agenda—all the while functioning as a means for monitoring the implementation of the Core curriculum.

Even without substantial data of this kind, Core has been sold as a "research-based" reform. Hirsch ensured teachers at the national meeting in 2004, "The Core Knowledge movement is based on deep principles that really have been established by the best scientists" (Buras, 2004; see also Hirsch, 2006). What is meant by "best science," however, is the foundation's understanding of research in cognitive psychology and neurophysiology, alongside measurements of educational performance that are standardized and solely quantitative in nature. Collecting this "scientific" data is nonetheless a rising priority for the foundation, and Core Knowledge schools will be increasingly expected to provide it (CKF, 2003d; see also Wang, Haertel, & Walberg, 1997).

WHAT ELEMENTARY TEACHERS NEED TO KNOW

The foundation would like to create a cadre of Core Knowledge teachers, not only by issuing resources that will potentially direct teacher implementation of Core, but through plans to influence preservice teachers in schools of education. In a letter to the editor of *Common Knowledge*, Thomas Berg, a professor of education at the University of Northern Iowa, reflected in 1999 on the influence of Hirsch's work on his student teachers. These student teachers, he regrets, are enrolled in "a teacher education program...that has been influenced by many of the current 'innovative' theories about which Professor Hirsch has been thoroughly critical." Berg goes on to argue:

> We must establish teacher education programs that will prepare our graduates to develop cultural literacy.... The Core Knowledge movement currently exists, by and large, outside of the institutions which can do the most to implement the changes that are needed. The time has come to...begin to develop model teacher

education programs which prepare our students to develop Core Knowledge in their own classrooms. (p. 8)

Funded by the conservative John M. Olin Foundation, the Core Knowledge Foundation demonstrated its agreement with Berg's assessment by coordinating the development of eighteen college course outlines detailing "What Elementary Teachers Need to Know" (CKF, 2002; Davis, 2002; Hitchcock, 2002). None of the syllabi are for courses in education—a decision based on Hirsch's belief that progressivism in schools of education has sacrificed academic content by focusing on child-centered pedagogy. The syllabi radically recenter the allegedly displaced content by specifying what elementary teachers need to know in history and geography, composition and grammar, literature, biology, chemistry, and math. The foundation (2002) explains:

> This program is premised on the belief that what teachers need ... is a detailed knowledge of the subjects they intend to teach.... Pedagogy might be addressed ... by incorporating a pedagogical element into the subject-area courses. If the pedagogy courses are added on [as separate courses], there will probably not be room for too many of them, since so many hours will need to be spent on the subject areas. (p. 8)

The pedagogical element recommended for subject-area courses would be a "mini-practicum" where "future teachers" could focus on "translating an adult's knowledge of a subject into an effective teachable unit for young children" (p. 9). In some institutions, the foundation explains, arts and sciences professors could organize, supervise, and assess the practicum without education faculty; another scenario would be a collaborative effort between arts and sciences faculty who would teach the content area and education faculty who would oversee the practicum—a sort of "lab period" attached to the lecture part of the subject-area course.

The foundation acknowledges that existing teacher education programs may wish to supplement subject-area courses with "select courses in pedagogy, class management, child development, and educational theory." In the case of pedagogy courses, the foundation stresses that they should be "grounded in principles derived from cognitive psychology and research" (CKF, 2002, p. 4). Regarding educational theory courses, the foundation "would be pleased if [those] required as part of the program included consideration of some of the writings of E. D. Hirsch," though Hirsch's work "might be taught in tandem with other, possibly dissenting voices in education" (p. 9). Clearly, the foundation's teacher education program has been developed against the specter of educational progressivism; it is marked by Hirsch's call for "solid content" and his critique of skill-based and child-centered education.

Seeking to strengthen ties between teacher education programs and Core Knowledge, the foundation suggests that institutions of higher education might ask, "Are there Core Knowledge schools or other schools in the area that might be willing to partner with the...university and provide sites for students teaching?" Universities may even inquire, "Would it be worthwhile for students in the program to have, as a culminating experience, some training provided by the Core Knowledge Foundation?" (2002, p. 11). Cleary, the foundation aims to extend its realm of influence by contributing to the establishment of a corps of Core Knowledge teachers.

To promote this agenda, the foundation sponsored several ads in the *Chronicle of Higher Education*. This led the foundation to join Boston University School of Education in applying for a grant to support a trial of the program. The grant was not obtained, but had it been, the university planned to partner with the Chelsea Independent School District, which would have been "the laboratory for seeing how the new teacher training would prepare teachers for real classroom settings" (CKF, 2003e, p. 15). Meanwhile, "institutions using or considering using the syllabi" are asked to notify the foundation, so it "can assess the distribution and spread of the syllabi" (CKF, 2002, p. 5). In due time, the foundation seeks to discipline not only existing Core Knowledge teachers, but those who will become teachers. By inculcating preservice teachers with "appropriate" content through a program that is nothing short of a *Core Knowledge Sequence* for elementary and middle school educators, the foundation hopes the nation's students will be more likely to learn the specified knowledge.

IMPLICATIONS

This combination of mechanisms—textbooks, teacher handbooks, new implementation standards, tests, and even a nascent teacher education initiative—is intended to reshape the Core Knowledge movement. The influence of these interventions on the balance between autonomy and discipline is of central importance. Core Knowledge teachers appreciate a level of independence and professional respect, but the historic lack of Core resources has contributed to the intensification of their labor. The foundation wants to win the consent of diverse communities and mobilize widely, but curricular deviance must be managed and disciplined if the official vision is to be more fully realized. Taken together, these recent initiatives will likely heighten the foundation's ability to steer the movement, even if at a distance. This leads me to suggest that the balance of forces in the movement and the overall political character of this reform will most reflect neoconservative imperatives. Consider the following:

- Although Core content guidelines are sufficiently canonical, the initial lack of Core Knowledge resources created a space for more radically inclusive mediations of the curriculum. The greater the availability of Core resources that standardize the delivery of content, the more likely the implementation of Core will align with official aspirations, especially in those class-rooms and schools in which teachers heavily depend on those resources. The fact that the Core Knowledge Foundation has partnered with Pearson Learning to produce and distribute Pearson Learning-Core Knowledge History and Geography Textbooks (Hirsch, 2002) speaks to the potentially pervasive use of such resources in Core classrooms. In fact, the Ameri-can Textbook Council (2006), which provides information on textbook adoptions, noted Core textbooks among the most widely adopted elementary social studies texts in the nation. In 2006, moreover, the Core Knowledge Foundation organized a Core Knowledge National Sales Conference to mobilize "a full-fledged [commission-based] sales force bringing the Core Knowledge message and materials to schools nationwide" (Garvin-Kester, 2006b). Based on budgetary considerations, the effort to "represent Core Knowledge publications on the national textbook market" will begin in Chicago and New York City, but will likely be expanded if those cities respond as anticipated (CKF, 2006a).
- The intensification of labor associated with implementing the curriculum independent of Core resources, combined with the overall lack of elementary-level resources pertaining to Core's literary and historical content, will likely engender greater dependence on Core Knowledge resources.
- In light of new implementation standards, the closer a school is tied to the Core Knowledge Foundation and the higher its status (friend, official, or model), the more disciplined will be its implementation of the curriculum. The foundation's agenda may differ in significant ways from a school's agenda, but the foundation is the certifying institution and it is guided

by a rather particular understanding of what counts as Core Knowledge.

At the very same time, however, existing tensions within the Core Knowledge movement might actually increase as the foundation pushes forward its managerial effort. Thus, while greater discipline may render the movement more unified and even more neoconservative in character—potentially taming more progressive elements—it may also weaken the movement by compromising the commitment of particular communities to Core for reasons ideological, cultural, or professional in nature. For example, schools that seek to blend Core with parallel cultural programs may come to find Core too restrictive in its implementation requirements. Alternatively, teachers who embraced Core because of the flexibility it allowed and creativity it inspired may come to see Core as just another standardizing reform in an age of accountability and withdraw their support. Rightist multiculturalism—that is, the effort to engineer a compromise that simultaneously satisfies the neoconservative agenda while also authentically appealing to subaltern groups *and* ensuring that their investments conform to particular exigencies—is a delicate and thorny process; unfortunately, it is one for which neoconservatives may be particularly prepared in light of historic roots, which have produced an "in-between" politics suited for striking compromises and building alliances.

Of course, we should not assume that neoconservative commitments and those of subaltern groups are always at odds. As I and others have argued, the politics of traditionally marginalized groups are often contradictory, retrogressive in particular ways, or even staunchly conservative (Apple & Buras, 2006; Buras, 2007a, 2007b; Dillard, 2001; Dyson, 2005). As such, the level of compromise required to bring such groups into neoconservative-inspired reform efforts may be less than expected. Recall here the African American principal who applauded Core Knowledge and expressed relief that the students of color in her urban school were studying the "classics" rather than Afrocentric curricula.

Core Knowledge history textbooks (Hirsch, 2002), which I analyze in the next chapter, must be understood in light of the movement's trajectory and emerging managerial impulses. It is crucial to determine precisely how Core content gets constructed in these materials, which will be used ever more widely, and to think about how the texts might appeal to disparate groups.

4

THE DISUNITING OF AMERICA'S HISTORY
Core Knowledge and the National Past

People who have called this approach a collection of "mere facts" or called it names such as "Eurocentric" and "elitist" have not bothered to find out just what is in the Core Knowledge Sequence.

E. D. Hirsch in *Common Knowledge*, the newsletter of the Core Knowledge Foundation (2001a, pp. 3–4)

Writing in the *Harvard Educational Review* [Kristen Buras], accused Hirsch of posing "serious threats to a social order already unjust and unequal." Apparently the theorists who attack Hirsch completely ignore the substantial content on ethnic minorities to be found in the Core Knowledge Curricular Sequence.

Lucien Ellington and Jana Eaton in the Thomas B. Fordham Foundation book, *Where Did the Social Studies Go Wrong?* (Leming, Ellington, & Porter, 2003, p. 83)

Written history is always more than merely innocent story-telling, precisely because it is the primary vehicle for the distribution and use of power.

Alun Munslow in *Deconstructing History* (1997, p. 13)

THE FACTS OF HISTORY

In 1926, HISTORIAN CARL BECKER provocatively asked, "What are historical facts?" Responding to this question before the American

Historical Association, he articulated a tenet that challenges the philosophy of history embraced by so many neoconservatives today:

> The present influences our idea of the past, and our idea of the past influences the present. We are accustomed to say that "the present is the product of all the past."...But it is only a half truth. It is equally true...to say that the past (our imagined picture of it) is the product of all the present. We build our conceptions of history partly out of our present needs and purposes. (1955, p. 337)

Although Becker made his remarks nearly a century ago, they remain at the center of debates around the production of historical knowledge. Indeed, the assertion that present-day contexts and competing ideologies shape the writing of "legitimate" history is one often vehemently denied by traditional, or modernist, historians and their neoconservative allies in education. Hirsch (1996) argues that education is a technical rather than a political matter, and that the "facts" of history "are not and should not be subjects of controversy" (p. 37). Yet clearly, neoconservatives have engaged in a cultural politics focused on defending particular conceptions of the national past against the perceived threat of "ethnic loyalism" and forms of so-called divisive multiculturalism (Hirsch, 1992b; Leming, Ellington, & Porter, 2003) as well as the alleged danger posed by relatively recent developments in historiography, including both new histories from below and postmodernist histories (Himmelfarb, 2004). In 2004, the United States Department of Education "destroyed more than 300,000 copies of a booklet designed for parents to help their children learn history after [Lynne Cheney] complained that it mentioned the National Standards for History, which she has long opposed" because they are "not positive enough about America's achievements and paid too little attention to figures such as General Robert E. Lee, Paul Revere and Thomas Edison." For Cheney, the history standards, sometimes used to guide textbook development, represented "politicized history" (Alonso-Zaldivar & Merl, 2004, p. 1). Her complaints and the actions of the Department of Education were not viewed, by comparison, as an ideological intervention.

The above episode is not an anomaly. Just 2 years later, Florida Governor Jeb Bush signed an omnibus education bill into law (H.B. 7087e3) that provided the following mandate for teaching history in public schools:

> American history shall be viewed as factual, not as constructed, shall be viewed as knowable, teachable, and testable, and shall be defined as the creation of a new nation based largely on the uni-

versal principles stated in the Declaration of Independence. (cited in American Historical Association, 2007, para. 1)

Even more striking is the dictate embodied in an earlier version of the bill, which was removed from the final version: "The history of the United States shall be taught as genuine history and shall not follow the revisionist or postmodernist viewpoints of relative truth" (para. 2). In this case, history is again asserted to be a straightforward and uncontested account of the past—one, notably, that aligns with the "universal principles" stated in the Declaration (which stipulated, it is often forgotten, that "whenever any Form of Government becomes destructive of [unalienable rights], it is the Right of the People to alter or abolish it"). Apparently, the people do not have the right to alter particular views of the past, at least not without being called ideologues, revisionists, or relativists. Those defending the "facts" are again portrayed as non-constructionist and genuine.

All of this speaks to a series of ongoing debates in historiography, a field that cannot be disconnected from classrooms, including Core classrooms, where such work influences what students learn and do not learn about the past. It is instructive therefore to consider the development of these debates. A good part of the conflict is over what constitutes historical fact as well as what constitutes legitimate historical scholarship. In *The Disuniting of America: Reflection on a Multicultural Society*, Arthur Schlesinger (1992) asserted:

> The Anglocentric domination of schoolbooks was based in part on unassailable facts. For better or for worse, American history has been shaped more than anything else by British tradition and culture.... To deny this perhaps lamentable but hardly disputed fact would be to falsify history. (p. 53)

He had more to say along these same lines, which I share in order to make a fundamental point about the epistemological nature of the conflict:

> It may be too bad that dead white European males have played so large a role in shaping our culture. But that's the way it is. One cannot erase history. These humdrum historical facts, and not some dastardly imperialist conspiracy, explain the Eurocentric slant in American schools. (p. 122)

Regarding those who contend that these "unassailable" and "humdrum" facts are better understood as evidence of European male hegemony in knowledge production than a reflection of historical truth and who challenge such facts by writing women's history or advocating Afrocentric history, for example, the following warnings are offered:

> The ethnic enclaves [have] developed a compensatory literature. Inspired by group resentment and pride, this literature very often succumbed to the Platonic temptation of "noble lies." (p. 55)

> Cultural pluralism is not the issue. Nor is the teaching of Afro-American or African history the issue; of course these are legitimate subjects.... The issue is the kind of history that.... Afrocentric ideologues propose for American children. The issue is the teaching of *bad* history under whatever ethnic banner. One argument for organizing the school curriculum around Africa is that black Africa is the birthplace of science, philosophy, religion, medicine, technology, of the great achievements that have been wrongly ascribed to Western civilization. But is this in fact true? (pp. 75–75)

> The use of history as therapy means the corruption of history as history. (p. 93)

> Formulating these critiques as a question, Schlesinger asks: "Is it really a good idea to teach minority children myths—at least to teach myths as facts?" (p. 80)

His final conclusion is quite clear:

> Our schools and colleges have a responsibility to teach history for its own sake—as part of the intellectual equipment of civilized persons—and not to degrade history by allowing its contents to be dictated by pressure groups, whether political, economic, religious or ethnic.... If we now repudiate the quite marvelous inheritance that history bestows on us, we invite the fragmentation of the national community into a quarrelsome spatter of enclaves, ghettos, tribes. (Schlesinger, 1992, pp. 137–138)

Schlesinger's comments reflect a rather intense history of exchanges that are at their root about issues of epistemology, historical consciousness, and the character and reality of the past. For him and other neoconservative defenders of tradition, histories from below—that is, histories centered on long-ignored aspects of the past as experienced by oppressed groups—threaten to balkanize and disunite the nation. Even worse, according to this contingent, this kind of history threatens to mythologize the past by presenting falsehoods as facts. In the end, new histories from below do not represent "real" history. They instead degrade the nobility of the discipline and compromise the stability of the nation.

A decade after the publication of Schlesinger's now classic diatribe, Sheldon Stern—an historian who developed the U.S. history syllabus for the Core Knowledge Foundation's (2002) teacher education initiative—issued a report card for the Thomas B. Fordham Foundation on state standards for U.S. history. He had the following to say about the nature of the old history and the alleged monopoly of the new:

> The once-dominant approach to the American past, which disregarded or trivialized the lives and contributions of women and minorities, has been replaced for some time now by a new, more inclusive and diverse history....
>
> However, instead of correcting yesterday's distortions by presenting a balanced and complete national history for American students, state standards and curricula often replace old distortions with new ones. In classrooms all over the U.S., the struggle to include those previously excluded has frequently produced an equal and opposite reaction...requiring the exclusion of those previously included. Today's students can readily identify Sacajawea and Harriet Tubman but often can barely discuss Washington or Jefferson—except as slave owners. Political history has been all but abandoned in American schools and textbooks, but politically correct distortions, half-truths, omissions, and lies are thriving. (Stern et al., 2003, p. 13)

It is quite plain that Schlesinger's assertions continue to powerfully resonate with neoconservatives and remain the bedrock of the foundations with which they affiliate.

I could explain these tensions over "good" and "bad" history or "fact" and "fiction" by outlining the various theories of historical knowledge that feature prominently in the philosophy of history. Alun Munslow (1997) does a fine job of this when he responds to the question: Can empiricism legitimately constitute history as a separate epistemology? Each school of thought naturally presents a different answer. The *reconstructionist* approach is founded on the notion that "the historian's work is the 'rational, independent, and impartial investigation' of the documents of the past" (p. 20). In short, writing history is understood as an empirical act that has little to do with present-day concerns or ideology; historians, simply put, can reconstruct the past through direct access to archival records unmediated by interpretation. This approach most characterizes Hirsch's position. In comparison, the *constructionist* approach, often associated with various forms of new history, presumes that the historian's "beliefs and commitments cannot be suspended, but that this does not diminish the value of our historical understanding"

(p. 24). In fact, writing history in this tradition is often part of a broader political commitment to oppressed groups; such practitioners acknowledge their role in constructing history, while also respecting general standards of evidence. Finally, the *deconstructionist* approach, usually identified with postmodernist modes of history, is yoked to the idea that "there is no ultimate knowable historical truth, that our knowledge of the past is social and perspectival." Notions such as "real-unreal, fact-fiction, truth-untruth" are believed to have little relevance since language can never do more than imperfectly signify and mediate our access to the realities "out there" (pp. 25–26).

Again, exploring these theories and discerning their implications for the writing of history are crucial tasks. Some of this will be undertaken later in the chapter after analyzing Core Knowledge textbooks. To go no further, after all, would imply that these debates are "merely" theoretical. They are not. If we are to truly grasp not only the debates but the historical forces and contexts that gave rise to the narratives embodied in Core textbooks, we must at least briefly investigate the whirlwind of events and struggles that have affected both the *making* and *writing* of history since the 1950s. In doing so, we may come to see that accounts of the past endorsed by neoconservatives, including those accounts in Core, are far more politicized than acknowledged.

HISTORIES OLD AND NEW

Consensus is a word often used by neoconservatives. Daniel Patrick Moynihan, as you may remember, originally suggested that *The Public Interest* be called *Consensus* to convey the belief that policy making required only technical knowledge rather than "ideological" maneuvering and argument. Similarly, Hirsch believes that the process of reaching consensus on a body of shared knowledge should not generate significant discordance. These sentiments are not unlike dominant understandings of history in the 1950s. Most historians of the period engaged in writing *consensus history*, which emphasized "continuity" and "stability" and portrayed the United States as "a relatively homogeneous society with a relatively conservative history" (Wiener, 1989, p. 402).

This epistemological orientation was undoubtedly encouraged during the era of McCarthyism, which powerfully influenced the discipline of history. As historian Jonathan Wiener (1989) explains:

> The attack on radicals and radical ideas proved to be effective in intimidating academics.... A chill spread across the intellectual landscape: avoiding controversy became prudent.... Faculty mem-

bers played it safe, avoiding topics in their teaching and research that might arouse the red hunters. The institutions of the history profession took part in the anticommunist hysteria. (p. 404)

Consensus history was the "old history" (not red, but red, white, and blue), and thus its predispositions were only exacerbated as the Cold War began. Nonetheless, by the late 1950s a second wave of "new history" emerged as "intellectuals leaving the Communist party joined with leading independent radical scholars" (p. 405); the first wave had officially begun just before the turn-of-the-twentieth-century under James Harvey Robinson (1912; Stearns, 1993) and was continued by his student, Charles Beard, although outside the halls of academia a competing tradition existed much earlier, as evidenced by Frederick Douglass' *Narrative*. The new history was not the man's but the lion's history. At the University of Wisconsin-Madison in 1959, students studying with historian William Appleman Williams, including now well-known critical education scholar Stanley Aronowitz, founded *Studies on the Left*—an organ of the new history. Its student editors proclaimed that existing notions of "objectivity" conveyed the view of "the scholar satisfied with—or browbeaten by—things as they are" (in Wiener, 1989, p. 408). The founders of another new history journal, *Radical America*, would describe the profession of history as "a gentlemen's clubhouse" with an "upper-class tone" and a penchant for "dry monographs, usually accessible only to other historians...and patriotic textbooks, written in a manner that is very careful not to disturb anyone's comfortable notions about the status quo" (in Wiener, p. 425). Clearly this cohort articulated a view of history that chafed against the dominant disciplinary paradigm, one they argued only served corporate leaders and other powerful segments.

The most significant impetus for writing the new history, however, was the new history that was *being made*. Indeed:

> The rise of the antiwar movement, the civil rights movement in the South, and the wave of ghetto rebellions...shattered the consensus school's assumption that in the United States the fundamental problems had been solved..... [Such opposition] suggested a different sense of how history was made: not simply by elites, from the top down, but in the interaction of social groups holding power in different forms.

Befittingly, the second wave of new history would be dubbed "history from the bottom up," and it took much of its cue from these grassroots movements (Wiener, 1989, pp. 412–413).

The new history evoked quite a strong reaction from traditional historians wedded to the old consensus history. The *American Historical Review*—among the most preeminent journals in the field—published scathing critiques of the work being done by practitioners of the new history. A groundbreaking book by Linda Gordon in women's history provoked a reviewer to clarify, for instance, that "history and political polemics have different rules" and to bluntly conclude "this is not history" (in Wiener, 1989, pp. 426–427). Yet another piece in the journal was dedicated solely to attacking the radical new histories and their authors, who were said to have "a contempt for pure history," which should be "allowed to speak for itself." Such work was said to have emerged not from "the natural dialogue of the discipline," but from "the outside cultural and political world" (p. 428).

It is not difficult to see the origins of the critiques raised by Schlesinger and others about what counts as historical fact and as history. Early on, new histories were written off as ideological constructions compromised by present-day preoccupations and politics. Not without irony, Schlesinger's own book, *The Vital Center*, which was mentioned in chapter 1, was itself a contributor to the anticommunist ethos of the 1950s. This fact should cause pause in light of his call for objectivity in the profession and his attack on politicized tracts that pollute the discipline. It appears that traditional, reconstructionist historians are more constructive than they imagine. Whatever the case, the new history slowly gained greater parlance among traditionalists, with Richard Hofstadter, a founder of consensus history, ultimately asking: "Whose participation in a consensus really counts? Who is excluded from the consensus? Who refuses to enter it? To what extent are the alleged consensual ideas of the American system…actually shared by the mass public?" (in Wiener, 1989, p. 429) More than anything, these shifts reveal that what counts as history is itself a product of history—a recognition that would appear to undermine Hirsch's own discussion of "consensus research" in education, the "inherent stability" of literate culture, and "agreement" on the "basic facts" of history. But this has not shaken the views of Hirsch or kindred scholars of the old history.

As one example, take Gertrude Himmelfarb, who might well be considered the "mother of neoconservatism" as her husband, Irving Kristol, has been deemed its "father." In her treatise on history, *The New History and the Old: Critical Essays and Reappraisals*, Himmelfarb (2004) predictably (and partly rightfully, I think) attacks the newest history—postmodern history, especially "hard" versions—for denying "the possibility of arriving at any truths about the past" (p. 16), for producing works that "not only read more like fiction than history but actually are, to one degree or another, fictionalized," and for liberating historians "from the fetish of facts" (p. 23). For the original new history, she reserves a host of other criticisms: "Whereas the old [history] features kings, presidents, politicians, leaders, [and] political theorists, the new [history] takes as its subject the 'anonymous masses'" (p. 32). She explains that this kind of history, "in devaluing the political realm, devalues history itself." Himmelfarb continues:

> It makes meaningless those aspects of the past which serious and influential contemporaries thought most meaningful. It makes meaningless not only the struggle over political authority but the very idea of legitimate political authority, of political rule that is not merely a euphemism for "social control,"... of principles and practices that do not merely reflect (as Antonio Gramsci would have it) the "hegemony" of the ruling class. (p. 36)

Here again, there is no acknowledgment that what is considered "most meaningful" in history is contested and closely intertwined with the exercise of power. Most relevant to our analysis of Core history, perhaps, is Himmelfarb's strategic compromise. Her objection, she states, is not to new or "social history as such but to *claims of dominance*." Her objection is "not to social history as it may *complement or supplement traditional history* but to that which would supplant it" (italics added; p. 44). In terms of how this complementary relationship is to be established between the old and the new history, Core Knowledge provides a troubling but innovative model.

This momentous debate about history and the tensions and compromises it has engendered provide the background against which Core narratives of the national past must be understood. An analysis of the stories actually embodied in Core Knowledge history textbooks will be most informative.

CORE KNOWLEDGE AND THE *NEW* OLD HISTORY

History in schools has generally been taught in narrative form, a speech genre present in textbooks used by teachers and read by students. Regarding speech genres, Bakhtin emphasized:

> Utterances are not indifferent to one another, and are not self-sufficient; they are aware of and mutually reflect one another.... Each utterance is filled with echoes and reverberations of other utterances to which it is related.... Every utterance must be regarded as primarily a *response* to preceding utterances of the given

sphere.... Each utterance refutes, affirms, supplements, and relies on the others, presupposes them to be known, and somehow takes them into account. (in Morris, 1994, p. 85)

If each utterance contains "echoes and reverberations" of past utterances in related social fields and takes these into account, then we must keep in mind the broader conversations, debates, and contexts (see also Gee, 1999) relevant to the writing of Core Knowledge history. As we have seen, the trajectory of struggle between old and new histories—meaning history from above and from below—is most pertinent. Much of the neoconservative reaction, after all, has been driven by a desire to sustain a particular epistemological orientation to studying the past—one that centers on founding fathers and more powerful groups, and what they did to build the nation. Defending the tradition of old history against the onslaught of the new is what compelled Schlesinger (1992) to warn of the disuniting of America. "The militants of ethnicity," he wrote, "now contend that a main objective of public education should be the protection, strengthening, celebration, and perpetuation of ethnic origins and identities." Sounding the alarm, he continued, "Separatism, however, nourishes prejudice, magnifies differences and stirs antagonisms.... The result can only be the fragmentation, resegregation, and tribalization of American life" (pp. 17–18). New histories focused on subaltern groups, and conflict rather than consensus, were to blame. In turn, historians of long ignored pasts—those of African Americans, Asian Americans, women, immigrants, the working class, and so forth—defended such work as legitimate and overdue (Foner, 1997, 2002; Stearns, 1993; Wiener, 1989).

This is the legendary debate in which Core history texts are embedded and to which they "respond." Unlike additive multiculturalism in which "one half of a page here and one half of a page there" discusses subaltern groups (McCarthy, 1998, p. 115), Core Knowledge history, I will argue, represents a strategic innovation that moves beyond additive multiculturalism to something that I have termed the "*new* old history."[1] By this, I mean that Core texts reflect to a *greater degree* the tendencies of *both* the old and the new histories, and that the relationship between these traditions within Core is more *complex* than the additive approach that has characterized so many school texts over past decades (e.g., see Zimmerman, 2002). I will provide select illustrations and wish to emphasize that the illustrations provided reflect the broader patterns that I found in the many Core history texts that I analyzed (see appendix A for a more extensive discussion of methodology).[2] In offering these illustrations, I aim to show how Core texts as *new* old history are themselves contributors to the "disuniting of America's history."

More to the point, the pattern that I document (see also Buras, 2006) is one in which both elite and subaltern groups are recognized within Core history texts, but their recognition is premised on two main conditions. First, reflecting the old and the new, the pasts of groups above and below are narrativized, but *not in relation* to one another: elites are powerful but they do not exercise power over any group; subalterns are oppressed but they do not live amid oppressors. Second, the pasts of groups above and below are narrativized *in relation* to one another through a frame that stresses *consensus* (the bulwark of old history) and overshadows or ignores conflict and power (pivotal to new history). Moreover, it is the major storyline that reflects the old history, while the minor storyline "takes into account" and "echoes" the new history. Similarly, images in the texts generally respect these conditions. Core narratives do not represent what has been called *integrative* (Said, 1988) or *synthetic* history (Bender, 1989); this does not mean a total history, but rather any number of partial histories in which "groups interact to make national politics and culture" and do so in "a continuing contest...to define both themselves and the nation as a whole" (Bender, pp. 198–199). Rather, the *new* old history constructed through Core texts is simultaneously (although not equally) integrative and disintegrative, as it conditionally unites and disunites elite and subaltern realms of experience. In this way, it constitutes a strategy of rightist multiculturalism at the epistemological and curricular level.

Significantly, Hirsch (2001a) has asserted that "people who have called this [reform]...'Eurocentric' and 'elitist' have not bothered to find out just what is in the Core Knowledge Sequence" (p. 4). What is more, his supporters at the Fordham Foundation (Ellington & Eaton, 2003) and elsewhere have echoed this defensive posturing. An educational commentator in *Forbes*, for example, complained:

> Typical of the ongoing rants against Hirsch's theory is that of...Kristen Buras. She contends that Hirsch is "delegitimizing the demands of oppressed groups for representation and redistribution." Teaching the basics, say Hirsch's opponents, could deprive minorities of knowledge of their own cultures and traditions. (Summers, 1999, p. 70)

As a response to these claims, I shall closely examine how Core represents the basics of "our" national past, all the while keeping in mind that "Every written history is a selection and arrangement of facts   And the selection and arrangement of facts...is always an act of choice, conviction, and interpretation" (Beard, 1934, p. 220). The point, then, is to assess what kind of selection and arrangement of "facts" characterizes

Core Knowledge school history—facts that Hirsch believes "should not be subjects of controversy."

TURN OF THE CENTURY IMMIGRANTS

Before even turning a page, one cannot help but notice that Core school history, despite Hirsch's criticism of "ethnic loyalism," is framed in terms of identity politics. Upper grade textbook covers, for example, do not feature unifying images, such as the American flag, that generally appear on the fronts of other widely adopted elementary social studies textbooks (e.g., American Textbook Council, 2006; Houghton Mifflin, 2007; McGraw-Hill, 2006; Pearson Learning, 2004).[3] Rather a collage that includes not only a president and a general, but a Native American and an immigrant adorns Core covers. A flip through the series further suggests that the national past is a story of diverse groups, from Mount Rushmore presidents and civil rights leaders to industrial giants and workers. Yet the deep structure of the narratives and the connections and disconnections they foster raise serious questions about the legitimacy of this appeal.

First consider the second- and sixth-grade texts on immigration (Hirsch, 2002). In the second-grade reader, immigrant life is depicted through a major storyline focused on *suffering* in the old country and *success* in the new country. Students are told that millions "moved" because they were "looking for a better life in a new country" (p. 2). In Ireland, people "did not have potatoes" and "went hungry" (p. 3). Even on their way to the new country—students read—immigrants were "poor" and "had to sleep on the floor of the boat" (p. 5). By contrast, they arrived in a more promising nation where they "went to schools" (p. 4), "helped to build the first railroad" (p. 10), "went to the Great Plains to farm" (p. 11), and, for the most part, experienced success and mobility. The text ends with several immigrant success stories, which serve to reinforce the dominant storyline. "Andrew Carnegie was born in Scotland," but he "worked hard" in America and "became successful" (p. 12). Albert Sabine came from Poland and "worked" to discover a cure for polio—a cure "used all over the world" (p. 13). Similarly, Irving Berlin "was born in Russia" and "worked as a singing waiter" after coming to the United States, but ultimately became famous after writing "God Bless America" (p. 14). That song captures the overall thrust of the account, as second graders are left with a visual image of Berlin singing the praises of his new country. Although overshadowed by the major storyline, a minor storyline does exist. In this other storyline, success in the new country is less certain. Students are informed that some immigrants "lived in crowded cities" and that "large families had to live in only one or two rooms" (p. 8). As a whole, the narrative unevenly blends, but blends nonetheless, the older patriotic history with the newer history of dreams deferred.

This account of a generally harmonious transition to life in the United States is sustained by disuniting groups from one another. Immigrants encounter a new country largely uninhabited by native-born citizens; they have few relations with dominant groups. For example, the text indicates that immigrants "lived in their *own* neighborhoods," but who lived in the other neighborhoods and the reasons for segregation are not specified. In such neighborhoods, the story continues, immigrants "could speak *their familiar* language" (italics added; Hirsch, 2002, p. 10). But to whom was their language was unfamiliar? Chinese workers "helped to build the first railroad," "were strong and brave," and "worked seven days a week" (p. 10). But who was helped by their work and for whom did they labor? The work of Chinese immigrants occurs in a vacuum and is explained by personal character rather than capitalist relations with railroad magnates. On only one occasion does the text explicitly address relations between immigrants and another group—namely, immigration officials: Doctors on Ellis Island "checked" the health status of immigrants (p. 7). In this instance, the association is depicted neutrally, with no mention of the intimidating, panoptic component of that experience.

In sum, this text depicts immigrant relations with an amorphous "United States" as positive and devoid of conflict, and ignores that their experiences were shaped by the actions of groups with particular economic, racial, linguistic, religious, and national affiliations. Absent such evidence, it appears that nativist citizens and legislators never sought to restrict the immigration of specific groups, whether the Chinese or southern and eastern Europeans. Industrialists never sought to exploit immigrant labor, whether on the railroads or in the garment industry. As a rendering of the past, this narrative most reflects consensus history, with the Carnegies, Sabines, and Berlins portrayed as representative of immigrants generally. Much less attention is given to immigrant struggles from below. Put another way, immigrants are given extensive attention in Core history, but the selective use of evidence actually frames subaltern experience from above. There are certain pasts not included in this lesson.

For the most part, visual images serve to reinforce the written text. The cover of the reader depicts European immigrants on a ship moving toward the Statue of Liberty, which appears yet again in a subsequent frame alongside a grand picture of the Ellis Island facility. In this way, immigrants confront symbols rather than native-born groups consti-tuted as historical actors. Moreover, opportunities to work and succeed are depicted through images such as a thriving storefront where Asian men busily transact and a portrait of Carnegie dressed in a bow tie and suit. This visual record of the past rarely deviates from the major storyline, offering up just a single photo of an immigrant family in tight living quarters. Much as the written word, the images represent only particular views or "facts." While the Statue of Liberty and Ellis Island—the first points of contact for European immigrants on the East Coast—are shown, Asian immigrants are less frequently pictured, and there are no images of Angel Island on the West Coast.[4] European female immigrants are most often shown arriving with or tending to children and are visually absent as members of the urban manufactur-ing class, which would, of course, require a relational history in which factory owners are made visible.

Indeed, dominant individuals and groups do not appear in illustra-tions, with one exception. A black and white photo of a teacher amid immigrant students accompanies the text: "Most people who came to the United States did not speak English. They had to learn this new lan-guage. Some went to schools like this one" (Hirsch, 2002, p. 4). In the same picture, two American flags hang above the students and each has been color-enhanced in red, white, and blue. In this way, the written text and visual image interact to convey the idea that learning to speak English is what it means to become "American." Interestingly, there are two more recent images at the end of the text. One shows immigrants of color "becoming citizens" as they take an oath to "obey the laws of *our* country" (italics added; p. 15). The next and last image is of predomi-nantly white citizens waiting in line at a voting booth decorated with an American flag. There is thus a subtle native-born presence—Americans who speak English and are white—but there is virtually no interaction between native-born and immigrant groups.

The sixth-grade text on immigration is also a complex composite of old and new. It is worth noting that this particular text is twenty-one pages long and seems at first to be an extensive exploration of immi-grant experience during the mid-nineteenth and early twentieth cen-turies—far more extensive than other textbooks I have encountered. Much like the second-grade reader, the major storyline is one in which immigrants are *pushed* to emigrate due to terrible conditions in the homeland and are *pulled* toward America, the land of opportunity. The old country was a place, one Irish immigrant says, "where there will be nothing for us but to lie down and die" (Hirsch, 2002, p. 244). In contrast, the United States is generally presented in a positive light. When the subaltern speak in this text, it is usually to hail America's greatness. This is illustrated by the inclusion of seven long excerpts from the letters of European immigrants, one right after the other. "Listen to the voices of these earlier immigrants," the text reads, "and you will have no trouble understanding why a struggling European farmer or town worker would consider giving up everything and moving." From the pens of immigrants, it is submitted to students: "One sees no poor here.... One cannot discern any differences between the cobbler's wife and the wife of a prominent gentleman" (p. 245). There is, however, a minor storyline too. In this storyline, success in America is not absolute. Students read that "living conditions for most immigrants in American cities were simply dreadful" (p. 249). Notably, far fewer immigrants in the text speak about this.

This is history from below in that the voices and experiences of immigrants are centered, but the narrative is actually more complicated. It is only European immigrants who speak—Asian immigrants are virtually absent—and when they do, they are only "allowed" to speak in ways that support the major storyline. The minor narrative on hardship and inequality in America is consistently undermined by its relationship to the broader narrative. This occurs through a process that includes *acknowledgment, qualification, comparison*, and *affirmation*. First there is an acknowledgment of immigrant struggle: "Making a living in the city was not easy.... Usually [immigrants] wound up with the hardest jobs, the longest hours, and the lowest pay" (Hirsch, 2002, p. 254). Then after a paragraph or two on pay and working conditions for immigrants, and a quote from "someone" who wrote that "the streets [of America] were not paved with gold" and that it was immigrants who "were expected to pave them," the text indicates:

> Hard as life may have been for them, however [qualification], these new Americans knew they were far better off than they had been in their native lands [comparison].
>
> In time, many learned new skills and improved their earnings. They were able to afford better housing.... Within one generation, or sometimes two, many of [their] children were entering the fields of medicine, education, business, [and] law [affirmation]. (p. 255)

In this way, the minor storyline, and the history of immigrant struggle that it represents, is consumed by an affirmative narrative of success and consensus in the United States.

One of the most telling instances in which experience from below is reframed from above relates to persecution in the old country and the opportunity to become American in the new. Early on, students read that many immigrants:

> had been persecuted in their native lands simply because they spoke a different language, had different customs, or followed a [different] religion.... They weren't allowed to have newspapers or books in their own language, or to get very far in school or in work unless they gave up their language. (Hirsch, 2002, p. 253)

Yet later these same tendencies are described as desirable in the United States and are actually a core part of becoming American. With regard to first-generation immigrants, the question is posed, "Did living in their own neighborhoods, and reading newspapers in their own language slow down the process of becoming American?" It was the third generation, the text lauds, that felt "fully, comfortably American," something facilitated by the fact that "foreign language newspapers no longer existed" and few in this generation still felt "torn between the ways of the old and the ways of the new" (p. 262). In short, immigrants flee persecution for a similar experience called "becoming American," only this experience is portrayed as positive.

Significantly, the major storyline is sustained through a non-relational history. Rather than confronting immigration officials, the captains of industry, or native-born citizens, immigrants mainly encounter geographic locations (e.g., New York City), the American nation (e.g., new world), disembodied forces (e.g., mood of the country, American ways, demands that the government limit who entered), symbols (e.g., Statue of Liberty), institutions (e.g., Americanization programs), and unidentified presences (e.g., those who would take down the welcome sign). Only 20 of 170 references to dominant individuals or groups correspond to actors embodied with specific attributes of class, race, religion, language, or national origin; among these few are an official on Ellis Island, skilled workers born in America, a Congressman, and Protestants. On the whole, this is not a narrative in which subaltern and dominant groups relate or interact—each as identified, embodied groups. Even when the narrative turns to nativism, students are told that some "Americans" favored immigration, while others were troubled by those unlike "themselves" (Hirsch, 2002, p. 258). The "mood of the country" and "nativist sentiment" are far more present than "Protestants" who "called for laws" to stop immigration. One drawing does depict violence against the Chinese, but the caption says that "riots...resulted in the beating of Chinese immigrants." The text later explains that "those responsible" were rarely punished (p. 259).

CIVIL RIGHTS LEADERS AND ABOLITIONISTS

In second grade, students read a Core history text dedicated to civil rights leaders, particularly African Americans. Then, in the fourth grade, American reformers are studied, with one segment of the text dedicated to abolitionists (Hirsch, 2002). Old and new, above and below, are also conditionally incorporated into these narratives.

The major storyline in the text on civil rights leaders is that all Americans worked to ensure equal rights. In tension with this is a minor storyline that some groups did not have equal rights. More specifically, this story unfolds as utterances on black experience alternate with ones on white benevolence. Thus, the text indicates that Mary McLeod Bethune, whose parents "had been slaves," believed that "every black child should get an education." She "started a school" for African American girls with whom she is pictured. In this narrative frame, Bethune's experience is raced; she seeks to equalize educational conditions for *black* children (Hirsch, 2002, p. 4). Next appears Eleanor Roosevelt who "wanted to help others" (p. 5). Bethune and Roosevelt, finally, are shown together in a photo as they relate to one another with smiles. Students read that they "worked together to help all American children get a good education" (p. 6). In this frame, Bethune's racial struggle is transformed into a cooperative effort with Roosevelt to help all *American* children.

This pattern persists as the narrative continues: "White people played in the major leagues and black people played in the Negro leagues," but Branch Rickey, the white manager of the Brooklyn Dodgers, "still wanted Jackie Robinson" to play on his team (Hirsch, 2002, pp. 7–8). Martin Luther King "wanted integration," but at the Lincoln Memorial, he spoke to thousands who "wanted a better life for all Americans." Students are told that King knew Gandhi had freed his country "without violence" (pp. 12–13). These alternating discourses—one focused on unequal conditions and the other on cooperative relations and an "all American" effort to ensure equality—are only reinforced by the textual images. Jackie Robinson and Branch Rickey are pictured together shaking hands and smiling. Martin Luther King is pictured at the Memorial with the statue of Lincoln elevated behind him—itself an image of nonviolent relations as Lincoln "watches over" King.

Notably, this narrative is simultaneously non-relational and relational. Unequal conditions prevail in the minor storyline, but Africans Americans never encounter whites exercising power in direct or explicit ways. It is nonetheless the case that violent southern segregationists did not work to help "all" Americans. And the struggle for integration saw much violence—namely that perpetrated by whites against blacks. Yet all of this is absent within a non-relational frame that manages to convey a story from below of the black civil rights struggle, only without malevolent whites. At yet another point the text explains: "Black people had to sit at the back of the bus. Rosa Parks broke the law in Alabama. She would not move to the back of the bus to give a white man her seat" (Hirsch, 2002, p. 10). Accompanying these words, however, is a photo that shows Parks sitting *in front* of a white man who is calmly seated and does not attend to her presence. It thus seems that Parks was able to address unequal treatment without tension, much less arrest. The "read aloud" in the teacher guide—meant to be read by the teacher to the class—does on occasion allude to conflictual relations, for example, announcing that "Rosa Parks got arrested on the bus" and said she "was tired of being pushed around" (p. 14). But these representations are not reflected in the written or visual text that students directly engage. Instead, subaltern and dominant racial groups only meet within a consensual frame. The minor storyline on inequality, as lived from below, is subverted by a story in which blacks have cooperative relations with benevolent whites.

Much of this is reflected in the fourth-grade text on abolitionists. Just as the major storyline on civil rights is that all Americans worked together to ensure equality, the principal storyline here is that white abolitionists worked to achieve freedom for slaves, alongside black abolitionists who appear to have played a complementary but more minor role. Related to the major storyline, which emphasizes the common cause of whites and blacks, is a minor one that conveys that although some slaveholders were "kind" and freed their slaves, other slaveholders did not want liberation for enslaved blacks; white benevolence, in other words, coexisted with some level of opposition to equal rights for all.

The narrative thus begins with a discussion of early presidents who "felt slavery was wrong and believed it would end in time," although all except John Adams "owned slaves." It next turns its focus to "kind owners" who freed their slaves, including George Washington and a slaveholder from North Carolina whose four "reasons" for doing so are given a thorough airing:

> Every human being...is entitled to freedom. My conscience condemns me for keeping them in slavery.... The golden rule directs us to do unto every human creature, as we would wish to be done unto....I wish to die with a clear conscience.

There is a more subtle acknowledgment that malevolent slaveholders existed—that is, "those who were not interested in hearing the abolitionists' message." For the most part, though, it is benevolent whites—regretful and renegade slaveholders and abolitionists—who take center stage. White abolitionists, the narrative proceeds, "thought that once masters understood how sinful it was for one person to own another, they would give up their slaves, just the way that North Carolina slaveholder did" (Hirsch, 2002, p. 328). To a significant degree, the major storyline on white abolitionists is actually reinforced by the minor storyline on slaveholders, most of whom appear more compassionate than cruel.

Most prominently featured is William Lloyd Garrison, the period's leading white abolitionist, whose photo takes up the *entire lower half* of a page and is positioned right next to an enlarged picture of his newspaper's masthead—*The Liberator.* This visual image (read: Garrison-white man-liberator) thus serves to reinforce the main textual narrative. Frederick Douglass, whose writings and activism have been a crucial part of new histories from below, is only secondarily mentioned in Core as "another important abolitionist." Moreover, in comparison to Garrison's *Liberator,* the name of Douglass' newspaper, *The North Star,* is not even offered. In this way, traditions of black abolitionism are simultaneously recognized and marginalized within the narrative—ultimately creating the impression that freedom was struggled for by whites for blacks rather than those efforts occurring within the context of slave resistance and black abolitionism. Interestingly, it is mentioned that because Douglass escaped from slavery, those who listened to his lectures "knew that he was talking from real experience." Yet readers are not given the opportunity to hear the voice of Douglass or those who might speak from "real" experience. Instead, they are informed that it was abolitionists—presumably white—who "believed deeply in *their* cause," "kept working to achieve freedom *for* the slaves," and "told their listeners about the cruel treatment" (italics added; Hirsch, 2002, p. 329). All in all, this text assumes the elements of the new history—in this case, it partly alludes to an unequal and conflicted past in which whites and blacks struggled over slavery—but develops a narrative that accentuates consensual white-black relations and even the voices of dominant groups.

One problematic feature of this narrative is the way in which white abolitionists are credited with a position that actually characterized early black abolitionist efforts. Students are told: "Abolitionists weren't just saying they didn't like slavery. They were saying that the country should do something about it—abolish it, not at some time in the distant future, but *now, right away*" (Hirsch, 2002, p. 329). In fact, this was not the position of white abolitionists before the 1830s. During previous decades, most white abolitionists advocated gradual emancipation, compensation to slaveholders for freed slaves, and the colonization of free blacks elsewhere. In 1816, the American Colonization Society—a white antislavery organization—formed and it advocated precisely this position. It was free blacks—not white abolitionists—who early argued that abolition should be immediate, that no compensation should be offered, and that plans for colonization should be rejected. They began forming their own antislavery organizations—almost 50 existed by 1830—and their own papers, such as *Freedom's Journal* (Stuckey, 1987; Wright, 1993). The absence of such facts—abolitionist traditions did exist within the African American community—facilitates a view that whites nearly single-handedly fought for black freedom and that without their benevolence, the institution of slavery might never have been challenged.

All of this is reinforced when pupils read that "the flame of antislavery feeling had never burned strongly in the South" and that by the early 1800s, it had "flickered out and died." It was this flame, they learn further, that "abolitionists wanted to light...again" (Hirsch, 2002, p. 328). Here again, when one writes that "antislavery feeling never burned strongly in the South," one can only be speaking of white sentiment. If one considers evidence of daily slave resistance and documented uprisings (see Blassingame, 1977), clearly antislavery feeling always burned strongly in the South.

It is undoubtedly striking to see attention dedicated to abolitionism in this fourth-grade text. It is not simply mentioned as one reform in a list of many, as is often the case. Upon closer reading, however, it becomes evident that this narrative, with its connections and disconnections, constitutes a highly Eurocentric tale about white benevolence and black freedom. It seems more than appropriate to reflect on the opening words of the first edition of *Freedom's Journal*, which read: "We wish to plead our cause. Too long have others spoken for us" (see Wright, 1993, p. 198). This wish is precisely what gave rise to new histories. In Core, the new "complements" the old (to use Himmelfarb's word), and the "speaking for" continues. Abolitionism is a subject worthy of extended study, but in which tradition? Overall, this narrative places the greatest emphasis on harmonious white-black relations. It is notable that few specifics are given on the nature of life under slavery—the very institution that made abolitionism necessary. Rather than peopling the story with representative slaveholders and slaves and at least partly detailing the record of savage mistreatment and resistance that bound them, especially as a preface to discussing abolitionism, readers of this history are notified that enlightened slaveholders and white abolitionists were the unequivocal partners of black abolitionists in the collective quest for freedom.

EARLY PRESIDENTS

Finally, let us turn our attention to kindergarten and fourth-grade texts on early presidents, with some added focus on Thomas Jefferson—a figure we already know has been constructed quite differently in Core classrooms before these texts were produced. In kindergarten, students are presented with a big book on the Mount Rushmore presidents (Hirsch, 2002). A single storyline drives this book. According to text in the teacher guide, which is meant to be "read aloud" to students alongside the book, these presidents are worthy of "honor" because they were "honest, smart, fair, and brave" individuals (p. 5). Each is presented positively and in generally biographical rather than more broadly political terms. In the book, an image of a young boy writing by candlelight helps convey that George Washington "liked to learn" (p. 5). Students are also told that he was a "surveyor" and the "leader of the army." Abraham Lincoln "was born in a log cabin," "read books by light from a fire," and "spoke out against slavery" (pp. 11–13). Along with an old photo of a very young boy, the book explains that "Little Teddy Roosevelt was often sick," although he later became "a Rough Rider in the army" (pp. 14–15). The latter statement is accompanied, of course, by a photo of Roosevelt astride a horse. With such minutiae at its center and much emphasis on personal attributes and the desire to learn and grow, one cannot help but conclude that the book is more intended as a form of character education for youngsters than an historical primer on the politics of the presidency.

As for Thomas Jefferson, children read that he "played the violin," "built his house, called Monticello," and said that "all men are created equal" (Hirsch, 2002, pp. 8–10). An historic image of Jefferson's home graces a page of the book, revealing a large, well-manicured yard on which two European American women are strolling. The "read aloud" in the teacher guide further informs students that Jefferson was a "fine planner and builder" and that he wrote the Declaration of Independence and "treated everyone the same" (pp. 11–12). Clearly, this rendering of Jefferson is more in line with the heroic narrative taught in the suburban Core school earlier mentioned than the portrayal of Jefferson as a slaveholder as taught in the urban one. The fact that enslaved blacks do not appear in the photo of Monticello further masks issues of race and effaces particular pasts. In this text, Jefferson does not exist as a figure who exercises power, especially state power, in relation to certain groups. The idea that everyone was treated the same, in fact, is introduced at the very beginning of the "read aloud" which asks:

> Who can become President? Can a farmer become President? Yes—George Washington was once a farmer. Can an inventor become President? Yes—Thomas Jefferson was an inventor. How about a store clerk? Yes—Abraham Lincoln worked in a store when he was young. How about a cowboy? Yes—Theodore Roosevelt once worked as a cowboy. (p. 5)

While it may be true that a cowboy can become president—we must not forget George W. Bush—the notion that a farmer or store clerk can just as easily become president hardly constitutes a factual historical lesson. To depict Washington as simply a farmer and to overlook that he was the richest man in the country is to use facts so selectively that myth, more than historical understanding, is generated.

The "read aloud" continues, explaining that Jefferson's father, grandfather, and teachers "taught him to be good and honest" (Hirsch, 2002, p. 10). Students are also informed that in parenting his own daughter, Jefferson made certain she knew her schedule: from eight to ten o'clock in the morning, "music practice," from ten to one, "dance or draw," from one to two, "write letters," and thereafter dedicate time to "read French" and "read English and write" (p. 11). This pattern continues for other Mount Rushmore presidents mentioned in the "read aloud," including Washington who in a notebook "wrote the rules of good behavior that his teacher had taught him" (p. 7), Lincoln who owned a bible and "read it over and over" (p. 14), and Roosevelt who was often sick but "grew up to become a strong man" (p. 16). Once again, the emphasis on educational discipline, character development, and individual effort and mobility is evident. With such a biographical depiction of political leaders, one wonders how students are prepared to participate in a "discussion" of "why they think Thomas Jefferson was a popular president," an activity recommended in the teacher guide (p. 12). So little, after all, is said about the history of his and other presidencies.

In fourth grade, students encounter a unit on early presidents in which Jefferson is also obviously covered. The biographical line here is less central, as the major storyline is one of statecraft: "President Washington and Congress had laid a solid foundation for a healthy new government of the United States" (Hirsch, 2002, p. 294). The minor storyline, by comparison, acknowledges that this new government did not always serve the interests of all people, although few specific examples are offered. The first year, the text explains, "Congress decided to create three executive departments," the Department of State that "was supposed to help the President in his dealings with foreign countries," the War Department that "was in charge of defending the country," and the Department of the Treasury that "was expected to collect taxes, pay bills, and take care of the government's money" (p. 293). The founding and functioning of these departments occur, however, in a vacuum. No connections are made, for example, between the War Department and the treatment of Native Americans, or the Department of the Treasury, the monied interests of government officials, and a history of related protests, such as Shays' Rebellion. The Whiskey Rebellion is noted as an episode during which taxes were contested, but students are likewise instructed that Washington "felt that the law was the law" and thus "put on his old general's uniform and led 13,000 troops... to put down" the rebellion. This showed that "the new government could not only pass laws, but also make people obey them." Such action, in the end, "left a bitter taste in the mouths of many farmers" (p. 296). That bitter taste is virtually the only one mentioned in the narrative on early presidents.

This relatively fraternal storyline continues with Jefferson, a president whose "main interest... was in making life better for all" (Hirsch, 2002, p. 302). That dominant storyline chafes only slightly against a more minor one in which Jefferson was not quite able to improve life for everyone. Thus in reading this narrative, students learn that Jefferson, unlike Alexander Hamilton, "wanted America to remain mainly a nation of small farmers" (p. 295) and that on the day he took office, "he was dressed in a plain suit, like those worn by plain citizens" (p. 303). The text goes on:

> When Jefferson had to go anywhere outside the President's House, he rode on horseback by himself—no splendid presidential coach.... [He] did these things because he wanted to make a point. In a republic, all are equal. No one should have privileges above anyone else. (p. 304)

Students learn, in fact, that Jefferson "viewed slavery as evil" and had earlier "tried to get Virginia to pass a law that children born to slaves would be automatically free at birth," a proposal that was rejected but still stands as "one of the great 'might have beens' in our history" (p. 303). This utterance establishes a consensual relationship between Jefferson and enslaved blacks. It does so by neglecting to note that Jefferson likewise believed that after emancipation, free blacks "should be colonized to such a place as the circumstances of the time should render most proper" and that "vessels [should] at the same time [be sent] to other parts of the world for an equal number of white inhabitants" (Peden, 1982, p. 138). Jefferson "owned many slaves," students are told, but even this statement is brought into alignment with a consensus narrative through the qualification, "as nearly every well-to-do southern family did." Jefferson's exchange with Benjamin Banneker—a free black from Baltimore who surveyed the Federal City—is also discussed. Banneker "reminded Jefferson of his own words... that all men are created equal" and asked him how he could "continue to hold slaves." Again moving to positively align Jefferson with Banneker, the text indicates that Jefferson "agreed that slavery was wrong," though "he had no good answers to Banneker's questions" which "troubled [him] to the end of his days" (Hirsch, 2002, p. 303).

Students also learn that Jefferson had a positive relationship with the western farmer. This affiliation was fostered through Jefferson's "greatest achievement" as president—the Louisiana Purchase (Hirsch, 2002, p. 304). Through the Louisiana Purchase, Jefferson was able to secure access for western farmers to the port city of New Orleans, without which "farmers would not be able to get their crops to market." Even better, he "doubled America's territories at a cost of a few pennies an acre," an act deemed "the biggest bargain in American history" (p. 305). Framing this narrative is an image of the Louisiana Purchase—that is, a map denoting the newly bought territory, eastern states, and major river systems in North America. In the end, Jefferson is able to "make life better" for farmers, even if his efforts on behalf of blacks were well-intended but unheeded by a reluctant state legislature. In this narrative, Jefferson, the political figure, for the most part has consensual relations with farmers and African Americans. Those he enslaved are notably absent from yet another picture of Monticello—this time, a present-day photo. A picture of a plow that Jefferson invented also adorns the page, although again, those who most likely used the plow at Monticello (i.e., slaves) are not discussed. Much as Jefferson's slaves do not make an appearance in this text, neither do Native American groups appear on the map of the Louisiana Purchase. In this regard, the narrative is a non-relational one. Jefferson's low-cost bargain, his regard for farmers, and the link between his vision of nation and landed expansion (McCoy, 1980) are never associated with Native Americans and what the Louisiana Purchase "cost" them. The chapter ends by noting that "explorers [soon] went to see for themselves" what Jefferson had bought, but concludes, "that is a story for another time" (p. 305).

A THOUGHT EXPERIMENT: FACT OR FICTION IN CORE KNOWLEDGE?

The *new* old histories in Core represent only one way of writing about the national past. Saying this, though, is likely to evoke what has become a relatively standard neoconservative response. Indeed, when the issue of multiple and competing historical accounts is raised, neoconservatives play the "relativism" card. By this, I mean they assert that newer multicultural histories constitute an attack on truth and position every culture and every past as equally worthy of recognition. Writing on multicultural social studies education, for instance, Ellington and Eaton (2003) warn that "social studies instructors at all levels should reject the... notion that all cultures are equal" (p. 87). They also caution:

> Teachers should not assume the role of social activists who dwell upon the negatives in our society and urge students to struggle against various oppressors. Rather, our students should be taught to develop their own interpretations and analyses of history and culture after becoming thoroughly grounded in evidence-based studies that do not represent the views of one ideologue or another. (p. 88)

The degree to which multiplicity leads to relativity in history is a debatable issue, as are issues pertaining to the role of ideology and evidence in the writing and teaching of history. As the foregoing analysis revealed, Core Knowledge history is not a disinterested account of the past or a neutral rendering a historical "facts." Like all knowledge—historical or otherwise—Core represents a selective tradition. We might wonder, then, on what basis Core history might be distinguished from other possible historical accounts, since all represent only a part of the whole. Indeed, if we are to critically assess the selection and use of facts in Core history and interrogate which facts are allowed and not allowed to inform the national narratives in these textbooks, then we need to make clear the grounds on which determinations might rest. If criticisms are raised about the "facts" in Core, does this mean that we have fallen victim to relativism or ideology, as neoconservatives so often charge? Beyond this, if a given account of the past is based on facts, on what grounds can the account be criticized as lacking in truth? Are there other selections and arrangements of facts that might be "more" true than those presented in Core? In order to confront these questions, which will inevitably be raised by proponents of Core, it might be helpful to undertake a thought experiment. This thought experiment will allow us to think through the theories of history that were introduced at the beginning of this chapter, but to do so in a way that more forth-rightly relates to Core history and the specific questions just noted.

The modernist or reconstructionist position on historical analysis is best captured by Leopold von Ranke's well-known proclamation that historians "show how it really was." In this view, as observed earlier, the historian is capable of analyzing evidence from the past in a manner unmediated by present-day conceptions. It is believed that the application of scientifically disciplined methods to the study of the past enables one to discover the objective truth of history (Southgate, 2001). Indeed, this is what Hirsch would have us believe he has done (or at least those historians on whom he relied in creating the Core history textbooks).[5]

This stance has been challenged by postmodernist scholars—some of whom have launched a wholesale attack on modernist assumptions surrounding historical objectivity and truth. Indeed, ideology and the weight of the present are believed to figure so centrally that writing about the past is deemed an impossible task. Keith Jenkins (1997), for example, has argued that "the idea of a historicized past existing independent of our variously present-day constitutive concerns is an absurd one." According to him, "all we have are our versions" of the past (p. 61). Interestingly, Jenkins' (1999) recollection of his initial interest in history in the mid-1960s is quite Rankean (or we might say Hirschian):

> I trusted that the study of history that I was then embarking on would give me such knowledge and give it to me straight. In those early days I thought getting historical knowledge was getting together a lot of facts and information about what really happened in the past.

Significantly, he continues, "I remember being disoriented in the extreme by my first sustained contact with varieties of historical interpretation" (p. 11). This disorientation was slowly resolved by Jenkins' development of a radical postmodernist position that declared historical interpretation to be nothing more than a reflection of the subjectivity of the historian in contemporary context. Jenkins (1997) thus asserted:

> *All* the characteristics alleged to belong to 'the past' belong to us.... The whole modernist...ensemble [of academic histories] now appears as an ultimately self-referencing, problematic expression of our various interests, an ideological discourse *per se* without any real access to the past. (p. 61)

In other words, what has traditionally counted as historical narrative is merely our version of the past with no association to any real referent.

Jenkins' assertion that history can never be more than a reflection of the historian's ideology and context is followed by another assertion—this one related to the association of the historian to evidence of the past (e.g., traces in the archives). Regarding this relationship, Jenkins (1997) claims the following:

> The past is utterly promiscuous: it will go with anybody—Marxists, Whigs, racists, feminists.... The past has no resistance of its own; the past as such doesn't exist *historically* outside of historians' textual constitutive appropriations, consequently, being constructed by them it has no independence to resist them at the aesthetic "level of signification." The historicized past *itself* thus contains nothing independent of us that we have to be loyal to;...no facts we *have* to respect. (p. 64)

No facts we have to respect? According to Jenkins, historians may attribute whatever meaning they wish to the evidence with impunity. The evidence, in turn, can play no role in determining the legitimacy of one story over another; this is because the evidence cannot speak for itself, rather the historian speaks for it. And whatever the historian says can be no more than a self-referencing—never an evidence-referencing—act. Such a dismissal of the role of evidence due to absolute subjectivism (or ideology) leads to a highly relativistic view of the past. Importantly, this postmodernist critique of modernist understandings of history actually sounds very much like the critique neoconservatives raise about new multicultural histories, although clearly the critiques are being raised for very different reasons and applied more narrowly by neoconservatives. While postmodernists like Jenkins submit that *we cannot* apprehend the past due to ideological and linguistic limitations, neoconservatives contend that *some* of us—that is, practitioners of the new history—*will not* apprehend the past due to an *unwillingness* to shed ideological commitments. Whatever the reasons for or parameters of this critique, I want to argue for a *qualified* modernist position that allows the historian to (1) avoid the extremes of naive objectivism (Ranke's "show how it really was") and absolute subjectivism (Jenkins' "all we have are our versions"), and (2) mediate truth claims in relation to competing narratives while still conceding the influence of the historian/ideology/present on the writing of history. This position will provide the grounds for assessing the "facts" of Core history.

In this regard, it is essential to recognize that earlier practitioners of the new history, including Charles Beard (1934) and Carl Becker (1955), likewise problematized the ideal of objectivity embraced by modernist historians. Writing in 1934, Beard underscored:

> Has it not been said for a century or more that each historian who writes history is a product of his age, and that his work reflects the spirit of the times, of a nation, race, group, class, or section?...Every student of history knows that his colleagues have been influenced in their selection and ordering of materials by their biases, prejudices, beliefs, affections, general upbringing, and experience.

You may recall Beard putting it this way: "Every written history...is a selection and arrangement of facts, of recorded *fragments of past actuality*. And the selection and arrangement of facts...is always an act of choice, conviction, and interpretation" (p. 220). Unlike those who conclude that subjectivity renders knowledge of the past beyond reach, Beard recommended that historians respond to the dilemma posed by ideology by continuously employing the scientific method, the method by which "particular phases of history once dark and confused have been illuminated by research, authentication, [and] scrutiny" (p. 226). At the same time, Beard contended that "the historian is bound by his craft to recognize the nature and limitations of the scientific method and to dispel the illusion that it can produce a science of history embracing the fullness of history...as past actuality" (p. 227).

For Jenkins as well as neoconservative critics of the new history, the writing of history is the writing of the present *absent* the past, or the substitution of current ideology for the reality of history. Just think here of Schlesinger's (1992) references to the new history as a falsification of history, bad history, or a noble lie. In contrast, Beard argued that history is "[contemporary] thought about past actuality, instructed and delimited by history as record and knowledge" (p. 219). Such an understanding of history challenges Jenkins' and neoconservatives' conceptions in that it affirms the force of present-day thinking in shaping the historical narrative while also insisting that the narrative be simultaneously rooted in the historical record. Becker (1955) stated it this way: "Our imagined picture of the actual event is always determined by two things: (1) by the actual event itself insofar as we can know something about it; and (2) by our own present purposes, desires, prepossessions, and prejudices" (p. 336). He emphasized that "the proper function of erudite historical research is to be forever correcting the...image of the past by bringing it to the test of reliable information" (p. 339). Both Beard and Becker thus held that historical knowledge was possible as long as one grasped that every narrative will only partially reflect the fullness of the past, recognized the influence of present concerns in constructing the past, and disciplined one's choice, arrangement, and interpretation of facts by close and methodical scrutiny of existing evidence. The insight that the present influences historians' constructions of the past is important. But Beard and Becker argue that there is more: There *are* facts that we need to respect.

Educational historian Carl Kaestle (1992) echoes and refines many of the arguments forwarded a half-century earlier by Beard and Becker. Unlike many historians of that era, Kaestle stresses that "most historians today would make very modest claims about certitude and truth in [their] statements about the past" (p. 361). Compared to the skepticism of Jenkins and many neoconservative critics of new history, Kaestle argues that claims about the past are possible because historians can rely on particular standards of evidence. Rather than eschewing the role of ideology in shaping interpretations of evidence, he argues that theories "about social structure, social change, and human nature, whether from economics, sociology, political economy, or anthropology" can act as an "external source of standards of truth for historians" (p. 362). More to the point, Kaestle believes that:

> Using theory more self-consciously and creatively, historians can create a dialog [sic] between it and their data, each informing the other. Social theories, then, can help us decide how to seek the truth and can shape our answers. (p. 363)

More directly, there are a number of standards internal to the profession of history that can help historians "know when they know," including "consonance of micro- and macro-levels of analysis, synthesis of contradictory claims, and reinforcement across regions or nations" (p. 366). While "new perspectives in women's history, minority history, radical history, and gay history" have "further diversified the truths promoted in contemporary history," Kaestle insists that we need not conclude that "contrary propositions are equally valid." Standards provide "some sense of better or worse ways of arguing, more-viable and less-viable generalizations about the past" (p. 362). While Kaestle's argument does not resolve the issue that standards themselves can be contested, it does suggest that a mechanism exists for judging the truthfulness of particular narratives in relation to evidence.[6] Even McNeill (1986), who argues that all history is part myth and that "truths are what historians achieve when they bend their minds as critically and carefully as they can to the task of making their account...credible...to an audience that shares enough of their particular outlook and assumptions to accept what they say," concludes the following: "This does not mean that there is no difference between one mythistory and another. Some clearly are more adequate to the facts than others" (p. 19). Along similar lines, John Ibbett (2003) argues that we have an "obligation to the past," an obligation that requires respect for the object (i.e., evidence) and that necessarily constrains the stories that can be told (p. 61). Ultimately, therefore, recognizing that views of the past are plural and shaped by position does not mean that all views of the past are equally legitimate or substantiated—a tenet reflected in the Statement on Standards of Professional Conduct issued by the American Historical Association (2007).[7]

The question thus becomes how adequate Core history is to the facts, how adequate the accounts when brought to the test and breadth of evidence. All histories are partial but I contend that some partialities are more problematic than others, some more or less "true" than others. The choice and deployment of facts in Core (some of which are themselves questionable *as facts*) and the processes of inclusion and exclusion that shaped the narratives serve to mask particular aspects of the past and create a most inadequate form of mythistory. In short, the *new* old history in Core Knowledge is to a significant degree fictionalized history, even as it constitutes a powerful innovation in the exercise of hegemony.

Thinking of the Core history texts analyzed in this chapter, a number of illustrations come to mind. It may be true—a *fact*—that Andrew Carnegie climbed the ladder of success as an immigrant, but to disproportionately highlight "immigrant success stories," to allow only certain voices to speak by repeatedly referencing the letters of immigrants who comment on equality in the United States, to construct a narrative that for the most part leaves out the hard evidence on immigration officials, nativist citizens, legislators, and so on, is to make fact into fiction. To acknowledge but then qualify the oppressive circumstances of immigrants in the United States by continuously comparing living conditions in the new country to those in the old is hardly to let the facts speak for themselves (e.g., "Usually immigrants wound up with the hardest jobs.... [But] these new Americans knew they were far better off than they had been."). To construct a visual image of the civil rights struggle through a series of pictures that depicts whites and blacks as having *only* harmonious relations or to represent the civil rights struggle from below while *negating* the presence of segregationists is to create a most egregious form of mythistory. Depicting early presidents as eager readers, well-behaved pupils, and strong men to be honored, with so little discussion of how they administered government for an entire country, may constitute one kind of character education, but it surely does not constitute adequate political history or history education. Clearly, the facts of history are the subject of controversy—and should continue to be. Engaging in the process of analyzing competing accounts, thinking critically about multiple forms of evidence and the balance of existing evidence, debating the implications and truth of histories (in the plural), and relating multiple accounts to one another is what it means to be *historically literate*.

The line between fact and fiction is not always so clear. Despite Hirsch's fixation on facts, some level of fiction in writing and teaching history is actually deemed officially acceptable by the Core Knowledge Foundation. Mary Beth Klee, who founded a Core Knowledge school in New Hampshire and acted as its principal for five years, has written on teaching history in elementary schools. One of her articles, "Wisdom on Woe: How to Teach the Worst in World History" (1995) was published in *Common Knowledge*, the foundation's newsletter. It also appears among select articles ("favorites") catalogued on the foundation's website as "offer[ing] the Foundation's views" (Core Knowledge Foundation, 2007b; for Fordham Foundation writings, see Klee, 2003; Stern et al., 2003). In that piece, Klee says that in teaching history:

> We have the chance to inspire children with stories of great deeds, of heroic efforts to overcome seemingly insurmountable odds, of varied peoples and cultures. At the same time, we face a challenge, for the story of civilization is not all sweetness and light. There is also a dark side to human history: the undeniable record of evil, tragedy, and suffering. (p. 1)

She recommends that teachers "choose the stories in which virtue is rewarded, evil is punished, good comes from evil, love transforms hate." This, she argues, will give children the gift of "moral order," something that meets their developmental and emotional needs (p. 3). Attempting to clarify her position, she questions:

> Am I saying that we should make it a sanitized world? Leave out all the bad stuff? No—though when dealing with young children, "leaving out" does not constitute censorship or lying: on the contrary, it is the responsibility of adults to make well-reasoned choices.

While it is difficult to deny the point that there are concerns that need to be taken very seriously when educating especially young children, issues of inclusion, exclusion, and representation are no less complicated at this level; the choices made have rather significant ethical and political implications that cannot be written off as a result of devel-

opmental needs. In fact, the history that students learn is closely tied
to the development of their identities and their sense of the world, as
neoconservatives are very aware. It is equally tied to the development
of often retrogressive strains of nationalism, although Klee does not
address this. Truth-telling and lying, as we have seen, are not such simple matters.

Interestingly, Klee (1995) goes on to ask: "What shall we choose to
emphasize or downplay in our attempt to give meaningful shape to the
disordered record [of the past]?...How shall we tell a story that could
be told in many different ways?" (p. 4). Her recommendations are illu-
minating and reveal a good deal about the underlying epistemological assumptions associated with Core history education. For instance,
she details what she calls the basic categories of historical thought,
including: "humanity's quest to record great deeds," "the human quest
to understand where we came from (religion)," "the ongoing drive to
tell stories that in some way explain the world (mythology)," and "how
people are governed and govern themselves" (pp. 4–5). Such categories
are not neutral. Indeed, putting great deeds, religion, mythology, and
government at the center of teaching history creates not only an "interesting" combination of elements, but points toward a rather particular way of viewing the past. One can imagine, in fact, any number of
other modes of historical thought that might be added or given priority.
Focusing on the small deeds of common men and women (as opposed
to great deeds), struggles for justice and equality and civil disobedi-
ence (as opposed to government), the quest to understand where we
came from through a history of science (as opposed to religion), or to
explain the world through oral history or archival traces (as opposed
to myths) would call for a very different kind of historical thought and
education.

"When history is appalling and we must address it," Klee (1995)
writes, then "let tragedy be tragedy, and let bad guys be bad guys, but
set tragedy and evil in the context of hope" (p. 6). Again, some of this
advice seems pedagogically wise. She is right when she warns against
an overemphasis on historical empathy, which can often lead down the
road of not simply understanding the reasons for particular tragedies,
but ultimately justifying them. "If in our historical studies with children we encounter principles or practices that blatantly violate human
rights and dignity," she stresses, "then we can and should convey that
we understand why they did this, but we think it's wrong!" (p. 8) At the
same time, however, the suggestion to frame the past within a narrative
of hope and progress in order not to "overburden" children and thereby

promote "despair and loss of hope" would seem to foreclose possibilities for studying admittedly difficult but profoundly important matters. Without a sense of contradiction, Klee admits this is the case. She expresses concern regarding particular pieces of children's literature on Hiroshima, war in Yugoslavia, and American slavery, explaining:

> What distinguishes these books and others like them are the graphic horror and the endings, which are devastatingly bleak, devoid of hope. This is "reality," we are told. The idea is that by reading this sort of material at an early age, we will raise a generation so acutely sensitive to the dangers of war or social injustice that as adults they will ensure peace and justice. The question is: will the children's spirit survive this kind of darkness? (p. 9)

One wonders, then, are such subjects off limits? Is it not possible to engage young children in historical study of these realities, or can we only offer readers that depict consensus, justice, and progress?

In another piece, which similarly addresses the question of what can be done in historically educating early elementary students, Klee (1999) further reveals the epistemology that underlies Core lessons on the past. "What is history," she ponders, "if not a large collection of good stories?" One could, of course, wryly answer that history is a collection of good and not-so-good stories, but this is really not the point. The point is the disproportionate emphasis placed on the "good" in history, as this makes it difficult to tell particular kinds of stories about the past. "Regale them with tales." "Revisit the daring deeds." Make history classes "entertaining," Klee advises (p. 39). It is suggested that one way of doing this is through children's literature:

> In history "stories" are not limited to dramatized accounts of fictional or real figures. Teachers should feel free to use the fine works of nonfiction available too. The movement of ancient Greece toward government by its citizens is a great story, but it is not yet a great storybook. Consequently, it can be approached...with selections from some of the many, fine nonfiction books. (p. 40)

The act of granting teachers the permission to use works of nonfiction to teach history should be, on the face of it, utterly unnecessary. In other words, it is the use of fiction to teach history that should potentially concern us and require justification. But this is not the case; instead, nonfiction is what one uses when a great story has not yet become a storybook.

Again, this slippage between fact and fiction in history education requires careful thinking. As Cynthia Ozick (1999) points out in her reflection on fictional works and historical texts:

> The aims of imagination are not the aims of history. Scholars are nowadays calling historiography into radical question.... But even under the broken umbrella of contemporary relativism, history has not yet been metamorphosed into fable.... To whatever degree, history is what is owed to reality. Imagination—fiction—is freer than that; is freed altogether. Fiction has the license to do anything it pleases.... It can alter history; it can invent a history that never was, as long as it maintains a hint of verisimilitude.... History is rooted in document and archive.... The rights of fiction are not the rights of history. (p. 23)

While such delineations allow little room for the inevitable role of ideology in the construction of history, Ozick's central point about the unrestricted liberties of fiction and the unyielding obligations of history to evidence remains important and troubles any call to "regale [students] with tales," at least when those tales are presented as history. It is instructive to note that Frederick Douglass' narrative of his life as a slave, which in the opening chapter I indicated had been recently added to Core curriculum resources, has been included as an extension of the *Core Classics* series, which are *literary* works. This may not seem like an important distinction, until one recognizes that this means a primary source on slavery will sit alongside works of fiction such as *Treasure Island* and *Pollyanna*.

There is also another component to all of this that should not be overlooked. Klee developed a character education program—one endorsed by the Core Knowledge Foundation—called *Core Virtues*. The *Core Virtues* program is aligned with the Core curriculum and is based on what are called "consensus virtues" such as civility, courtesy, respect for the rights of others, loyalty, willingness to defer gratification, and a general concern for justice (Ellington & Rutledge, 2001, p. 43). Time and time again, the notion of consensus makes an appearance, as though "we" all agree on what constitutes virtuous behavior. The two main avenues for instilling these virtues include history and English, with an emphasis on "real life and fictional heroes and villains, famous speeches, and political and social controversy and reform [that] calls the students' attention to the hard choices individuals make that either benefit or harm society" (p. 42). This surely sounds good, except when one considers as an example the dose of character education represented in the Core text on Mount Rushmore presidents. Rather than dealing with fundamental political dilemmas and the challenges of forming and sustaining a just government, it seems that students are instead encouraged to be civil, study hard, and defer gratification so that they, too, can be upwardly mobile and perhaps even become president one day. It is not a matter of teaching or not teaching virtues in and through history, as every account has underlying ethical implications even if these are not made explicit. It is a matter of whose stories we tell (and how), which virtues are on offer, and how students ultimately come to see the national past and its relationship to present-day circumstances.

Within Core Knowledge and within other neoconservative circles, there has been much talk of the uses and abuses of history, particularly when it comes to progressive educators and new left historians. I hope to have demonstrated that Hirsch undoubtedly ab/uses history for purposes of his own. In light of neoconservative concerns over cultural cohesion and political stability, these ab/uses are closely tied to nation-building and are rooted in a kind of nostalgia or yearning for a national past that never quite existed. Boym (2001) writes:

> Nostalgia (from *nostos*—return home, and *algia*—longing) is a longing for a home that no longer exists or has never existed. Nostalgia is a sentiment of loss and displacement, but it is also a romance with one's own fantasy. (p. xiii)

From this vantage point, neoconservative representations of the past must be at least partly understood in connection with the sense of loss and displacement generated by progressive movements in the 1960s that shook the status quo in the discipline of history and the daily life of nation.

Interestingly, the term *nostalgia* first arose in the field of medicine and was invented by Swiss doctor Johannes Hofer in 1688. "Among the first victims of the newly diagnosed disease were various displaced people of the seventeenth century... [including] Swiss soldiers fighting abroad" (Boym, 2001, p. 3). Plagued by recollections of their homeland, soldiers treated by Hofer reportedly suffered from nausea, loss of appetite, fever, suicidal tendencies, and other maladies. Though a "curable disease," Hofer seemed "proud of some of his patients" for he viewed their nostalgia as "a demonstration of the patriotism of his compatriots who loved the charm of their native land to the point of sickness" (p. 4). In fact, Boym reveals:

> Since the eighteenth century, the impossible task of exploring nostalgia passed from doctors to poets and philosophers. The symptom of sickness came to be regarded as a sign of sensibil-

ity or an expression of a new patriotic feeling. The epidemic of nostalgia was no longer to be cured but to be spread as widely as possible. (p. 11)

With the development of a federal state and the heightening of Swiss nationalism in the nineteenth century, "what used to be an individual emotion expressed by sick soldiers and later romantic poets and philosophers turned into an institutional or state policy" (p. 14). Thus, nostalgia did not solely reside in the mind of the individual or the physical body but permeated the body politic. Many traditional historians have undeniably supported nostalgia as a state policy—one surely, if sometimes unofficially, implemented in Core schools and others.

Nostalgia, it should be noted, can assume different forms. Most pertinent here is restorative nostalgia:

> This kind of nostalgia characterizes... nationalist revivals all over the world, which engage in the... myth-making of history.... [Yet] invented tradition does not mean... a pure act of social constructivism; rather, it builds on the sense of loss of community and cohesion and offers a comforting collective script for individual longing.... This transformation [of fatality]... can be politically manipulated through newly recreated practices of national commemoration with the aim of reestablishing social cohesion, a sense of security and an obedient relationship to authority. (Boym, 2001, pp. 41–42)

Hirsch and other neoconservatives are clearly engaged in a restorative project of myth-making and nation-building. What makes them particularly powerful is the way in which their politicized battles over history and educational reform are fought through a discourse that pits fact against fiction, truth against ideology, good history against bad, cohesion against disunity, and past against present. This discourse is utilized by Klee (1999) when she insists:

> The question is not what incidents and characters from the past explain my understanding of the present but what was the past like? It is clearly the case that historical context unfolds from point *a* to point *b*, and not from point *z* to point *y*.... Teachers must resolve to walk away from the twentieth-century vantage point... and lead their charges back to the land of long ago and far away. (p. 38)

Having accessed a past allegedly untainted by present-day vantage points, students need only to unthinkingly consume "historical facts."

Klee believes it is possible in the early grades "to be fairly formulaic about teaching history" (p. 39). Once a story is told, the teacher might use a "fact-packed, historical tune" to "ingrain information in such a way that [students] can easily retrieve it" (p. 42), followed by a good project to "help young children [further] internalize the new historical knowledge" (p. 43). Finally, there is testing through weekly "quiz bowl," which includes "multiple-choice questions (with three possible answers) for each team" (p. 50). The teacher guides associated with Core Knowledge history textbooks follow just this kind of formula. Clearly, though, there is more to it than storing information; particular understandings are being restored or perhaps, more accurately, the nation is being *restored*. Rightist multiculturalism, which the *new* old history in Core exemplifies, has facilitated this project.

CORE HISTORY AND THE NEW HEGEMONY

When traditional historians first attacked the new history, they sought to defend particulars "truths" about the national past and feared that history from below might expose the fragility of consensus (Wiener, 1989). Decades later when Schlesinger (1992) raised concerns about the disuniting of America, it was the new history that he blamed for fragmenting the nation. In reality, it was the old history that divided the nation as it failed to recognize "we the people," or to bring together multiple groups in a relational narrative of nation-making, when writing about the past. The new history, if anything, was the more integrative history—one that sought to write a past that included a broad array of groups in the story of nation-building.[8] In light of the increasing power of various social movements from below and struggles to redefine the past, the old history no longer constituted an effective epistemology for maintaining hegemony. Additive history, which left the old history largely intact but incorporated the voices of traditionally marginalized groups by peripherally "mentioning" them within or even alongside the dominant national narrative, emerged next and, for awhile, may have even appeased particular groups (Zimmerman, 2002). As new history has advanced as a discipline and demands for cultural recognition have persisted, however, additive history has come under powerful criticism by still misrepresented and underrepresented groups (Ladson-Billings & Tate, 2006; Ladson-Billings & Gillborn, 2004; McCarthy, 1998; Yosso, 2006). Neoconservatives, in particular, have increasingly recognized that denunciations of multicultural history would no longer suffice and that a reconfigured, more responsive compromise with subaltern groups was strategically necessary. Returning to the old history was clearly no longer an option and additive history lost a good deal of its power to appeal to those groups wanting more than token representation.

The *new* old history, which Core has pioneered, represents one dimension of a new strategy for generating subaltern consent for neoconservative-inspired educational reforms by more thoroughly embracing and exploiting cultural impulses from below. This distinctly modernized strategy is best described as rightist multiculturalism. As demonstrated, Core Knowledge history texts provide a more comprehensive focus on subaltern groups, whether immigrants or civil rights leaders, while partly retaining the old focus on consensus. When experiences from below are narrated, a disuniting of America's history occurs, meaning that histories of oppression are documented without histories of domination. The melding of histories occurs only within a frame of consensus when groups relate harmoniously. Whatever the case, the striking appearance of the subaltern in Core history, even if conditional, represents a novel, more comprehensive way of writing the past in school history texts. The *new* old history, I want to make clear, does not represent the horizon of a truly integrative critical multicultural historiography, one which takes seriously that "no matter how one [tries] to extricate subaltern from elite histories, they are different but overlapping and curiously interdependent territories" (Said, 1988, p. viii). As a dimension of rightist multiculturalism, this kind of history instead appropriates the subaltern past in order to secure a particular kind of national future, one that leaves undisrupted the balance of cultural power and thus continues to benefit already powerful groups.

A "return" to the old history, Glazer (1997) said, "would no longer do," though moving beyond additive history could certainly do Core Knowledge one better. This strategy might actually have the power to mobilize both dominant and subaltern groups around Core without either group feeling that its interests or history are being undercut. It is useful to remember Ravitch's (1996) declaration: "You, as teachers and leaders of Core Knowledge schools, must foment a revolution" (p. 11). I have suggested that those of us dedicated to more progressive conceptions of democracy, whether political, economic, or cultural, need to think about how precisely the revolution is being fomented. Groups from below may seek to redefine Core, but they are also surrounded by a network of very powerful neoconservative forces from above that will try, at every turn, to make and remake the movement and to write and rewrite the pages of history in ways that support dominant interests. The degree to which rightist multiculturalism will succeed in serving those interests is the question of the day.

5

CORE LESSONS ON THE POLITICS OF NEOCONSERVATIVE SCHOOL REFORM

The Ocean Hill-Brownsville dispute would become the defining battle in a cultural war that raged in New York City during the 1960s, and continues to affect the city [and the nation] today.... The debate began with a basic educational question: Why did black pupil achievement levels in the New York City public school system lag behind those of whites? It soon grew to embrace the legitimacy of black lower-class culture, the validity of "middle class" values and their relevance to the black community, and the ability of traditional models of cultural pluralism to speak to all segments of the city's population.

> **Jerald Podair in *The Strike That Changed New York*
> (2002, p. 48)**

What the future holds for these attempts to build a truly multicultural conservative movement, despite internal difficulties and disagreements among its members, is a pressing political question.

> **Angela Dillard in *Guess Who's Coming to Dinner* Now?
> (2001, p. 23)**

PRESSING QUESTIONS

THE FOREGOING ANALYSIS OF CORE KNOWLEDGE addressed a number of pressing political questions. In asking these questions, my intent has not simply been to gain a more critical understanding of Core

135

Knowledge as an educational reform, although surely there is merit in doing so. It is estimated that "more than 1.2 million students have used parts of [the Core] curriculum" (Thomas B. Fordham Foundation, 2003a). It is difficult to think of a comparable educational reform that has inspired such missionary zeal among its supporters and that has continued to gain adherents over the course of some 20 years. Investigating the dynamics of such an effort, along with the benefits and costs it entails, is bound to teach us any number of crucial lessons about the fears and aspirations embraced by different communities, the epistemologies that shape curriculum development and implementation, and the complexities of building reform movements in education.

Core Knowledge is also a part of something much larger: a complicated history of struggle to define and redefine our common sense around issues of culture, diversity, civil rights, economy, and nationhood. That is, Core represents not only a school-based intervention, but a new—cutting edge, if you will—hegemonic strategy founded on a dramatic redefinition of multiculturalism. The power of this strategy—rightist multiculturalism—has not been fully appreciated by either all segments within neoconservatism or other groups on the broader right. Its combination of elitist and populist sensibilities is striking, and its rather notable embrace (even if that embrace is highly conditional and at times exploitive) of the very diversity that has led other culturally conservative fractions to predict America's undoing has enabled it to "succeed" in ways that are truly concerning. Understanding the politics underlying this hybrid constellation and pondering what it may mean for narrowing as well as expanding the conditions necessary for culturally democratic schooling is tremendously important.

In the end, then, Core Knowledge is both foreground and background. Core itself has concrete effects on communities when adopted as a reform, but it also participates in and compounds the effects generated by the many neoconservative and rightist efforts that are simultaneously being undertaken, whether through the destruction of history education materials by Lynne Cheney and her allies in the Department of Education, battles over state standards, or the testing regime of the No Child Left Behind Act that reduces education to the elemental work of bubbling in the appropriate "facts" on standardized tests. In light of this, our consideration of the lessons that might be learned from Core will require moving back and forth from the specific meanings of the reform to its farther-reaching implications for equality and for cultural and economic democracy. It will also require moving back and forth from past to present, so that hindsight informs our assessments.

THE OCEAN HILL-BROWNSVILLE CRISIS

In an earlier chapter, which contextualized Core Knowledge through a partial history of neoconservatism, I mentioned that I would examine the Ocean Hill-Brownsville crisis of the 1960s—one that involved fundamental issues of cultural recognition. Admittedly, it may seem odd to begin the conclusion of a book about the politics of contemporary school reform by thinking historically. But as Jerald Podair, an historian noted for his documentation of this crisis, reminds us: "Multicultural curricula, affective learning techniques, non-competitive instructional environments, community-based educational systems—all trace their roots to the Ocean Hill-Brownsville experiment" (2002, p. 151). So many of the heated debates to which Core Knowledge responds—those pertaining to the legitimacy of cultural forms associated with different groups, competing conceptions of pluralism and their relationship to curriculum and national identity, and disparate views on the very meaning of and pathway to equality—were central to this historic episode. As such, revisiting Ocean Hill-Brownsville may actually help to cast Core in a new light and point toward a number of insights regarding neoconservative educational efforts in the current moment.

In the late 1960s, African American community members in the Ocean Hill-Brownsville section of Brooklyn undertook an educational experiment involving community control of curriculum and governance in local public schools. They were responding, in part, to the ongoing resistance of whites to school desegregation. In Jackson Heights—a predominantly white, middle-class neighborhood in Queens—for example, residents formed the Parents and Taxpayers (PAT) group in 1963 to defend "neighborhood schools" against various desegregation initiatives apathetically instituted by the New York City Board of Education. Podair (2002) explains: "Observers often remarked on their passionate desire for upward mobility and their contempt for those whom they perceived as lacking in this quality. More often than not, the objects of their disdain were black" (p. 26). Indeed, it was this kind of resistance (over 100 PAT chapters were established across New York City) and the conditions that continued to prevail in schools attended by black students (some classes had as many as 55 students, for instance) that drove the community of Ocean Hill-Brownsville (and even Kenneth Clark, the social scientist whose research was pivotal to the *Brown* decision in 1954) to instead prioritize the betterment of conditions in segregated schools through community control. As Clark put it during an exchange with the city's mayor, John Lindsay:

> The central Board of Education has certainly not been respon-
> sive to the cries of Negroes and other deprived groups in the city
> for desegregation. After the deprived people stopped asking for
> desegregation, they just asked for the same degree of control over
> the quality of their schools which people in the suburbs have and
> which middle class people even in our city have. (in Podair, 2002,
> p. 37)

Lindsay agreed with Clark on the issue of community control, but for
very different reasons. He wanted to avoid the "riots" that plagued other
urban centers during the mid-1960s and believed that some degree of
decentralization could help accomplish this (Podair, 2002).

Among other supporters of the Ocean Hill-Brownsville experiment
were organized black educators. The African American Teachers Association, initially an organization within the United Federation of Teachers (UFT), saw in community control the promise of both transforming
an educational system that had failed black children and increasing the
number of black teachers, who represented only 8% of the teaching
force in New York City. However, the UFT, which consisted primarily of Jewish and Catholic teachers who had fought for access to professional credentials, recognition of the union, fair compensation, and
ultimately opportunities to ascend the administrative ladder as principals and bureaucrats, at first rejected community control. They feared
it would undermine not only their progress, but the power of the Board
of Education with which the union had finally consolidated its relationship and on which its own power partly depended. Some of this was
rooted in good sense, as Jews had earlier been denied entry into many
domains of employment and had found the "objective," "merit-based"
examinations and job security of civil service employment, particularly in the school system, conducive to their advancement. Much of
the opposition nonetheless reflected a gradual shift of the UFT from its
democratic socialist origins. The Teachers Guild out of which the union
grew had represented democratic socialism for educators since the
1930s, and Albert Shanker, the president of the UFT, had been a member of the Young People's Socialist League, but the union had slowly
moved to a more conservative, pro-establishment stance. "Such a rank-
and-file body—careerist, upwardly mobile, and skittish about blacks,
both inside and outside the school system—could hardly be expected
to be sanguine about a community control doctrine that threatened
their professional lives" (Podair, 2002, p. 45). Equally significant, while
Ocean Hill-Brownsville community members and the African American Teachers Association anticipated the chance to reconstruct curric-

ulum along lines that centered African American experience, the UFT viewed community control as "antipluralist, antidemocratic, and even totalitarian in its implications" (p. 46).

As for African American community control advocates, they sought to challenge prevailing "culture of poverty" arguments—all of which blamed educational problems in the black community on supposedly deficient cultural forms, backward values, and welfare dependency— and to reveal the "shallowness and fraudulence of the core 'middle-class' values of the city" (Podair, 2002, p. 49). Such culture of poverty arguments, as I explained in chapter 1, were epitomized and circulated in reports by Daniel Moynihan and James Coleman on the causes of black underachievement. Parts of the Coleman Report were first given a broader airing in *The Public Interest*, where "the solution [to racial inequality]... was to remove poor children from the 'culture of poverty' of their homes and communities, and immerse them in the saving, middle-class values, and predominantly white world of their school and teachers" (p. 55).

At the same time, community control advocates also eschewed the moderate cultural pluralism that dominated the schools of New York City, a kind of pluralism that:

> defined expressions of ethnic identity, within common boundaries, as the essence of "Americanism" itself.... Ethnicity did not need to disappear, but merely bow in the direction of broad cultural unity.... It sought to recognize the contributions of various ethnic and racial groups to a "common" culture with a Western, European-based core. (Podair, 2002, pp. 56–57)

Instead, they embraced a more progressive, or radical, version of pluralism that legitimized black culture and experience, and aimed to create a curriculum more "relevant" to the historically marginalized students who would study it. The African American Teachers Association argued, for instance, that "if teachers showed respect for the culture of lower-class black students, made instruction relevant to their lives outside the classroom, and accepted them as they were, they would respond as they had not for the UFT teachers" (p. 168). In short, calls to adopt more cosmopolitan or universal affiliations as human beings were not understood as serving the interests of the African American community, which suffered discrimination not as individuals but as a group (Podair, 2002; see also Buras & Motter, 2006).

Finally, African American supporters of community control wished to bypass and later reinvent the professional examination system. They asserted, with good reason, that the system was not nearly as fair or

merit-based as the UFT claimed. Indeed, African American candidates regularly "failed" the oral expression component of such exams
as assessors consistently penalized them for what they deemed "poor
pronunciation" (Podair, 2002, p. 51).

Interestingly, it was the potential opportunity to expand its multimillion-dollar compensatory educational program, known as More Effective Schools (MES), which inspired the UFT to temporarily reverse its
position on community control and to offer its support. Criticized from
the beginning as elitist by much of the African American community,
MES was viewed by the UFT as the solution to culture of poverty issues.
It would better the life chances of black students by remedying their
"deficiencies," putting more teachers in each classroom, hiring reading
specialists, extending class hours, and offering related early childhood,
cultural enrichment, and after-school programs. The curricular structure underlying these compensatory initiatives, however, represented
precisely that brand of cultural pluralism that community control
advocates hoped to replace. The proposal for MES in 1964, for example,
called for instruction "to reflect the contributions of various groups to
our common culture" (Podair, 2002, p. 57). On some level, even this
approach was at the time more progressive than the skewed and scarce
coverage of black history in officially approved New York City school
texts. Nonetheless, its more troubling aspects were exemplified in the
work of the UFT's Committee on African American History, which
attempted to subsume black history within a Western narrative that
constructs all group experience as comparable to that of European
immigrant groups (Podair, 2002)—a narrative that continues to be
contested even today (e.g., see Cornbleth & Waugh, 1999). The centrist
curricular vision of the UFT was likewise illustrated by a social studies lesson taught by a white teacher during the Ocean Hill-Brownsville
experiment:

> The plan for the lesson asked: "How is America divided on the
> question of civil rights?" It divided a hypothetical "American
> Highway" into three lanes—two narrow ones for left- and right-
> wing "extremists," and a wide "center lane." Discussion questions
> included "What happens to America when either the right or left
> lane becomes more crowded?" and "Why is the key to peace and
> happiness found in observing moderation in things?" (Podair, p.
> 58)

This centrist approach, which marginalized and often ignored black
cultural forms and foreclosed the teaching of more critical histories,
was challenged in *Freedomways*—a journal that Shirley Graham, the

wife of W. E. B. Du Bois, began in 1961. One principal, Edward Weaver, wrote in its pages that compensatory education and the culture of poverty theory undergirding it was:

> ...a condescending approach to the culture of black people with no effort to structure dignity for their life-style, linguistic habits and behavior, but rather designed to produce white middle-class conventional behaviors.... [It] proposes that the black ghetto child become a super-child, lifting himself through reading and language skills to a nobler and greater world of the future. (in Podair, 2002, p. 61)

In comparison to such an education, black school activists "demanded that the curriculum balance discussions of ancient Greece and Rome with those of the African Ashanti culture, and the American, French, and Russian revolutions with Marcus Garvey, Malcolm X, and Stokely Carmichael." The head of African American education in Ocean Hill-Brownsville, Keith Baird, put it this way: "We aren't concerned with putting one culture over another, but with supplying the missing pages of black culture" (p. 67).

As Podair (2002) reveals, even before the Ocean Hill-Brownsville crisis occurred, significant questions were already under debate, including "Were lower-class black children 'culturally deprived?'" and "Was a pluralism that sought to dilute the force of racial and ethnic particularism through expressions of broad cultural unity merely a perpetuation of white dominance and black marginalization?" (p. 69) The crisis that ensued in Ocean Hill-Brownsville began in December 1966 when a black parent from the neighborhood was not allowed to voice her concerns at a central Board of Education meeting because her name failed to appear on the official list of speakers.

What resulted was a sit-in during which a "People's Board of Education" was formed to hear parents' grievances about the schools. The People's Board next passed a resolution that demanded community control of public education in New York. By early 1967, neighborhood activists had boycotted the local board and formed their own. Ironically, their board received the support of the UFT, which hoped it might be able to obtain greater investment in its MES program in the schools of Ocean Hill-Brownsville. Sandra Feldman was sent by the UFT to assist the independent board in gaining recognition and resources from the central Board of Education. Getting "more" of the same, however, was not the kind of reform that the residents of Ocean Hill-Brownsville had in mind. Rather, they wanted much deeper changes in the culture, knowledge, and history represented in schools and a greater voice in the educational decision making that so affected their children. Ultimately, "white teachers viewed the educational system as one that, while flawed, had helped them, and would help anyone wishing to work hard. Black parents saw the system as a failure" (Podair, 2002, p. 77).

The Board of Education, for political and economic reasons, decided to support a limited experiment in community control and granted Ocean Hill-Brownsville status as an experimental site in spring 1967. Teachers would still be assigned by the central Board and competitive exams would still guide the hiring process, although the local board could make curricular decisions within the overarching framework set by the Board and State Department of Education. The planning council of Ocean Hill-Brownsville began drafting its community control plan over the summer, a process that did not include UFT members who were on break. By September, it had a unit administrator, Rhody McCoy, an elected local board that consisted of mostly poor black women who had previously been involved in the schools, and an operational plan that gave the local board control over hiring, curriculum, and budgeting. Not without significance, the plan failed to include MES in any of its schools. When the UFT members of the planning council returned that fall, McCoy asked that they approve the summer's decisions. At that point, the UFT broke its ties with the local board. Moreover, the union went on strike in September for better wages, more MES funding, and a "disruptive child" provision that would allow teachers the discretion to remove such students from their classrooms. This strike began the truly downward spiral of relations between Ocean Hill-Brownsville residents and the UFT, as the former viewed the action as a racially-motivated attack on the schools and the community (see Podair, 2002).

In May 1968, nineteen white teachers in Ocean Hill-Brownsville received letters that terminated their employment and instructed them to report to the central Board for reassignment to other schools. The UFT decided to fight the move legally as a violation of due process, but when teachers attempted to return to the schools, African American residents and teachers blocked their way. Escorted by police in the following days, the teachers tried to reenter the schools, but were eclipsed when the local board closed public schools throughout the neighborhood. When the schools next reopened their doors, UFT-affiliated white teachers in Ocean Hill-Brownsville collectively walked out for the remainder of the school year. *Commentary*, under the leadership of Norman Podhoretz, was the first journal to support the UFT, while whites throughout the city rallied for the union. Diane Ravitch would later criticize the politics of black educational activists in Ocean Hill-Brownsville in *The Great School Wars* and in *Commentary*, especially their failure to "perceive a viable alternative to separatism and for putting the interests of [their] own group above the interests of the whole community" (2000b, p. 378). Clearly, fundamental political realignments were underway between middle-class Jews, who had often aligned with African Americans around the cause of civil rights but increasingly viewed themselves as unambiguously white, and their Irish and Italian Catholic counterparts in the city (Podair, 2002; see also Goldstein, 2006).

Come September, a day-long citywide strike occurred. With the local board of Ocean Hill-Brownsville and the union agreeing to arbitration of the teacher transfer issue, UFT teachers returned to work. They were told this time to report to the auditorium of one of the neighborhood schools for an "orientation session" where some fifty community members waved sticks and threw bullets at them. Returning rather shaken to their respective schools later in the day, no teaching assignments were given, instigating yet another walkout for two weeks. Returning yet again to the schools—this time with a promise from the Board of Education that classroom assignments would be given—assignment were once more withheld and another strike ensued. At that point, Shanker demanded an end to the Ocean Hill-Brownsville experiment. Things only worsened as anti-Semitic materials surfaced in Ocean Hill-Brownsville, some utilizing quotes from the *Protocols of the Elders of Zion*. A number of UFT supporters acted no better, as they screamed "nigger scab" at a black teacher reporting to work in Ocean Hill-Brownsville (Podair, 2002; see also Pritchett, 2002).

By November 1968, UFT teachers had returned to their positions under police escort while the district was placed under the command of a state trustee until things settled. In March 1969, the local board was reinstated; by this time, though, most white UFT teachers had left the district. Moreover, a sector of New York's Jewish community had shifted to the right, with their support for social welfare programs significantly dropping and their fear of and anger toward blacks rising. The following month the state legislature passed a final decentralization law that ended the community control experiment in Ocean Hill-Brownsville (Podair, 2002). Although the experiment was officially over, the long-term consequences of the struggle would influence educational debates and efforts for decades to come, including Core Knowledge (for a more extensive discussion of consequences, see Goldstein, 2006; Podair, 2002).

CORE LESSONS ON CULTURAL DEMOCRACY

In many respects, the issues at the center of the Ocean Hill-Brownsville crisis relate fundamentally to Core as an educational reform. A number of actors in and commentators on the crisis, including Shanker, Feldman, and Ravitch, would later come to endorse Hirsch's notion of cultural literacy and even sit on the Core Knowledge Foundation's board of trustees. Aside from such lineal connections is the ideological tissue that links this episode to Core. The More Effective Schools program, an early compensatory educational measure rooted in theories of cultural deprivation, may be viewed as a predecessor of Core Knowledge. More Effective Schools, much like Core, sought to uplift black students allegedly mired in a culture of poverty by providing them with the "enrichment," or knowledge, needed to integrally participate in the "common culture" of the nation. It was premised on a notion of pluralism that emphasized unity over diversity and that sought to quell more critical understandings of race by advancing a narrative of shared history, ethnic progress, and the Americanization of identity. For many of the white teachers in the UFT, middle-class values and cultural forms were the indubitable route to upward mobility. Upward mobility, in turn, meant that equality had been attained and the civil rights agenda fulfilled. We might think here of Hirsch's promise that the inculcation of common·knowledge represents the new civil rights frontier, as formerly culturally illiterate students are given access to "literate" culture and thus the cultural capital needed to ascend the ladder of mobility and ultimately participate as "equals" in the marketplace of America. "Public education in a democracy," says Hirsch, "has no more right to segregated knowledge than to segregated schools" (1999a, para. 4). Moreover, he urges, "Improving the effectiveness and fairness of education through enhancing both its content and its commonality has more than educational significance. The improvement would...diminish the economic inequalities within the nation" (1996, p. 238).

Dissenting from this view of equality and civil rights were the African American residents of Ocean Hill-Brownsville. Rather than embracing MES as an educational reform in the interest of their children, they opted for a curriculum that centered the cultural forms of poor, urban blacks and that connected learning to issues of core importance within racially oppressed communities. Recall the words of community activists, who demanded that the curriculum balance discussions of the American revolution with lessons on Malcolm X. Indeed, "supplying the missing pages of black culture" seemed to be the frontier of the civil rights movement in Ocean Hill-Brownsville.

The segregation of knowledge was surely understood as a monumental problem, but the answer was not to be found in making dominant culture equally available to all at the expense of black culture. Instead, the answer was to be found in diversifying what counted as knowledge and integrating heretofore segregated forms of knowledge and culture into a necessarily reconstructed school curriculum. In this case, equality was defined first and foremost in cultural terms, although clearly there were economic dimensions to the educational vision articulated by black activists (e.g., controlling the educational budget). At the deepest level, there may even have been the hope that defending the legitimacy of African American culture might itself facilitate upward mobility, as discriminatory assessments of black students and teachers, too often based on the derogation of black cultural forms, would be challenged and their accompanying economic barriers deconstructed. Such thinking reflects the arguments made by Nancy Fraser (1997) that issues of cultural recognition and economic redistribution do not always constitute separate spheres, but are often closely intertwined—something to be explored shortly.

More than anything, I believe that knowledge of this history should compel us to assess Hirsch's claims about Core with tremendous caution. Whose interests are most served by the Core Knowledge curriculum? At what costs? I want to say strongly upfront that there are many elements of good sense in Hirsch's critiques of education. As one example, his call for a common curriculum constitutes a powerful response to historic patterns in which one kind of education was offered to some students and another kind of education to others. Even today, this persists in the form of educational tracking, which results in particular students receiving a college preparatory education while others receive a vocational one. It is equally clear that poor students and students of color are generally on the receiving end of the latter (Oakes, 2005).

Having said this, I still think it is imperative to unpack the call for curricular commonality and the underlying definition of equality that Hirsch and many Core supporters endorse. At least officially, Core Knowledge represents a fairly narrow view of what constitutes equality, respect for civil rights and, more profoundly, *cultural* democracy. In the case of Core, the desegregation and "democratization" of knowledge mean neither the critical integration of multiple forms of knowledge nor an ongoing conversation about what constitutes the constantly evolving, always debatable epistemologies in classrooms and schools. Instead, integration under Core is unidirectional and the bounds of cultural recognition are actually rather limited. More specifically, particular groups of students (e.g., poor, of color, Spanish-speaking) are invited into the realm of dominant forms of knowledge. The reverse, however, is not the case. Traditionally privileged students (e.g., middle-class, white, English-speaking) are not expected to engage, in substantive ways, cultural forms that have generally been placed outside the canon. As to not overstate the point, I acknowledge that Core has supplied *more* of the "missing pages" of black and other subaltern cultures and histories than has typically occurred in the past. However, the issue is not simply more, but more of what? As I have shown, the pages of Core history selectively filter the "facts," often to the point of lapsing into nostalgic fictions about "our" national past. Nonetheless, those pages do include a *new* old history that takes more seriously demands for cultural and historical acknowledgment of traditionally oppressed groups. Again, this is part of the appeal of Core and with good reason. But this should not muddle our ultimate assessment. Core Knowledge is not the incarnation of democratic schooling in the cultural sense or, for that matter, the economic sense.

On the face of it, this criticism may seem unwarranted since Hirsch's stated goal is to provide all students with equal access to knowledge, especially those forms needed for economic mobility, which he perceives to be the lifeblood of democracy. Part of the confusion, I contend, lies in how democracy gets defined. Democracy is not solely a political or economic concept. It is just as centrally a cultural one. Any truly credible democratic project is multidimensional—it includes both a struggle for "economic redistribution" as well as a struggle for "cultural recognition"—and these dimensions are deeply interconnected. This argument is powerfully made by Fraser (1997):

> It should be axiomatic that no defensible successor project to socialism can simply jettison the commitment to social equality in favor of cultural difference. To assume otherwise is effectively to fall in line with the reigning neoliberal commonsense. This is not to say, however, that one should cling to socialist orthodoxy and eschew the politics of recognition altogether. On the contrary, critical theorists should rebut the claim that we must make an either/or choice between the politics of redistribution and the politics of recognition. We should aim instead to identify the emancipatory dimensions of both problematics and to integrate them into a single, comprehensive framework. (p. 4)

One illustration Fraser provides in support of her democratic theory centers on race. "Race," she asserts, has "both a political-economic face and cultural-valuational face." She continues:

Its two faces intertwine to reinforce each other dialectically, moreover, because racist and Eurocentric cultural norms are institutionalized in the state and economy, and the economic disadvantage suffered by people of color restricts their "voice." Redressing racial injustice, therefore, requires changing both political economy and culture. (p. 22)

In short, both the cultural and economic fronts must be taken seriously. They are two sides, equally important, of the same coin, which is not to say that they pose identical concerns, that their remedies are the same, or that dilemmas do not arise when trying to pursue change on both fronts (see Fraser, 1997). It is simply to say that one cannot be reduced to the other and that each merits attention as we grapple with how to actualize unfulfilled freedom dreams (Kelley, 2002) and utopian visions (Real Utopias Project, 2007).

Without hesitation, I should make clear that I am taking up these issues for two sets of reasons. The first relates to the arguments made by Hirsch and other neoconservatives who advocate cultural assimilation with little regard for the genuinely undemocratic, oppressive aspects of such a pursuit and who wrongly believe that the interests of democracy are best served by a "common culture." Failure to appreciate the full significance of subaltern cultural recognition to democracy (they do grasp the importance of strategically recognizing marginalized groups to maintain power) is compounded by an equally problematic view of the free market and capitalism: We are told that the embrace of a common culture translates into upward mobility, as though the actually existing economic structure is organized for distributive justice rather than constituting a hierarchical regime of class relations premised on a sustained and unequal allocation of resources. What is more, cultural recognition and economic redistribution are decoupled in neoconservative argumentation, so that the devaluation of particular cultural forms within schools and throughout the nation, miraculously, has little effect on the way in which members of culturally marginalized groups fare in the economy. Clearly, the notions of democratic life that inform neoconservatism need to be troubled.

But I am also taking up these issues for a second set of reasons. These pertain not to neoconservatives, but to those on the left who contend that cultural struggle is epiphenomenal, or a distraction from the "real" problem of economic exploitation and the fight for redistribution. I agree with Fraser (1997) that pitting redistribution against recognition creates a "false antithesis," one that has "structured an increasingly bitter split between 'the social left' and 'the cultural left' in the

United States" (p. 3). These tensions are explored in a collection edited
by Zeus Leonardo (2005), one in which critical theorists and critical
race theorists seek to articulate the relationship between class and race.
Yet the specter of orthodoxy haunts the dialogue, as some lament that
"post-Marxists," or "radical multiculturalists," have been "eager to take
a wide detour around political economy" and "assume that the principal political points of departure...must necessarily be 'cultural'" (Scatamburlo-D'Annibale & McLaren, 2005, p. 141). For those "invoking the
well-worn race/class/gender triplet which can sound, to the uniniti-
ated, both radical and vaguely Marxian," the following clarification is
offered: "It is not [radical]. Race, class, and gender, while they invariably
intersect and interact, are not co-primary" (p. 145). Instead, the conclusion is reached that race:

> is not an adequate explanatory category on its own and that the
> use of "race" as a descriptive or analytical category has serious
> consequences for the way in which social life is presumed to be
> constituted and organized. The category of "race"—the concep-
> tual framework that the oppressed often employ to interpret their
> experiences of inequality "often clouds the concrete reality of
> class, and blurs the actual structure of power and privilege." (p.
> 148)

As one who associates with neo-Marxist traditions, I fully agree with
and respect the argument that a politics of cultural recognition should
not *replace* concerns over political economy. What I do not understand,
as someone who likewise associates with critical race and insurgent multicultural traditions, is why an emphasis on race and culture blurs the
"actual" structure of power. The racial and cultural vision that guides
Core is part of a very real power structure with immense and concrete
consequences for the cultural integrity and identities (not solely the
relations of production and pocketbooks) of oppressed communities.
The effort to grasp the implications of Core and neoconservatism for
cultural democracy is not a misguided, post-Marxist undertaking.
It is an undertaking, as Gramsci knew from his own involvement in
cultural work (Fiori, 1970) and as Fraser (1997) has pointed out in her
own theorizing, which has independent merit. At the very same time,
it must—I repeat, *must*—be part of an economic critique that addresses
how the neoconservative vision reinforces economic subordination,
relies on a false assessment of capitalism, and actually legitimizes state
disinvestment by demonizing particular racial and cultural groups as
state-dependent welfare recipients mired in a "culture of poverty," as
"drains" on the economy, as economic-subordinates-by-choice in a

functional meritocracy, and, in the final analysis, as disposable. The cultural and the economic are interlocking—no doubt—but I also want to make certain that the cultural is taken utterly seriously as a co-primary part of the democratic project by both the right and the left.

Allow me, then, to focus for a moment on the cultural dimensions of democracy and to then underline their relevance to political economy. This recasting of democracy is a key part of making visible the limitations of Core and the neoconservative stance on culture, economy, and the state.

Regarding issues of cultural recognition, Fraser (1997) asserts that cultural domination undermines the democratic project and suggests that part of the remedy lies in "upwardly revaluing disrespected identities and the cultural products of maligned groups" and "recognizing and positively valorizing cultural diversity" (p. 15). This conceptualization of cultural democracy is antithetical to dominant notions of what it means to belong to a nation-state. Much democratic theorizing, in fact, is plagued by the contention that the state must rest on a uniform cultural tradition. Robert Dahl (1998), for instance, discusses what he calls "conditions favorable to democracy." He claims that democracy is "more likely to develop and endure in a country that is culturally fairly homogeneous and less likely in a country with sharply differentiated and conflicting subcultures" (pp. 149–150). Dahl goes on to explain assimilation as a possible solution to the multicultural "threat." Speaking of turn-of-the-twentieth-century immigrants and their descendants, for example, he states in positive terms that assimilation "was mainly voluntary or enforced by social mechanisms (such as shame) that minimized the need for coercion by the state" (p. 152). What is striking is the belief that any democratic nation could find justification—if necessary—for such coercion. When cultural differences cannot be reconciled, he concludes, the formation of independent political units in which cultural groups "possess enough autonomy to maintain their identity" is a solution (p. 155). Understood in this way, multiculturalism is the problem rather than undemocratic structures that fail to recognize diverse cultural forms (see Buras & Motter, 2006; Torres, 1998).

Instead, it is imperative to recognize that diversity does not inherently undermine community or democracy—whether local, national, or global in scale. Fraser (1997) reminds us that there has always been a "host of competing counterpublics," whether "elite women's publics, black publics, or working-class publics" (p. 75). Moreover, she insists that "this need not preclude the possibility of an additional, more comprehensive arena in which members of different, more limited publics talk across lines of cultural diversity" (p. 84). For those who would argue that multiple publics undermine a broader sense of national community, it is important to remember that "people participate in more than one public, and that the membership of different publics may overlap" (p. 84). In this way, community is understood as something that consists of multiple belongings at multiple scales, with bonds at a plethora of levels creating all sorts of unities (see also Buras & Motter, 2006). Such a vision also allows the space necessary for "subaltern counterpublics" to develop oppositional discourses and strategies that challenge dominance, with due recognition that not all subalternities are "virtuous" or "progressive" (Fraser, pp. 81–82; Apple & Buras, 2006).

Regarding issues of economic redistribution, Fraser (1997) emphasizes that economic exploitation, marginalization, and deprivation undermine the democratic project, but she does not presume that staking out a path of "upward mobility" is the solution, as neoconservatives do. Rather, she argues that the remedy for economic injustice "might involve redistributing income, reorganizing the division of labor, subjecting investment to democratic decision making, or transforming other basic economic structures" (p. 15). In other words, Fraser joins the social left in critically assessing the problematic of capitalism and is cognizant that the prevailing political economy requires fundamental restructuring. The rift with neoconservatives is rather obvious: They romanticize capitalism, which they believe functions as a meritocracy as long as one has the cultural capital valued by the marketplace. Recollect, for a moment, Hirsch's assurance regarding the economic fruits of assimilation: "We know it works."

In the final analysis, I believe that reconceptualizing democracy as a radical cultural-economic project can contribute to shaping more emancipatory identities, schools, and nations, ones that neither urge the "exchange" of cultural recognition for economic redistribution nor falsely assert that such an exchange is unproblematic, seamless, or even feasible under capitalism. Such dubious propositions merit aggressive critique in light of the aforementioned interconnections between cultural and economic spheres (Fraser, 1997) and in light of the unequal power relations that characterize the neoliberal state and global capital (Davis, 2006; Harvey, 2005; Saltman, 2007). In the end, a world of difference exists between conceptions of national identity and educational reform premised on a common culture and valorized marketplace, and insurgent multicultural visions based on the recognition of diversity through ongoing negotiations over knowledge and collective identity as well as transformation of cultural and economic structures of power.[1]

Is it not the innovative nature and strategic novelty of Core to skirt deeper issues of cultural recognition and economic redistribution while concurrently using the language of multiculturalism and even building a relatively multicultural alliance around its agenda? In response, we need to be asking: Precisely which legacy does Core draw upon when it comes to multicultural democracy and the pursuit of equality?

"THOU SHALL NOT STAND IDLY BY": CORE KNOWLEDGE AS THE CIVIL RIGHTS FRONTIER?

Reflecting on the disparate meanings and traditions associated with "Jewish" identity and the perennial struggle against oppression, Michael Apple (1999) recalls:

> I remember a picture that had importance in my family. It was a reproduction of a painting by Ben Shahn. It was of two hands, a white one reaching down and clasping the other one which was black. It was as if the black hand was attached to someone who was drowning or falling and the white one was saving it. Across the top of the painting were words in both Hebrew letters and English. They said "Thou Shall Not Stand Idly By." These words speak to the realities of the oppressive conditions of the racial state in which we live. To be black is often to be the other, to be subject to repressive economic and cultural conditions.... However, in that picture are other messages. "We"—the anointed ones, the ones with the best social conscience, the ones who too have experienced centuries of repression—will lift "you" up. Our task is to make this society better. We know the path; we will help you along it.... The hidden text is one that contains a crucial sense of the importance of intervention into oppressive social relationships, of reaching out, of real action. Yet it is combined with (more than?) a hint of arrogance, of certainty in the rightness of one's position, and of which group should be in leadership in joint struggles against oppression. (p. 40)

Thinking back to the position of the UFT in the Ocean Hill-Brownsville crisis, one can see how the image described above captures visually the cultural sentiments and political commitments of many of the Jewish and Catholic white teachers. Partially embedded in their actions was a desire to "not stand idly by." More Effective Schools was their intervention, or the "hand" they extended to poor African American students. At the same time, their sense of the path to equality—and even the very

meaning of civil rights implicitly invoked—contained within it powerful elements of cultural elitism, even as it sought to create a space for
marginalized students in the wider society and future of the nation. In
contradistinction, those students, their parents, and their black teachers
embraced a different concept of which pathway best served the interests
of the African American community and who should be in leadership.

Hirsch mirrors the interventions of UFT teachers through his efforts
around Core Knowledge. Often framing Core in terms of fighting racial
oppression and making democracy real, he is more than a little pre-
sumptuous when it comes to the cultural agenda he lays out. In a somewhat haunting, though surely unintended, bow to the Shahn image,
a recent Core Knowledge book on reading instruction (Davis, 2005)
includes on its front cover a picture of a white hand holding a ring with
two keys. Grasping the keys from below are two separate hands—one
black and one white. While this image, by contrast, contains both a
black and a white hand being "helped" by the keys to reading and educational success, the hand offering the keys remains white. This is a
visual snapshot of a good part of the official Core Knowledge agenda:
white "helping" black to learn, assimilate, and rise.

This is where we must begin to understand how Core is contributing
to the reconstruction of common sense around issues of cultural diversity and political economy, the meaning of civil rights, and the shape
of a just democratic order. Mica Pollock (in progress) makes clear, for
example, that "what specific policies and concrete practices are racially
discriminatory or even racially harmful, and what specific ways of
equalizing opportunity for students of color...are even acceptable or
even desirable, remain highly controversial." Despite the complexities
and debates, Hirsch positions Core as the embodiment, if not the actu-
alization, of an uncontested definition of equality and civil rights. Yet
Core hinges on the troubling cultural equation that informed *Brown
v. Board of Education*: that segregation damaged the identities and life
chances of black children, not white ones, and that black children stood
to gain by sitting alongside white children in classrooms. Delivering the
opinion of the Supreme Court, Chief Justice Earl Warren (1954) wrote:

> Segregation of white and colored children in public schools *has a
> detrimental effect upon the colored children*.... A sense of inferior-
> ity affects the motivation of a child to learn. Segregation with the
> sanction of the law, therefore, has a tendency to [retard] the edu-
> cational and mental development of *negro children* and to deprive
> them of *some of the benefits they would receive* in a racial[ly] inte-
> grated school system [italics added].

The impulse of *Brown* was unidirectional and compensatory, as were integration proposals that sought to bus black children to white schools, but almost never the reverse (for more on the costs of integration ideals for African American education, see Bell, 1995; Siddle Walker, 1996).

On the other hand, the impulse of critical multiculturalism and Black Power were something quite different; cultural integrity was asserted in ways that deconstructed the false position of superiority given to privileged white students and dominant forms of knowledge. Relying on rightist multicultural strategies, Hirsch has responded to the impulses of *Brown* and Black Power by positioning Core in-between discourses of cultural deficiency and civil rights, in-between "Americanism" and "ethnic loyalism," in-between the old history and the new, in-between autonomy and discipline, in-between cultural reaction and cultural recognition. In doing so, Core urges us, pushes us, to think about culture and democracy in specific ways—ways that tend to reinforce patterns of cultural disrespect and pressures to assimilate—and to overlook other understandings. We are being schooled to avoid the radical lanes, left and right, of the American civil rights highway, and to join the wider lane of moderation, which, we are told, promises peace and happiness.

To some, the claim that Core is part of a broader project aimed at reconstructing our common sense around culture and economy may seem overblown. After all, Core is just one of many educational reforms. However, as the theories of Antonio Gramsci remind us, every struggle is inherently an educational one and each contributes something to the legitimization or delegitmization of certain worldviews. Gramsci emphasizes that the educational relationship:

> should not be [understood as] restricted to the field of the strictly "scholastic" relationships by means of which the new generation comes into contact with the old.... This form of relationship exists throughout society as a whole and for every individual relative to other individuals. It exists between intellectual and non-intellectual sections of the population, between the rulers and the ruled, elites and their followers, leaders and led, the vanguard and the body of the army. Every relationship of "hegemony" is necessarily an educational relationship. (Hoare & Nowell Smith, 1971, p. 350)

Power is exercised and contested, in other words, not only or even mainly through brute domination, force, or a *war of maneuver* (although there is certainly enough of that going around), but also through an ongoing *war of position*, meaning that in ways small and large the terrain of struggle between unequally empowered groups is often defined by cultural and ideological interventions aimed at generating consent for particular worldviews and structures of power (Buras & Apple, 2006; Hoare & Nowell Smith, 1971). From above, the war of position is fought by building on the elements of good sense embedded in the everyday conceptions of subaltern groups, while redefining these in dominant cultural directions. Core Knowledge, it must be understood, is one front on which such a battle is being fought. In calling for schools to provide the same curriculum for all students, Hirsch expresses his faith that all children can learn and that the challenge is not one of potential, as has so often been argued, but one of access to so-called literate culture. It is an understandably compelling argument and to make it is to begin to reconstruct the way we might think about equality in schools.

Recognizing that multiculturalism has been assumed and appropriated by the right is far from insignificant. Reminding us that cultural battles are complicated, ongoing, and always have many sides, some of the communities that have adopted Core have redefined it in often unanticipated ways, ones that may serve interests very different from those envisioned by Hirsch and the Core Knowledge Foundation. In turn, the disciplinary mechanisms more recently adopted by the foundation may be understood as yet another maneuver from above to remedy deviance and ideological resistance from below. The balance of forces here is crucial to understand. Core does have its progressive moments, but there are good reasons to conclude that overall the alliance serves neoconservative ends more generally, even if not in each specific instance or classroom. Even if Core is reconstituted on the ground, diverse participation in this initiative lends wider legitimacy to the definitions of equality, civil rights, and democracy that neoconservatives aim to circulate and normalize. Not every individual contest can be won, but that does not mean the overall war of position will be lost by neoconservatives.

THE MULTICULTURAL RIGHT AND THE WAR OF POSITION

In fighting to secure neoconservative visions and power, many are already willing participants on the front lines. At a Core Knowledge school in one suburban town, for example, the strands of fear and elitism that partly run through Hirsch's vision and the Core Knowledge movement were clear before the school was even founded in the mid-1990s. More specifically, a group of largely white, middle-class parents sought to charter a Core school as more low-income students of color entered the district and as the district's strategic planning aimed to accommodate such diversity through curricular and pedagogic restructuring along presumably more progressive lines. Supporting the election of several "back to basics" candidates to the local school board, they circulated a paper, with obvious allusions to Hirsch, which detailed "What Every Voter Needs to Know." One passage read:

> What does it mean to "accept diversity?" Are all ideas, beliefs, cultures, and proposed social paradigms truly equal? In America, we feel a major benefit to schools over the years has been to transmit to our children the ideas and traditions we share as Americans. We share use of the English language, a history, life under a capitalist economic system, and government specified by state and federal constitutions. We do not want to minimize the racial problems our country strives to continue to overcome....However, we are dubious of educational goals that deflect us from the very important unifying role of the school and instead encourage ethnic, racial, and ideological balkanization of our students.

Moreover, the paper suggested that Hirsch's list of cultural literacy items should be made available to all teachers in the district and that teachers should take the list into account when formulating their teaching plans. In turn, some in the district aired frustration regarding the "basics" agenda and the apparent desire to stress "drills and memorization.... [and] a list of 5,000 words or phrases which are the 'distilled' residue of what 90 consultants thought people should know to be 'culturally literate.'" With the basics candidates ultimately elected, the parents next proceeded to charter a Core Knowledge school, which was soon criticized for excluding students of color. Indeed, at a heated school board meeting, one parent addressed the community, "describing the [school] as 'dangerous' and citing the deleterious effects Core [was] having on the common schools." Another parent explained that he was "tired of his tax money going to a segregated public school." Such instantiations of Core reveal a contingent firmly committed to the less democratic, more racially and culturally defensive aims of Hirsch's educational vision and more than willing to respond to the neoconservative call to educational arms. What is more, despite the above criticisms, the Core school attracted far more students than a progressive charter school in the same district, which meant that an increasing number of parents bought into the neoconservative arguments being made about diversity and an impending crisis in the district. Convincing such groups of the value of Core Knowledge as a reform has probably not been an exceedingly difficult task for the Core Knowledge Foundation (Buras, 1997).

The more interesting question, I have argued, is why traditionally oppressed groups have so often embraced Core with equal vigor. Relevant here is the work of Thomas Pedroni (2007b) in which the alliance between the right-wing, neoliberal Bradley Foundation and low-income African American parents around school vouchers in Milwaukee is examined. Although such parents offered their support for voucher schemes, Pedroni argues that they had not, in fact, "become right" politically. Instead, there was a distinct misfit between their reasons for endorsing vouchers, which had to do with a history of racism and inadequate resources in the Milwaukee public schools, and the neoliberal reasons given by members of the Bradley Foundation, which were rooted in critiques of a public school monopoly that stifled the ability of the market to function as a disciplinary mechanism for poorly performing state schools (see also Apple & Pedroni, 2005). Surely this tendency is likewise apparent in the Core Knowledge movement, meaning that there is a stream of traditionally oppressed communities that embraces Core not for the reasons noted by reactionary white suburbanites like those mentioned above, but for reasons that have to do with securing racial justice. This latter stream in the movement supports Core but does not embrace anything that resembles a neoconservative position on cultural demise or Western supremacy. The American Horse School on the Pine Ridge Indian Reservation, for example, teaches Core alongside a Lakota studies and language program.

At the same time, we would be remiss if we overlooked the appeal of neoconservatism *within* oppressed communities for reasons that do more firmly align with neoconservative ideology. As Angela Dillard (2001) eloquently points out, the right itself has become increasingly multicultural:

> American political conservatism can no longer be viewed, or accurately represented, as the exclusive preserve of white, male, and heterosexual persons with comfortable class positions. Rather, it has become a multicultural affair as the past few decades have witnessed the growth of readily identifiable conservative discourses within African American, Latino, and homosexual communities and among women. (p. 2)

This stream, too, is represented in the Core Knowledge movement. As Michael Apple and I have argued elsewhere, subaltern groups do not always speak in a progressive voice (Apple & Buras, 2006). There has been an understandable but dangerous tendency within critical multicultural circles to assume that particular kinds of consciousness correspond with particular kinds of identities. Indeed:

The embrace of dominant and even retrogressive forms by women or communities of color does not correspond with the way subalterns are supposed to believe and act. But this is exactly our point. Existing theories of cultural recognition, especially within education, have been largely premised on the assumption that a particular brand of consciousness is, by and large, always associated with subalternity—one that rejects dominant culture, resists assimilation, or refuses to perpetuate existing relations of unequal power. While it is the case that very real histories have contributed to the development of particular tendencies and sensibilities within oppressed communities, these are not always uniform or progressive, and they are mediated by multiple identifications based on class, race, gender, sexuality, language, "ability," and national origin.... It is crucial to account for the contradictions of subalternity. (p. 273)

In short, there are ideological debates and conflicts within subaltern communities. Members of any given community, moreover, have multiple affiliations, so that, for example, class can temper or reshape one's racial sense of self.

Some of this is explained by Dyson (2005) with regard to a speech made by Bill Cosby at an NAACP event marking the fiftieth anniversary of *Brown*. Cosby articulated harsh critiques that resounded with neoconservative sentiment. He accused poor urban blacks of "not holding up their end in this deal," especially when civil rights activists "marched and were hit in the face with rocks...to get an education, and now we've got these knuckleheads walking around" who "don't parent" and whose children "can't speak English" (pp. xi–xii). In short, Cosby went on to criticize this segment for dependency and cultural backwardness and for not raising themselves up after the sacrifices of civil rights pioneers. Importantly, Dyson stresses:

Cosby's remarks are not the isolated ranting of a solo rhetorical gun slinger, but simply the most recent, and the most visible, shot taken at poor blacks in a more-than-century-old class war in black America. His views are widely held among a number of black constituencies—it is not unusual to hear some black poor and working-class members themselves joining Cosby's ranks.... But Cosby's beliefs are most notably espoused by the *Afristocracy*: upper-middle-class blacks and the black elite who rain down fire and brimstone upon poor blacks for their deviance and pathology, and for their lack of couth and culture. (pp. xiii–xiv)

In comparison to the black elite, the *Ghettocracy*, according to Dyson, is "composed of single mothers on welfare, single working mothers, poor fathers, married poor and working folks, the incarcerated, and a battalion of impoverished children" (p. xiv). Without a doubt, the Afristocracy represents yet another stream in the complicated alliance around Core Knowledge, along with what might be alternatively called the *Latinocracy*, represented not by Cosby, but by figures such as Richard Rodriguez. Thus we might recall Sylvia Peters, the African American educational reformer who headed the initiative with several Core Knowledge schools in the largely low-income, black Sandtown-Winchester neighborhood of Baltimore and who lauded Core teachers for "recivilizing" the nation. Such discourses, as Dyson points out, unfortunately echo "the most vicious elements of the racial uplift philosophy," which "might have as easily veered toward the redemptive elements of uplift: focusing on elements of mass black culture that enable black folk to resist their oppressors, transcend their suffering, and transform their pain" (p. 202). Thus, while Pedroni (2007b) is absolutely correct that not all subaltern groups that participate in largely conservative educational initiatives have "become right," it is also a reality that some have not only become right, but have long embraced retrogressive ideologies and conservative positions. One of the real dangers, which Pedroni fully recognizes and which is likewise true of Core Knowledge, is that the presence of traditionally oppressed communities within neoliberal- and neoconservative-inspired educational reform efforts often helps to bolster the legitimacy of these efforts. Dillard (2001) puts it this way:

> By positioning themselves within the ranks of the Right as both diehard devotees and lukewarm fellow travelers, in both subtle and overt ways [conservative members of subaltern groups] have been steadily expanding the boundaries of the sayable. To be able to preface potentially racist and sexist remarks with the phrase, "As Thomas Sowell says...." or "As Linda Chavez has argued..." is to be able to cannibalize the moral authority of minority voices while skirting responsibility. (pp. 20–21)

Indeed, to have Richard Rodriguez speak at the annual Core Knowledge conference, where he vehemently demanded a common tongue, is something that makes Hirsch's ideological work that much easier. The same arguments that evoked such anger after the publication of *Cultural Literacy* (Hirsch, 1987) in the late 1980s can now apparently be forwarded with far less apprehension in light of the endorsements offered by neoconservatives of color. Along similar lines, the act of drawing upon and even misrepresenting the words of civil rights activist James Farmer to legitimize the Core curriculum represents a powerful, if sometimes duplicitous, method for waging a war of position. It is to invite or recruit the "other side" into the ranks of your battalion. Not every recruit will fully obey, of course, but that is the purpose of discipline, which the Core Knowledge Foundation stands ready to administer in palatable doses.

In the final analysis, we might learn something about the foundations of these peculiar alliances by closely examining Core as an instance—a relatively successful one—of neoconservative school reform. There are multiple streams—some rightist and some not—woven together in a somewhat tense network in which these very segments wrangle over the meanings not only of Core, but of inclusion, civil rights, equality, and democracy.

To better appreciate the slippage between the views of some of these groups, it may be useful to provide an illustration in which there are seemingly overlapping but distinctly different positions on the issue of equality in education. Often the question arises about what separates Hirsch's position from that of Lisa Delpit, an African American educator and scholar who has likewise raised concerns about particular aspects of progressive education in relation to students of color. In her now classic book, *Other People's Children: Cultural Conflict in the Classroom*, Delpit (1995) makes explicit her hesitations with open classrooms and process-oriented literacy education that places "fluency" over the teaching of formal writing "skills," explaining:

> Progressive white teachers seem to say to their black students, "Let me help you find your voice. I promise not to criticize one note as you search for your own song." But the black teachers say, "I've heard your song loud and clear. Now, I want to teach you to harmonize with the rest of the world." (p. 18)

One might legitimately ask: Is this not Hirsch's agenda—that is, to teach students of color to harmonize with the rest of the world? Yet there are major differences between the positions of Hirsch and Delpit. We need only to listen closely to Delpit's next words:

> I run a great risk in writing this—the risk that my purpose will be misunderstood; the risk that those who subject black and other minority children to day after day of isolated, meaningless, drilled "subskills" will think themselves vindicated. That is not the point.

... Students need technical skills to open doors, but they need to be able to think critically and creatively to participate in meaningful and potentially liberating work inside those doors. Let there be no doubt: a "skilled" minority person who is not also capable of critical analysis becomes the trainable, low-level functionary of the dominant society, simply the grease that keeps the institutions which orchestrate his or her oppression running smoothly.... We must insist on "skills" *within the context of* critical and creative thinking. (pp. 18–19)

Such words do not actually reflect the sentiments of Hirsch's words or views. More to the point, it is the critical and liberatory element that is utterly missing from his endorsement of harmonization with dominant cultural forms.

Delpit (1995) goes on to address what she calls a "culture of power," or the ways of talking, writing, and interacting that are required to enter into (and potentially change) the dominant culture. Again sounding a bit like Hirsch, Delpit emphasizes, "Children from middle-class homes tend to do better in school than those from non-middle-class homes because the culture of the school is based on the culture of the upper and middle classes." Yet again, this is where the similarities end. She continues, "Children from other kinds of families operate within perfectly wonderful and viable cultures but not cultures that carry the codes or rules of power" (p. 25). She even proceeds to declare, "I do not advocate that it is the school's job to attempt to change the homes of poor and nonwhite children to match the homes of those in the culture of power. That may indeed be a form of cultural genocide" (p. 30). A culture of *power*? Children from poor families of color operate within *perfectly wonderful* and *viable* cultures? Changing such cultures may be a form of *cultural genocide*? Nothing could be farther from the position advocated by Hirsch, who denies the role of power in defining what counts as knowledge and who describes the culture of power as a "common culture" unmoored from the traditions of any specific group, who refers to the families of working class children and children of color as "bad home schools," and who rarely gives a second thought to the idea that the notions of cultural deficiency and assimilation that he embraces might indeed contribute to the decimation of particular cultures.

When thinking about Core Knowledge, at least in its official incarnation, we would do well to reflect on a crucial question posed by Delpit:

I...do not believe that we should teach students to passively adopt an alternate code. They must be encouraged to understand the value of the code they already possess as well as to understand the power realities in this country. Otherwise they will be unable to work to change these realities. And how does one do that? (p. 40)

She moves on to reveal how one Native Alaskan teacher of Athabaskan Indian students simultaneously teaches students about "Our Heritage Language" and "Formal English." The teacher concentrates much of her initial energies "savoring the words, discussing the nuances" of the students' Indigenous linguistic tradition. She next goes on to tell students, "We're going to learn two ways to say things. Isn't that better? One way will be our Heritage way. The other will be Formal English" (p. 41). In short, this teacher puts these two traditions in critical dialogue with one another, ensuring that students both understand the value of their own culture and master the elements of the culture of power.

There is indeed evidence that particular Core Knowledge schools are doing precisely this—teaching students about Thomas Jefferson, for instance, but including critical elements of his biography and early presidential history, or teaching students Core Knowledge as it intersects with the cultures and histories of traditionally oppressed groups. As one African American principal (interestingly, the successor of the principal who praised the classical rather than African-centered approach of Core) explained, Core students study poems such as Walt Whitman's "I Hear America Singing," but also Langston Hughes' "I, Too, Sing America" (Achievement Alliance, 2007). In this way, the heritage of students might be taught in interaction with Core—the "Formal English" part of the curriculum. To the extent that this is done, Core has the potential to advance a progressive and even liberatory educational agenda. But we must also realize that even if this is done in particular instances, it does not change the fact that there are powerful neoconservative forces that do *not intend* for Core to be used this way and that *will continue* to attempt to advance their own cultural authority both in schools and in other social arenas. They will use the participation of oppressed groups in such reforms to establish wider consent for their vision. They will invoke definitions of multiculturalism and civil rights which render invisible more culturally democratic and radically transformative articulations. They will write and rewrite the pages of history to support particular and largely nostalgic understandings of the national past. And they will make every effort to discipline gross cultural and ideological deviance within Core and other related movements. Considering the ideological work that neoconservatives are doing around notions of culture, economy, and schooling, and the intense conditions of teaching that prevail in schools, the balance of forces in the movement will likely tend to favor neoconservative ends.

If the new hegemony is to be unsettled, a concerted and countervailing war of position must be fought to take back and revisualize yet again the meanings of equality and multicultural democracy.

A KNOWLEDGE DEFICIT OR A CULTURAL DEBT?

One counterhegemonic approach may be to interrogate the discourse around the knowledge deficit and to redirect the conversation toward a focus on the cultural debt, with an emphasis on forms of domination that have historically affected dispossessed communities. I want to think aloud about this for a moment. Hirsch (2006) chose to entitle his most recent book on reading, *The Knowledge Deficit: Closing the Shocking Education Gap for American Children*. Yet Ladson-Billings (2006) has challenged us to stop thinking in terms of deficit and the achievement gap and to begin thinking in terms of the "education debt" that has accumulated over time. The education debt refers to the economic, socio-political, and moral resources that we *should have been investing* to equalize education since the nation's founding. Part of this debt, I would add, is cultural, as Ladson-Billings (1994) recognizes in her own work on culturally relevant pedagogy (itself a lineal descendant of Ocean Hill-Brownsville and even much earlier critiques of destructive forms of mis-education). We must restructure curriculum and reform in ways that contribute to remedying this part of the debt. In the spirit of the radical pluralists of Ocean Hill-Brownsville as well as Fraser's radical democratic theory, this involves critically recognizing and upwardly revaluing the cultures and histories of diverse groups that have built and constituted the nation—those heretofore disparaged or excluded from the "core." This is dead serious work—for instance, two-thirds of the residents of New Orleans, mostly African American, remain displaced since Hurricane Katrina, while some 2,000 perished in the floodwaters. Despite the fact that the city was culturally and economically constructed on their backs, African Americans, especially poor and working class blacks, have been demonized and given no place in elite plans for building a new New Orleans—a strategy portrayed as "benign neglect" since removal will unravel the "culture of poverty" in which so many were supposedly mired before Katrina (Buras, 2005, 2007a, forthcoming). Macroaggressions like this necessitate making visible the deficiencies of prevailing conceptions of democracy, which too often exclude deeply felt issues of identity and cultural experience. In this regard, the notion of cultural debt, as opposed to deficit, is central to the war of position against neoconservative school reform.

It will not be an easy road. One of the early critiques guiding critical race theorists in the field of law was that more radical discourses on and visions of civil rights and racial justice had been mainstreamed, or taken up in ways that compromised their transformative potential: race consciousness was cast to the margins by "meritocracy" and "color blindness"; critiques of racism and white supremacy morphed into calls for "equal opportunity"; integration, at least as an ideal, took precedence over the equalization of resources and the interests of children of color (Crenwshaw et al., 1995). In the field of education, critical race scholars similarly warned:

> The current multicultural paradigm functions in a manner similar to civil rights law. Instead of creating radically new paradigms which ensure justice, multicultural reforms are routinely "sucked back into the system"; and just as traditional civil rights law is based on a foundation of human rights, the current multicultural paradigm is mired in liberal ideology that offers no radical change in the current order. Thus, critical race theory in education, like its antecedent in legal scholarship, is a radical critique of both the status quo and the purported reforms.... As critical race theory scholars we unabashedly reject a paradigm that attempts to be everything to everyone and consequently becomes nothing for anyone, allowing the status quo to prevail. (Ladson-Billings & Tate, 2006, p. 25)

I have a good deal of sympathy for this position. That very dynamic, after all, is precisely what accounts for rightist multiculturalism, which carefully strained away the critical elements of the multicultural project (e.g., cultural recognition, critiques of unequal power, transformation) and "sucked back into the system" what remained (e.g., cultural remediation, core knowledge as a civil right, integration into the existing order).

Past president of the Core Knowledge Foundation, Barbara Garvin-Kester, began an initiative before her departure in 2006, one "aimed at fostering the Core Knowledge mission in new venues" (Core Knowledge Foundation, 2006a, p. 4). This included reaching out to organizations and policymakers as disparate as the Fordham Foundation, National Alliance of Black School Educators, the NAACP, and National Council of La Raza. It is not surprising that Garvin-Kester (2006a) deemed Core Knowledge "a multicultural experience." "The time teachers and students should devote to particular subjects or topics in school presents a constant point of debate," she acknowledged, especially when it comes to "the historical and cultural contributions of ethnic groups." There is no reason to "despair," she reassures, because Core Knowledge supporters "have the basic curriculum that already recognizes these contributions," that is, "an agreed-upon framework of multicultural elements to introduce every American child to the contributions of diverse peoples who make up the mosaic of one unified nation" (para. 1). And besides, she reminds Core's beneficiaries:

> the *Sequence* is not intended to comprise the entire school curriculum; it presents only the common core of knowledge that enables children from all walks of life to master, fully, the language and background knowledge necessary to compete in the dominant U.S. culture and in the broader global workplace. (para. 2)

Teachers still have time, therefore, to address "local requirements." In the same breathe, she announces the foundation's release of *Grace Abounding: The Core Knowledge Anthology of African-American Literature, Music, and Art*—imagine that, two decades after the publication of *Cultural Literacy* and its corresponding, Eurocentric list. This is the reigning multicultural paradigm—a diverse mosaic but unified, local but also global, relatively binding but also *Abounding*. To pose a classic Marxist question: What is to be done?

Hirsch's advice to progressives is the following: "If it's social change you want, then acculturate first, so that everyone can argue in the same language. The cultural left are willing, for the sake of an ideal or even of a theory that hasn't been fully worked out, to risk condemning a generation to ignorance and to poverty" (in Hitchens, 1990, p. A32). Again, what is to be done? I propose that a crucial move consists of making visible the fact—yes, the fact—that the "theories" have been tested and that, contrary to neoconservative claims, they are not responsible for condemning a generation to marginalization. We have evidence that educators, just like the one that Delpit mentioned, are engaged in radically democratic educational work that reaches beyond the confines of cultural literacy and toward a remediation of the cultural debt we have been discussing. Positing that students from traditionally oppressed groups are knowledge deficient and then proposing a program of compensation strategically packaged as a civil rights intervention is a colonizing act. There is another way forward.

FROM CULTURAL LITERACY TO LITEROCRACY

Rather than allowing Hirsch and his neoconservative compatriots to colonize the meanings "cultural literacy" and "democracy," critical scholars, educators, and community activists need to widely circulate the counterhegemonic notion of "literocracy." Maisha Fisher (2007) defines literocracy as a critical "intersection of literacy and democracy," one which emphasizes "that language processes exist in partnership with action" (p. 4). She chronicles the Power Writers, a group of students in the Bronx—African American, Dominican, Puerto Rican, Colombian, El Salvadoran, West Indian, and "White" youth—who write and perform spoken word poetry with their teachers as part of a seminar in an alternative public high school. She explains: "The Power Writers and their teachers built a literocracy, a space in which each participant had an opportunity to access both written and spoken words while speaking his or her own truth" (p. 4). Through such pedagogy students were to move beyond their "ascribed lives," as one teacher, Joe, put it. "I want you to be literate in as many ways as possible" was his guiding philosophy (p. 5).

One powerful example of this is found in the way that teachers and students negotiate the relationship between "Standard English" and *Bronxonics*, a term that Joe invented to capture not only the "features in 'nonstandard' English but also...the cadence, style, and vocabulary used on some of the Power Writers' blocks in the Bronx, influenced by Spanish mixed with English and African American Vernacular English" (Fisher, 2007, p. 38). Fisher writes, "I became keenly interested in how Joe attempted to achieve a balance between preparing students for the world outside of the Bronx and preserving 'around the way' language so they could navigate their neighborhoods" (p. 38). What she witnessed was students writing and rewriting the world through their poetry, which built from their life experiences and community histories, incorporated 'around the way' language, but also drew upon sometimes unfamiliar and dominant forms of knowledge—words that Joe encouraged students to "fish for" and "catch." In doing so, students not only commanded what Hirsch calls common culture. They "redefined literacy to include their own words, voices, and faces around the table" (p. 83). One student's words expressed the profound implications of literocracy when she shared, "This poem is called 'Why do I write.'...I write because I had many unspoken words....I write not just because I'm a writer but because I am the words that I write" (Jennifer in Fisher, p. 66).

The significant differences between cultural literacy and literocracy are perhaps best illustrated in an exchange between Joe and one of the Power Writers, Manny. Manny initiated his work with the group by announcing, "I can't write." Months later, he shared a powerful piece of writing with his peers that reflected concerns about the in/significance of his life. In turn, Joe had this to say:

> In this house, we see ourselves as travelers. And for you to go from "My name is Manny and I can't write" to somebody who thinks about the world in such a complex way.... I claim you. I will always claim you. You mine. You are developing your mind, your desire to learn about the world. You used to be a boxer, and you used to be a knuckle master, and now you can master the word if that's what you want. (in Fisher, 2007, pp. 91–92)

To "claim" a student, to embrace the fullness of who they are biographically, linguistically, culturally, and so forth, and to simultaneously stand with them as they move beyond their "ascribed life" is a world apart from Hirsch's sense of mission: "My proposals are antitracking, antidiscrimination. They are designed to rescue the poor and the underclass" (in Hitchens, 1990, A32). To rescue, however, is not to claim—it is to assist one in abandoning who they are for what you want them to become. To claim is to recognize and value, while remaining permanently invested in the future course of the individual and the communities (in the *plural*) of which they are a part. As Fisher so eloquently explains: Joe's words to Manny "communicated that there was a relationship between literacy learning and developing one's full humanity" (p. 91). Commanding Core Knowledge in order to enter dominant culture and the marketplace has little to do with developing our fullest humanity or our highest democratic ideals. While Hirsch speaks of critical educators condemning children to marginalization, the Power Writing seminar was "a way for students of color to live outside the dismaying statistics of failure, poverty" (p. 99). I firmly believe that one of the most important things that we can do to battle the hegemony of rightist multiculturalism is to support and build such literocratic educational experiments and to widely share the counterstories (Solórzano & Yosso, 2002) that they represent. Such stories will teach us more than a few core lessons on the meaning of an education that develops one's full humanity rather than one which dictates living one's life as ascribed by the common—or more accurately, neoconservative—culture.

Appendices

A

METHODOLOGIES: GETTING TO THE CORE OF THE MATTER

For those interested in how I got to the core of the matter, this appendix details the various methodologies that were utilized, including review of historical research, content analysis, literature review, fieldwork, and discourse analysis. The protocol for the discourse analysis is provided. I also share the rationales and theories that guided my decision to use a particular method.

REVIEW OF HISTORICAL RESEARCH: CHAPTER 1

As my initial research on Core Knowledge proceeded, I assumed that Core constituted a conservative "reaction" to demands for cultural recognition articulated during the movements of the 1960s. This interpretation was shaped by one of the prevailing narratives on neoconservatism, which portrays the cultural new right as an oppositional group (or set of groups) bent on restoring those traditions of knowledge threatened by more recent progressive gains. Part of this is indeed the case. However, I became increasingly convinced that this account was not fully historicized. To what did the "neo" in neoconservatism refer? Here again, it was commonly assumed that what was new about this sect of conservatives was their desire and effort to restore the cultural order presumably threatened by the aforementioned movements. In other words, their conservatism was not new per se; instead, that which was new was their emerging reaction and their defensive agenda.

I began to do some digging and first discovered a book written by Peter Steinfels (1979) entitled *The Neoconservatives: The Men Who are*

Changing America's Politics. In this book, Steinfels explores "the road to neoconservatism" and reveals that many leading neoconservatives had actually been old leftists. That some segment of the cultural new right had originated on the old left was a significant finding, particularly in relation to contextualizing Core, which clearly had melded elements left and right within the movement.

Perhaps most revealing was the resonance between my own critique of Hirsch's educational vision and his underlying assumptions (Buras, 1999b) and Steinfels' (1979) discussion of the major tenets of neoconservative thought, including the assertion that "a crisis of authority" had "overtaken America and the West generally," that the crisis was "primarily a cultural crisis," and that neoconservatism needed to confront this crisis by insisting that "authority be reasserted." Although I had written "Questioning Core Assumptions" more than five years before reading Steinfels' book, his chapter on "What Neoconservatives Believe" and my piece in *Harvard Educational Review* on Hirsch's ideology were remarkably similar.

From that point, I continued to search for and read writings on the history of neoconservatism. Despite the relative scarcity of historiography in this area, I was able to formulate a substantive reading list that included both primary and secondary sources. A groundbreaking special issue of *American Jewish History* on American Jewish political conservatism, which had just come out in 1999, was very helpful. In addition to such secondary works, I also found and read a number of primary sources, including autobiographies and oral histories of leading neoconservative intellectuals, and archived issues of *Commentary*, *The Public Interest*, and *Dissent*, a journal established in response to the first two. In 2005, *The Public Interest* also put out a special issue to commemorate its last and fortieth year, which provided yet another window into some of this history. Since my reading focused on various streams within neoconservatism, including African Americans, the original writings of Thomas Sowell and Shelby Steele, for example, were consulted, while secondary works were simultaneously found helpful, particularly Angela Dillard's (2001) *Guess Who's Coming to Dinner Now?* Combined with readings on educational history, the above kinds of sources enabled me to write chapter 1 and to situate Core Knowledge within a longer and more complicated history.

CONTENT ANALYSIS: CHAPTER 2

It is fairly accurate to say that I performed a content analysis before writing and publishing "Questioning Core Assumptions" (Buras,

1999b), a portion of which ultimately became chapter 2. Although a fully systematic approach was probably not required in order to grasp the underlying assumptions that guided Hirsch (1996) in *The Schools We Need and Why We Don't Have Them*, I was quite methodical in my analysis of the book. It is essential to note that I did not simply read the book and then generate a list of assumptions. Instead, I read the book very carefully three times and took tedious notes the third time. These notes consisted of writing down words, phrases, and sentences from the book that appeared frequently, represented central ideas about culture and education, and seemed to coalesce around certain themes, which I had begun to discern during previous readings. These notes on the book's content, which totaled fifty pages, were then color coded for associations. Based on this, I was able to specify five major assumptions under which the notes variously fit. This was the process used to excavate the ideological underpinnings of Hirsch's educational vision as embodied in his most major work to date—*The Schools We Need* (1996). While not a full scale content analysis, the approach used to develop and write the original article was much more rigorous than just reading the book and writing a review of it. *Harvard Educational Review* did not publish it as a book review, in fact, but as an essay review, which is more comprehensive in its scope. This reflected my intent to use the book as a means for revealing the deeper ideology and vision on which Core was officially based and to situate the book and its content within a much broader educational and political project under the leadership of neoconservatives.

LITERATURE REVIEW AND
FIELDWORK: CHAPTERS 3 AND 5

Tracing the Core Knowledge movement in chapter 3 required years of work. I first began studying Core in 1997 as a master's student in the Department of Curriculum and Instruction at the University of Wisconsin, Madison. Over the next decade, including my tenure as a public high school history teacher and a doctoral student at Wisconsin, I slowly built up an archive of literature on Core—one going back to its origin in the late 1980s. This archive was comprehensive and included the full range of materials produced by the Core Knowledge Foundation, such as pamphlets, informational literature, the *Common Knowledge* newsletter (even before its days as an online publication), special and annual reports, informative videos, Core curriculum resources (e.g., *Sequence, What Your K–6 Grader Needs to Know* series, collections of Core Knowledge teacher-generated lesson plans, Baltimore Curriculum

Project lesson plans, Pearson Learning–Core Knowledge history and geography textbook series), articles by E. D. Hirsch, lists of Core Knowledge schools over the years and materials from school websites, studies commissioned by the Core Knowledge Foundation, writings by Core Knowledge school administrators, teachers, and advocates, and pieces on Core from local and national magazines and newspapers.

Moreover, I also did some fieldwork in a Core Knowledge school as a master's student in 1997. Although the school was unable to fully accommodate my research, I had the opportunity to speak with and interview key members of the school community, tour the school, and gather additional literature on the school from a community newspaper and a public library, where the school archived its newsletters. This enabled me to develop a portrait of the chartering of a Core Knowledge school in a suburban community, which I partly discuss in chapter 5, and to think through the political struggles surrounding the school. For a host of reasons, I was unable to complete a parallel study of an urban Core Knowledge school prior to publishing this book, so I decided against publishing the suburban portrait in its entirety. Additionally, I became increasingly convinced that such ethnographic work merited its own book. To this end, I encourage researchers.

In 2004, I attended the 13th annual National Core Knowledge Conference sponsored by the Core Knowledge Foundation. Held in Atlanta, the conference was attended by nearly 2,100 administrators, teachers, and parents from Core Knowledge schools across the nation. As a conference attendee, I was able to hear keynote addresses, observe Core Knowledge school performances and award ceremonies, witness teachers sharing and presenting Core lesson plans, listen to foundation representatives, principals, teachers, and parents participating in sessions, and review Core resources at the book exhibit. This experience helped me to better understand the complexities and dynamics of the movement and provided a set of conference-related documents and notes on which to reflect.

Taken together and collected over the course of nearly a decade, these resources provided a rich archive of data for writing about the growth of the Core Knowledge movement.

DISCOURSE ANALYSIS: CHAPTER 4

In chapter 4, I aimed to provide a nuanced understanding of the official Core curriculum through a critical discursive analysis of purposefully sampled material from history textbooks edited by Hirsch (2002) for

Core Knowledge schools. The questions at the center of this part of my research were:

How are diverse groups represented in the national narratives of Core Knowledge history textbooks, and how do associated teacher guides relate pedagogically to those narratives?

What does this analysis reveal about how the official Core Knowledge curriculum conceptualizes U.S. history and identity?

Focusing on how diverse groups are represented in these national narratives, I was guided by two theoretical traditions: first, critical educational theories that understand curriculum as selective in its content and reflective of struggles between differently empowered groups to define knowledge (Apple, 2000; Freire, 1993; McCarthy, 1998); and second, theories of history that recognize narratives of the past as constructions informed by particular ideologies rather than complete, fully objective accounts based on direct access to an archival record unmediated by interpretation (Beard, 1934; Becker, 1955; Kaestle, 1992; Kelley, 1993; Southgate, 2001).

Informed by these traditions and a methodology elaborated by critical discourse analyst James Gee (1999; see also Jaworski & Coupland, 1999), I prepared a subset of questions and codes based on my primary research question regarding the representation of diverse groups in Core textbooks (see concluding section of this appendix). More to the point, the codes facilitated the processing of selected historical narratives and enabled me to discern linguistic patterns—the presence or absence of dominant and subordinate groups, the existence of major and minor storylines that detail the nature of group experience, and the connotation of utterances that characterize relationships between groups. Based on the coded material, analytic memos noting significant patterns were written. These memos, placed alongside relevant debates in historiography pertaining to textual content as well as the literature on school history texts, informed the conclusions drawn about Core's depiction of national history and identity. In an effort to triangulate data sets, associated teacher guides were reviewed to assess how recommended pedagogic interventions reinforced, challenged, or transformed textbook representations.

More specifically, the guiding questions and codes that I prepared helped to facilitate the discursive organization, coding, and processing of the textbooks and review of the teacher guides. Printed materials were first carefully read and coded according to my questions and emergent theories about how language was functioning in the text. Once this process was complete and patterns had been discerned, the printed text was demarcated and discursively organized as a typed transcript and then coded in a more refined fashion. Informal notes based on the coded material were prepared and used to develop analytic memos that articulated responses to each of my guiding questions based on the data generated.

In sum, I examined all or significant portions of the following: immigration and citizenship (grade 2) and immigration (6); civil rights leaders (2) and American reformers (4); Mount Rushmore presidents (K) and early presidents (4); industrialization and urbanization in America (6); and exploring the west (1), earliest Americans (3), and Native Americans—cultures and conflicts (5). In making these choices, I considered the scope and organization of the curriculum and aimed to balance the various groups examined and the historical periods covered. Although I was unable to discuss all of the data that I generated and all of the texts that I analyzed, the patterns noted in chapter 4 are representative of the broader patterns that I found.

I also reviewed the teacher guides associated with any texts that I discursively analyzed from grades K–2, and read even those U.S. history texts for grades K–6 that I did not discursively analyze. Images in all discursively analyzed texts were also examined.

Before planning and initiating the discursive analysis, I completed a literature review of past textbook analyses and attempted to formulate a method that built upon the strengths and mediated against the weaknesses of earlier research (Alter, 1995; Anyon, 1983; Banks, 1969; Brophy, McMahon, & Prawat, 1991; Cobble & Kessler-Harris, 1993; Commeyras & Alvermann, 1996; Cruz, 1994; Ellington, 1986; Garcia & Sadoski, 1986; Garcia & Tanner, 1985; Hahn & Blankenship, 1983; Kretman & Parker, 1986; Potter & Rosser, 1992; Sleeter & Grant, 1991; Tetreault, 1984; Wade, 1993; White, 1988; Zimmerman, 2002). I completed further reading on the use of images in history textbooks, associated shortcomings, and issues surrounding the interpretation of visual images as historical texts (Burke, 2001; Dekker, 1996; Masur, 1998; Roeder, 1994, 1998; Trachtenberg, 1989; Wexler, 2000).

I closely analyzed an array of texts and reviewed associated teacher guides under the presumption that the rigor of the study would be heightened through the examination of multiple data sets. The various sources of data were used in a "triangulated" manner to assess the fitness of interpretations by taking note of the patterns and tensions within and across the data sets. Further, critical discourse analysis—with its close attention to linguistic details and patterns and an emphasis on grounding conclusions in those details—set the study apart from past textbook analyses that have been quantitative in nature and attended to the frequency of references (e.g., how many times women were mentioned) at the expense of analyzing the context and nature of the reference (e.g., how women were constructed in the narrative) and its relationship to historiography (e.g., how the narrative relates to broader debates about writing women's history). This last point is particularly important in that this study is distinguished by its grounding in historiography and related debates, its close attention to the use of visual images in history texts (another area that has often been approached only quantitatively rather than qualitatively), and its concern with issues related to history as a field of teaching (Cornbleth, 2000; Levine, Lowe, Peterson, & Tenorio, 1995; Levstik & Barton, 2001; Schweber, 2004; Vansledright, 2002; Wineburg, 2001). In addition, many past textbook analyses have failed to adequately define questions and coding schemes and to explain how it is that textual citations relate to or represent the broader text (see Wade, 1993). Gee (1999) has argued that validity in discourse analysis is largely a function of convergence—answers to research questions are compatible, coverage—the analysis is applicable to related sorts of data, and linguistic details—the analysis is tightly tied to details of linguistic structure. This study attends to each of these measures.

Below are broader questions that I kept in mind throughout the discourse analysis as well as specific questions that were asked of the texts and teacher guides, along with associated codes that I used.

BACKGROUND QUESTIONS

According to Core Knowledge curriculum materials and related literature, why should students study the past?

What conversations, debates, and contexts are relevant to understanding the construction of U.S. history in Core Knowledge texts? Are there associated tensions?

Which epistemologies shape Core Knowledge narratives of the past?

QUESTIONS WITH RELATED CODES

1. *Which* dominant and subaltern identities—whether individuals or groups—are represented in or absent from Core Knowledge United States history texts? (e.g., participants—nouns and noun phrases) How *specific* are references to dominant and subaltern groups? Are members of particular groups named? (e.g., use of proper nouns) With what frequency?

Ind–S	subaltern individual in text
Ind–D	dominant individual in text
Ind–S/D	individual whose status is either ambiguous in text, or both subaltern and dominant at the same time in text
Grp–S	subaltern group in text
Grp–D	dominant group in text
Grp–S/D	group whose status is either ambiguous in text, or both subaltern and dominant at the same time in text
Absent: ___	note made alongside text that indicates a significant omission, such as an individual or group either not mentioned or insufficiently discussed

Note on use of the terms *subaltern* and *dominant*: For the purposes of this study, I define as *subaltern* an individual or group in a subordinate position of power in relation to a more powerful individual or group within a given historical context. Alternatively, I define as *dominant* an individual or group in a position of power over another individual or group within a given historical context. I do recognize that both individuals and groups exist in relation to multiple axes of power and can occupy contradictory spaces of dominance and subalternity at the same time or one or another position of power depending on the context. These issues were dealt with as carefully as possible in both coding and analyzing data. At the same time, I contend that distributions of power have been structured in ways that are sufficiently stable to warrant the use of these categories in analyzing the past.

2. How are dominant and subaltern identities and experiences constructed in the narratives present in Core Knowledge United States history texts?

MajCM major cultural model, storyline, vision of the past, idea, or ideological frame that drives the historical narrative

MinCM an alternative, minor cultural model, storyline, vision of the past, idea, or ideological frame that shapes the historical narrative, but to a less significant degree than the major cultural model

S1, S2 . . . refers to associated parts of the storyline or macro-structure of the narrative

How are dominant and subaltern individuals, groups, cultures, actions, and experiences depicted or constructed through grammar, including adjectives, verbs, and satellites such as adverbial clauses?

For example, how are participants described (adjectives)? What did participants do or experience (verbs)? What was the nature of the action or experience (verb choice and satellites such as adverbial clauses)?

Adj/Vrb/Sat (Describe)   an adjective, verb, or satellite, such as an adverbial clause, that describes or characterizes dominant or subaltern individuals, groups, actions, or nature of experience; refers to microstructure of text

Note: Based upon guiding questions, a careful reading of the written text, and emergent theories about how language was operating in the text, the printed text was given an initial coding. Based on what was learned from this process (e.g., macrostructure of the story, choice and use of grammar), the printed text was next demarcated and discursively organized as a typed transcript, with relevant grammatical devices (i.e., adj/vrb/sat) underlined and characterized, and other codes also applied in a more refined fashion.

3. How are historical *relations* between dominant and subaltern groups represented (e.g., connotation of verb, order and relation of clauses in sentence)? When are agentic subjects present or absent (e.g., participants in sentence)? To what effect and what consequence?

Rel + : ___   relation depicted as positive, cooperative, equal

Rel – : ___   relation depicted as negative, conflictual, unequal

No Rel   groups are not discussed in relation to one another

Rel Other: ___ relation that does not fit into above categories (e.g., we/they)

What are the connections and disconnections within and across utterances of larger text? What are the effects or consequences? What forms of coherence or incoherence result?

4. From whose perspective is history told? And when? If the text is heteroglossic, how do the various social languages, grammars, and cultural models blend or conflict? Encourage or deny particular affiliations or understandings of the past?

> **Perspect I/E:** ___ notes perspective from which narrative is implicitly or explicitly told; note made each time there is a shift in perspective; include instances when narrative explicitly urges student to assume the view of a particular individual or group or when a quote represents a specific viewpoint

> *Note*: At times, this code may somewhat overlap with the MajCM and MinCM codes.

5. *How* are dominant and subaltern identities constructed in the visual images present in Core Knowledge United States history texts?

> **Source Y/N** yes, source of image is specified in text/no, source of image is not specified in text
>
> **Historical Y/N** yes, source is archival in nature/no, source is not archival in nature
>
> **Caption** caption is provided to explain meaning of or provide context for interpreting visual image—for instance, its original producer, character of the medium, or historic purpose or use of image
>
> **ImageWho** description of who is in image
>
> **Ind–S, Ind–D, Ind–S/D, Grp–S, Grp–D, Grp–S/D** _ _ ( ) __ indicates race, gender, (status such as child, immigrant, or other category), and class; Example: African American male child who is poor is coded AfM (C) Poor
>
> | | |
> |---|---|
> | **Af** | African American |
> | **As** | Asian American |
> | **E** | European American |
> | **L** | Latino/a American |
> | **N** | Native American |
> | **F** | Female |
> | **M** | Male |
> | **(C)** | Child |
> | **(I)** | Immigrant |
> | **Elite** | Elite or Upper Class |
> | **Mid** | Middle Class |
> | **Work** | Working Class |
> | **Poor** | Poor |

ImageWhat description of event, occurrence, condition, or
state of affairs depicted

Image/Text relation of visual image to the written text (e.g.,
does image reinforce, conflict with, or substitute for textual
discussion?)

Note: A chart was used to record this data.

6. How do the textbook narratives relate to historiography and
associated debates?
To what degree does the text reference *evidence* of the past?
Which evidence is included and excluded? To what effect?

Hist Evid notable information cited to support a point

Absent: ___ note made alongside text regarding the absence
of significant evidence when compared with historiography and associated debates

(?) inaccurate or gross misrepresentation of existing
historical evidence

References list of potential historical works that illuminate
historiography in a given area (e.g., turn-of-the-
century immigration)

Note: Again, these codes may partially overlap with those
related to coding dominant and subaltern individual and group
absences as well as those related to historical relations between
groups and the perspective taken in the text. Depending on the
nature of the text, these codes provide sufficient flexibility so
that the most appropriate code can be used, while also ensuring that there are enough tools to work with the data.

7. How do the teacher guides reinforce, extend, challenge, or
transform textbook constructions of dominant and subaltern
identities and experiences?

B

CORRESPONDENCE ON THE POLITICS OF ANTONIO GRAMSCI FROM *HARVARD EDUCATIONAL REVIEW*

SPENCER RESPONDS TO BURAS

To the Editors:

Your Spring 1999 issue of the *Harvard Educational Review* includes an Essay Review entitled "Questioning Core Assumptions: A Critical Reading of and Response to E. D. Hirsch's *The School We Need and Why We Don't Have Them*." The reviewer, Kristen L. Buras, tells us that her purpose includes locating Hirsch's work "within New Right politics" (p. 67) and "situat[ing] the book within the conservative restoration" (p. 67). Further, she describes Hirsch as "perhaps the most influential neoconservative voice over the last decade" (p. 69) and his educational program as inherently undemocratic and at odds with the achievement of social justice.

Yet Ms. Buras fails to mention a striking portion of *Schools* that directly challenges her Paulo Freire–based doctrine that political progressivism requires educational progressivism, and shows that another revered hero of the Left totally disagreed.

Hirsch writes, "In 1932, the Communist Antonio Gramsci, writing from jail (having been imprisoned by Mussolini), was one of the first to detect the paradoxical consequences of the new 'democratic education,' which stressed 'life relevance' and other naturalistic approaches over hard work and the transmission of knowledge" (p. 6). As Gramsci put it in his book *Education*:

181

182 • Rightist Multiculturalism

The new concept of schooling is in its romantic phase, in which the replacement of "mechanical" by "natural" methods has become unhealthily exaggerated. Previously pupils at least acquired a certain baggage of concrete facts. Now there will no longer be any baggage to put in order. The most paradoxical aspect of it all is that the new type of school is advocated as being democratic, while in fact it is destined not merely to perpetuate social differences but crystallize them in Chinese complexity. (p. 6)

Startlingly, Hirsch adds that at the time it was "Il Duce's educational minister, Giovanni Gentile, in contrast to Gramsci, [who was] an enthusiastic proponent of the new ideas emanating from Teachers College, Columbia University, in the United States" (p. 6).

What Gramsci saw, Hirsch continues, was that

to denominate such methods as phonics and memorization of the multiplication table as "conservative," while associating them with the political right, amounted to serious intellectual error....Gramsci held...that political progressivism demanded educational conservatism. The oppressed class should be taught to master the tools of power and authority—the ability to read, write, and communicate—and to gain enough traditional knowledge to understand the worlds of nature and culture surrounding them. Children, particularly the children of the poor, should not be encouraged to flourish "naturally," which would keep them ignorant and make them slaves of emotion. They should learn the virtue of hard work, gain the knowledge that leads to understanding, and master the traditional culture in order to command its rhetoric. (pp. 6–7)

As Hirsch sums up his own and Gramsci's views, "Educational progressivism is a sure means for preserving the status quo, whereas the best practices of educational conservatism are the only means whereby children from disadvantaged homes can secure the knowledge and skills that will enable them to improve their condition" (p. 7).

More and more progressives agree with Hirsch's and Gramsci's point as stated above. Examples include the politically liberal founders of Mathematically Correct, the nationwide organization of distinguished scientists and math professors, who promote rigorous teaching of traditional mathematics and rage at fellow liberals for patronizing and shortchanging poor children. Similarly, other liberal educators join in actively urging restoration of explicit phonics in teaching reading, as the calamitous results of whole-language teaching come to light. Hirsch himself is an ultimate example of a lifelong political progressive, much of whose entire purpose is greater social equity. And even his frequent adversary, leading progressive educator Howard Gardner, recommends for that purpose a core curriculum such as Hirsch's in his latest book, *The Disciplined Mind*. "Especially for disadvantaged children, who do not acquire literacy in the dominant culture at home," Gardner writes, "such a prescribed curriculum helps to provide a level playing field and to ensure that future citizens enjoy a common knowledge base" (p. 107). This is pure Hirsch, and Gramsci.

Kristen Buras's determined avoidance of this portion of E. D. Hirsch's book indicates a rigid ideological orthodoxy that impoverishes what might have been a more stimulating discussion.

Louisa C. Spencer
School Volunteer, P.S. 198
New York City

[Spencer is a member of the Core Knowledge Foundation's board of trustees.]

BURAS REPLIES

In 1979, Harold Entwistle published the book *Antonio Gramsci: Conservative Schooling for Radical Politics*. Despite Gramsci's "revolutionary political and social theory," Entwistle argued, "his prescriptions for curriculum and teaching method are essentially conservative" (p. 2). Significantly, Entwistle's book received tremendous criticism. In a review symposium by Henry Giroux, Douglas Holly, and Quintin Hoare (1980), Entwistle is admonished for misreading and misrepresenting Gramsci's work as well as failing to contextualize Gramsci's educational ideas either historically or with respect to Gramsci's overall body of thought. Regarding Entwistle's intentions, Holly contends, "The book will be seen by sophisticated readers for what it is—a polemic against 'neo-Marxism' and 'the new sociology [of education]'. Others, however, will not be so discerning. Real conservatives will derive much amusement out of a *communist* endorsement of their ideology" (p. 316). One of the less discerning, E. D. Hirsch (1996), credits Entwistle's book as being one of the primary texts providing him with "insights into Gramsci's ideas about education" (p. 274, n. 9). It may interest readers that such uncreditable and reactionary scholarship informed Hirsch's discussion of Gramsci (pp. 6–7) and contributed to the misappropriation referenced by Louisa Spencer.

I am disturbed by efforts to represent Gramsci as an educational conservative. Endeavors that decontextualize and misappropriate his work as a way of disciplining leftist educational initiatives do not constitute a serious engagement with Gramsci's life history (Fiori, 1965) or writings (Forgacs & Nowell Smith, 1985; Hoare & Nowell Smith, 1971). Thus, the remainder of my response entails a brief effort to counter Hirsch's claim that a correspondence exists between his own views (see Buras, 1999) and Gramsci's.

As a revolutionary in early twentieth-century Italy, Gramsci's vision of social justice required the radical transformation of civil society's cultural institutions, takeover the state, and absolute destruction of the capitalist economy. Even in the midst of Fascism, Gramsci never supported "bourgeois democracy"; rather, he strategically advocated its defense as a means to fend off dictatorship and *only* as an intermediate step in the ultimate conversion to communism (Fiori, 1965). In contrast, the central concern underlying Hirsch's work is a desire to promote "social equity" by having children passively absorb hegemonic culture ("common culture") in order to later participate in the capitalist economic relations ("marketplace") that Gramsci spent his life condemning. Clearly, Gramsci's revolutionary stance is at odds with Hirsch's emphasis on social stability and defense of the status quo.

Beyond conceptualizations of social justice, Gramsci and Hirsch also hold disparate views on the institutions of civil society, including schools. Gramsci stressed the involvement of such institutions in the production of hegemony—that is, their connection to the maintenance of bourgeois power through the generation of widespread "consent" for dominant worldviews—and he recognized the need to fight a "war of position" if alternative cultural forms were to acquire power (Hoare & Nowell Smith, 1971). Hirsch understands the school as a "technical" institution involved in the transmission of a "shared" culture that has been wrongly associated with "Eurocentrism" and other forms of dominance and power. For him, schools are not sites of cultural struggle.

In terms of intellectual activity and possibility, as well as the recognition of nondominant forms of experience, knowledge, and culture, the positions of Gramsci and Hirsch are divergent. Gramsci held that:

Each [person] ... carries on some form of intellectual activity, that is [s/he] is a "philosopher," an artist, a [person] of taste, [s/he] participates in a particular conception of the world, has a conscious line of moral conduct, and therefore contributes to sustain a conception of the world or to modify it, that is, to bring into being new modes of thought. (Hoare & Nowell Smith, 1971, p. 9)

Referring to this milieu as a popular or "folkloristic," Gramsci recognized working-class knowledge as valuable while avoiding its romanticization. It was essential, he believed, to distinguish "various strata" within it, thereby separating the "conservative and reactionary" elements while building on those "which consist of a series of innovations, often creative and progressive,...and which are in contradiction to or simply different from the morality of the governing strata" (Forgacs & Nowell Smith, 1985, p. 190). In fact, the role of Gramsci's "organic intellectual" was to assist in the "critical elaboration of the intellectual activity that exists in everyone," thus facilitating the development of a lucid counterhegemonic perspective (Hoare & Nowell Smith, p. 9). Most importantly, organic intellectuals could only accomplish this task by maintaining ties to their class origin (proletariat). Loss of these ties meant co-optation by the dominant hegemony and betrayal of the needs of their class. In contrast, Hirsch views those from nondominant groups as "deficient" in knowledge and in need of "compensation" by dominant culture. His goal is to disassociate them from their class of origin ("less-good-home school" or "local" surroundings) and to integrate them into the existing hegemony.

With respect to the place of dominant knowledge—in society generally as well as within schools—there is little coherence between their positions. While it is true that Gramsci did, to some extent, value the mental "discipline" he believed a traditional humanistic education could impart (a sort of discipline needed for the struggle), he strongly held that the proletariat should command dominant culture *only* to critique and transform it. For Gramsci, examining "folkloristic" conceptions against those of "national-popular" culture enabled a deeper comprehension of hegemony. "Folklore" he believed, "should...be studied as a 'conception of the world and life' implicit to a large extent in determinate [subordinate]...strata of society and in opposition...to 'official' [dominant] conceptions of the world" (Gramsci, quoted in Apitzsch, 1993, p. 140). Only this way could subaltern classes seek to untangle the complexities of intellectual domination and thus forge "a new common sense and with it a new culture...rooted in the popular consciousness" (Hoare & Nowell Smith, 1971, p. 424). Far from adhering to Gramsci's view of "official" knowledge, Hirsch desires that all citizens command dominant culture because he sees it as universal, believes it contributes to continual social cohesion, and contends that its alternative is the absence of culture itself.

Regarding pedagogy, too, their positions are dissimilar. Gramsci's pedagogy was based on the collaborative development of consciousness. He viewed the revolutionary party and other proletarian organizations as pedagogical in nature. For example, Gramsci insisted that organizing cultural associations for workers "would deal a fierce blow to the dogmatic and intolerant mentality created in the Italian people by Catholic and Jesuit education." Alternatively, "love of free discussion, the desire to discover the truth with uniquely human means" would be instilled (Forgacs & Nowell Smith, 1985, p. 23). Juxtaposing such cultural associations with "Popular Universities" offered by the bourgeoisie to the masses, Gramsci emphasized, "It is not the lecture that should interest us, but the detailed work of discussing and investigating problems, work in which everybody participates, to which everybody contributes, in which everybody is both master and disciple" (p. 25). By contrast, Hirsch's pedagogical ideal includes teacher-centered instruction focused on transmission of predetermined facts.

Ultimately, one must understand Hirsch's misappropriation of Gramsci for what it is: a crude attempt at disciplining the Left. Nearly twenty years ago, Holly (Giroux et al., 1980) concluded his review of *Antonio Gramsci: Conservative Schooling for Radical Politics* by stating, "We would do far better to read Gramsci than Entwistle" (p. 319). In the present moment, the same may be said of Hirsch.

Kristen L. Buras
Teacher, New York City

REFERENCES

Apitzsch, U. (1993). Gramsci and the current debate on multicultural education. *Studies in the Education of Adults, 25*, 136–145.

Buras, K. L. (1999). Questionning core assumptions: A critical reading of and response to E. D. Hirsch's *The Schools We Need and Why We Don't Have Them. Harvard Educational Review, 69*, 67–93.

Entwistle, H. (1979). *Antonio Gramsci: Conservative schooling for radical politics.* Boston: Routledge & Kegan Paul.

Fiori, G. (1965). *Antonio Gramsci: Life of a revolutionary.* New York: Verso.

Forgacs, D., & Nowell Smith, G. (Eds.). (1985). *Antonio Gramsci: Selections from cultural writings.* Cambridge, MA: Harvard University Press.

Giroux, H. A., Holly, D., & Hoare, Q. (1980). Review symposium [Antonio Gramsci: Conservative schooling for radical politics]. *British Journal of Sociology of Education, 1*, 307–325.

Hirsch, E. D., Jr. (1996). *The schools we need and why we don't have them.* New York: Doubleday.

Hoare, Q., & Nowell Smith, G. (Eds.). (1971). *Selections from the prison notebooks of Antonio Gramsci.* New York: International.

NOTES

CHAPTER ONE

1. The dilemmas and costs of assimilation to the American Jewish community and the related Jewish Renewal Movement are insightfully discussed by Eric Goldstein (2006).

CHAPTER TWO

1. Although it is true that teachers and students interact with materials in ways that lend credence to as well as undercut the credibility of textual narratives, I still contend that excluding such content from the knowledge deemed important in classrooms does have notable, if not indisputable, effects on student learning.
2. Authentic assessment refers to forms of testing, such as portfolio assessment, that evaluate the learning process by allowing students to demonstrate the development of knowledge over time through multiple, nonstandardized means.
3. "Dominant ways of knowing" refers to those ways of seeing the world that privilege the perspective of powerful groups while either marginalizing or ignoring alternative views. Cameron McCarthy (1998) explains, for example, that "American schoolchildren come to know the world as one made by European ancestors and white people generally" (p. 111).

CHAPTER THREE

1. Much like the partnership between Trinity and Hawthorne, preservice teachers at the University of Virginia, where Hirsch was a professor, participate in a practicum experience at Cale Elementary (Cale, n.d.). Revealing ongoing connections at all levels, the principal of Cale Elementary, Gerald Terrell, marked the end of his 26-year tenure in the school system by becoming the vice president and director of personnel and development of the Core Knowledge Foundation (Siler, 2001a).

CHAPTER FOUR

1. Gertrude Himmelfarb (2004) has used the terms *new* new history and *old* new history, and has written about Lawrence Stone's proposal for a new old history, but none of these usages correspond with my invocation of the term *new* old history.

2. I undertook a critical discourse analysis of purposefully sampled materials from the *Pearson Learning-Core Knowledge history and geography textbooks* (Hirsch, 2002). Readers should see appendix A for a more extensive discussion of my methodology, including the questions and codes that guided the analysis (Gee, 1999). The illustrations provided in this chapter reflect the patterns that I found more broadly in the many Core history texts that I analyzed, including all or significant portions of the following: immigration and citizenship (grade 2) and immigration (6); civil rights leaders (2) and American reformers (4); Mount Rushmore presidents (K) and early presidents (4); industrialization and urbanization in America (6); and exploring the West (1), the earliest Americans (3), and Native Americans—cultures and conflicts (5). I also reviewed the teacher guides associated with any texts that I discursively analyzed from grades K–2, and closely read all of the U.S. history texts grades K–6. Images in all discursively analyzed texts were also examined. In deciding which texts to analyze, I considered the scope and organization of the curriculum and aimed to balance the various groups examined and the historical periods covered.

3. This chapter does not reflect a comparative study of history textbooks, but rather a close analysis of Core Knowledge history texts. Nonetheless, my experiences as a former history teacher, knowledge of many of the textbooks in circulation, command of the literature on social studies and history textbooks and curricula, involvement in studies of other social studies texts, and informal examination of current texts lead me to conclude that Core does indeed represent a new and strategic multicultural compromise—one that moves beyond the more limited and additive multiculturalism that has characterized so many texts. Moreover, while some of the patterns of representation that I document may be reflected to lesser or greater degrees in non-Core history textbooks, it is also the case that Core history texts, unlike other texts, are connected to an educational reform movement that has been growing for two decades. This means that Core narratives have a certain parlance and level of support not typically associated with state-adopted textbooks, which are often criticized but rarely embraced with missionary zeal, as is Core. Finally, Core texts are part of a much more comprehensive set of strategies undertaken by the Core Knowledge Foundation and its neoconservative allies, whereas textbook publishers, although undeniably implicated in the definition of official knowledge and state standards, are less often directed by such a clearly defined agenda.

4. In this text, a total of 78 European immigrants are pictured, along with two images that include countless European immigrants. In comparison, only 19 Asian immigrants are featured in images, with one image of countless immigrants of color.

5. I learned at the annual National Core Knowledge Conference that the historians who collaborated on the series with Hirsch were hand-picked by the Core Knowledge Foundation. The foundation negotiated the right to choose its own consultants rather than using those that would normally be provided by Pearson Learning, the publisher of the Core Knowledge textbook series (Buras, 2004). I do not know which specific consultants were involved. Along these lines, it is noteworthy that neoconservatives Sheldon Stern (Stern et al., 2003) and Paul Gagnon (see Cornbleth & Waugh, 1999) prepared the American history and world history syllabi, respectively, for the Core Knowledge Foundation's (2002) teacher education initiative—What Elementary Teachers Needs to Know.

6. It is important to recognize that documents in the archives constitute only one form of evidence. Oral histories, cultural artifacts, and other fragments of the past must also be considered a part of the historical record and subjected to serious investigation. Even the study of longstanding traditions within communities can illuminate historical understanding.

7. Part of the Statement on Standards of Professional Conduct reads:

> Every work of history articulates a particular, limited perspective on the past. Historians hold this view not because they believe that all interpretations are equally valid, or that nothing can ever be known about the past, or that facts do not matter. Quite the contrary. . . . But the very nature of our discipline means that historians also understand that all knowledge is situated in time and place, that all interpretations express a point of view, and that no mortal mind can ever aspire to omniscience.

Regarding the aforementioned omnibus education bill on the teaching of history in Florida, the American Historical Association goes on to thereby emphasize: "It is right to teach students that every historian must work as accurately and honestly as he or she can. But it is simply wrong to tell them that any single account of history is simply 'factual'" (see American Historical Association, 2007).

8. I must emphasize my concern regarding the way in which multiculturalism in the United States, whether leftist or rightist, has traditionally been framed in terms of the nation-state. While national history is important and still quite relevant despite globalization (actually, the history of nation-states cannot be extricated from historic processes of globalization), I have also addressed the necessity of expanding the bounds of multiculturalism to include a critical cosmopolitan dimension (see Buras & Motter, 2006).

CHAPTER FIVE

1. Within the parameters of the current discussion, I cannot address my concerns regarding the limitations of framing the multicultural democratic project in mainly national terms. I have, however, discussed this elsewhere (Buras & Motter, 2006).

REFERENCES

Abrams, N. (2005). "America is home": *Commentary* magazine and the refocusing of the community of memory, 1945–1960. In M. Friedman (Ed.), *Commentary in American life* (pp. 9–37). Philadelphia: Temple University Press.

Achievement Alliance. (2007). It's being done: Capitol View Elementary [electronic]. *Common Knowledge, 20* (1).

Adams, D. W. (1995). *Education for extinction: American Indians and the boarding school experience, 1875–1928.* Lawrence: University Press of Kansas.

Alonso-Zaldivar, R., & Merl, J. (2004, October 10). Booklet that upset Mrs. Cheney is history. Common Dreams. Available: http://www.commondreams.org/headlines04/1008-05.htm

Alter, G. (1995). Transforming elementary social studies: The emergence of a curriculum focused on diverse, caring communities. *Theory and Research in Social Studies, 23*(4), 355–374.

American Enterprise. (1996). Eugene Genovese and Elizabeth Fox-Genovese [electronic version]. *The American Enterprise.* Available: http://www.taemag.com/issues/articleid.16285/article_detail.asp

American Federation of Teachers. (2003, March). American Federation of Teachers on Core Knowledge [bound compilation of articles]. Washington, DC: Author.

American Historical Association. (2007). Statement on the 2006 Florida education bill. Available: http://www.historians.org/perspectives/issues/2007/0703/0703aha6.cfm?pv=y

American Textbook Council. (2006). Widely adopted history textbooks. Retrieved July 17, 2007, from http://www.historytexbooks.org/adoptions.htm

Andrews, T. (Ed.). (1996). *The National Association of State Directors of Teacher Education and Certification manual 1996–1997.* Dubuque, IA: Kendall/Hunt.

Anyon, J. (1983). Workers, labor and economic history, and textbook content. In M. W. Apple & L. Weis (Eds.), *Ideology and practice in schooling* (pp. 37–60). Philadelphia: Temple University Press.

Apple, M. W. (1995). *Education and power*. New York: Routledge.

Apple, M. W. (1996). *Cultural politics and education*. New York: Teachers College Press.

Apple, M. W. (2000). *Official knowledge: Democratic education in a conservative age* (2nd ed.). New York: Routledge.

Apple, M. W. (2006a). *Educating the "right" way: Markets, standards, god, and inequality* (2nd ed.). New York: RoutledgeFalmer.

Apple, M. W. (2006b). "We are the new oppressed": Gender, culture, and the work of home schooling. In M. W. Apple & K. L. Buras (Eds.), *The subaltern speak: Curriculum, power, and educational struggles* (pp. 75–93). New York: Routledge.

Apple, M. W., & Beane, J. (Eds.). (2007). *Democratic schools* (2nd ed.). Portsmouth, NH: Heinemann.

Apple, M. W., & Buras, K. L. (Eds.). (2006). *The subaltern speak: Curriculum, power, and educational struggles*. New York: Routledge.

Apple, M., & Christian-Smith, L. K. (Eds.). (1991). *The politics of the textbook*. New York: Routledge.

Apple, M. W., & Pedroni, T. C. (2005). Conservative alliance building and African American support of vouchers: The end of *Brown's* promise or a new beginning? *Teachers College Record, 107*(9), 2068–2105.

Aronowitz, S., & Giroux, H. (1991). Textual authority, culture, and the politics of literacy. In M. W. Apple & L. K. Christian-Smith (Eds.), *The politics of the textbook* (pp. 213–241). New York: Routledge.

Ball, S. J. (2003). *Class strategies and the education market: The middle class and social advantage*. New York: RoutledgeFalmer.

Baltimore Curriculum Project. (2004a). Baltimore curriculum project: Draft month-by-month content lesson plans based on the Core Knowledge sequence. Available: http://www. cstone.net/~bcp/

Baltimore Curriculum Project. (2004b). Sample lesson packet: Eighth grade intermediate III. Baltimore: Author.

Baltimore Curriculum Project. (2007a). Baltimore curriculum project charter schools. Available: http://www.baltimorecp.org/charters.html

Baltimore Curriculum Project. (2007b). Baltimore curriculum project history. Available: http://www.baltimorecp.org/history.html

Banks, J. A. (1969). A content analysis of the Black American in textbooks. *Social Education, 33*(8), 954–957, 963.

Banks, J. A. (2004). Race, knowledge construction, and education in the United States. In J. A. Banks & C. A. McGee Banks (Eds.), *Handbook of research on multicultural education* (pp. 228–239). San Francisco, CA: Jossey-Bass.

Beard, C. (1934). Written history as an act of faith. *American Historical Review, XXXIX* (2), 219–229.

Becker, C. L. (1955). What are historical facts? *The Western Political Quarterly, VIII* (3), 327–340.

Bell, D. A., Jr. (1995). Serving two masters: Integration ideals and client interests in school desegregation litigation. In K. Crenshaw, N. Gotanda, G. Peller, & K. Thomas (Eds.), *Critical race theory: The key writings that formed the movement* (pp. 5–19). New York: The New Press.

Bender, T. (1989). Public culture: Inclusion and synthesis in American history. In P. Gagnon & The Bradley Commission on History in Schools (Eds.), *Historical literacy: The case for history in American education* (pp. 188–202). New York: Macmillan.

Bennett, W. J., Finn, C. E., & Cribb. J. T. E., Jr. (1999). *The educated child: A parent's guide from preschool through eighth grade.* New York: Simon & Schuster.

Benveniste, L., Carnoy, M., & Rothstein, R. (2003). *All else equal: Are public and private schools different?* New York: RoutledgeFalmer.

Berg, T. R. (1999). Schools of education must start training Core Knowledge teachers [letter to the editor]. *Common Knowledge, 12*(4), 8.

Blassingame, J. W. (Ed.). (1977). *Slave testimony: Two centuries of letters, speeches, interviews, and autobiographies.* Baton Rouge: Louisiana State University Press.

Bourdieu, P. (1984). *Distinction.* Cambridge, MA: Harvard University Press.

Boym, S. (2001). *The future of nostalgia.* New York: Basic Books.

Bring New Orleans Back Commission. (2006, January 17). Rebuilding and transforming: A plan for world-class public education in New Orleans [final presentation]. Available: http://www.bringneworleansback.org/

Brophy, J., McMahon, S., & Prawat, R. (1991). Elementary social studies series: Critique of a representative example by six experts. *Social Education, 55*(3), 155–160.

Buchanan, P. J. (2003, March 24). Whose war? [electronic]. *The American Conservative.* Available: http://www.amconmag.com/03_24_03/cover.html

Buras, K. L. (1997). Unpublished field data. University of Wisconsin, Madison.

Buras, K. L. (1999a). Buras replies [correspondence]. *Harvard Educational Review, 69*(4), 469–472.

Buras, K. L. (1999b). Questioning Core assumptions: A critical reading of and response to E. D. Hirsch's *The Schools We Need and Why We Don't Have Them. Harvard Educational Review, 69*(1), 67–93.

Buras, K. L. (2004, March). Field notes. Core Knowledge national conference, Atlanta, GA.

Buras, K. L. (2005). Katrina's early landfall: Exclusionary politics behind the restoration of New Orleans. *Z Magazine, 18*(12), 26–31.

Buras, K. L. (2006). Tracing the Core Knowledge movement: History lessons from above and below. In M. W. Apple & K. L. Buras (Eds.), *The subaltern speak: Curriculum, power, and educational struggles* (pp. 43–74). New York: Routledge.

Buras, K. L. (2007a). Benign neglect?: Drowning yellow buses, racism, and disinvestment in the city that Bush forgot. In K. Saltman (Ed.), *Schooling and the politics of disaster* (pp. 103–122). New York: Routledge.

Buras, K. L. (2007b). Neoconservatism. In D. Gabbard (Ed.), *Knowledge and power in the global economy: The effects of school reform in a neoliberal/ neoconservative age* (pp. 45–58). Mahwah, NJ: Erlbaum.

Buras, K. L. (forthcoming). *Can a city school the nation?: Reconstruction, race, and resistance in post-Katrina New Orleans.* New York: Routledge.

Buras, K. L., & Apple, M. W. (2005). School choice, neoliberal promises, and unpromising evidence. *Educational Policy, 19*(3), 550–564.

Buras, K. L., & Apple, M. W. (2006). The subaltern speak: Curriculum, power, and educational struggles [Introduction]. In M. W. Apple & K. L. Buras (Eds.), *The subaltern speak: Curriculum, power, and educational struggles* (pp. 1–39). New York: Routledge.

Buras, K. L., & Motter, P. (2006). Toward a subaltern cosmopolitan multiculturalism. In M. W. Apple & K. L. Buras (Eds.), *The subaltern speak: Curriculum, power, and educational struggles* (pp. 243–269). New York: Routledge.

Burke, P. (2001). Views of society. In P. Burke, *Eyewitnessing: The uses of images as historical evidence* (pp. 103–122). Ithaca, NY: Cornell University Press.

Cale Elementary School. (n.d.). Cale's programs. Retrieved January 4, 1998, from http://www.pen.k12.va.us/Anthology/Div/Albemarle/Schools/Cale/programs.html

Cheney, L. (1991). A conversation with Henry Louis Gates, Jr. *Humanities, 12*(4), 4–10.

Cobble, D. S., & Kessler-Harris, A. (1993). The new labor history in American history textbooks. *Journal of American History, 79*(4), 1534–1545.

Coleman, J. S. (1981). Coleman report on public and private schools: The draft summary and eight critiques. Arlington, VA: Educational Research Service.

Colorado Schools. (2003). Colorado schools grow through Holly Hensey's support [electronic]. *Common Knowledge, 16*(3).

Commeyras, M., & Alvermann, D. E. (1996). Reading about women in world history textbooks from one feminist perspective. *Gender and Education, 8*(1), 31–48.

Connell, R. W. (1993). *Schools and social justice.* Philadelphia: Temple University Press.

Core Knowledge Foundation. (1996a). ABC news "solutions" [video]. Charlottesville, VA: Author.

Core Knowledge Foundation. (1996b). Common misconceptions about Core Knowledge. Available: http://www.coreknowledge.org

Core Knowledge Foundation. (1996c). Core Knowledge in the schools as of Fall 1996 [brochure]. Charlottesville, VA: Author.

Core Knowledge Foundation. (1997). Core Knowledge professional development workshops [brochure]. Charlottesville, VA: Author.

Core Knowledge Foundation. (1998). *The Core Knowledge sequence: Content guidelines for gradesK–8*. Charlottesville, VA: Author.

Core Knowledge Foundation. (2000). *Core Knowledge K–8 guide: A model monthly topic organizer.* Charlottesville, VA: Author.

Core Knowledge Foundation. (2002). *What elementary teachers need to know: College course outlines for teacher preparation.* Charlottesville, VA: Author.

Core Knowledge Foundation. (2003a, March 1). Professional development workshops. Retrieved October 22, 2003, from http://www.coreknowledge.org

Core Knowledge Foundation. (2003b, August 25). Official Core Knowledge school application: Information for school year 2003-2004. Retrieved October 14, 2003, from http://www.coreknowledge.org/CKproto2/schools/schllst_O_app.htm

Core Knowledge Foundation. (2003c, September 15). Official Core Knowledge schools. Retrieved October 14, 2003, from http://www.coreknowledge.org/CKproto2/schools/schllst_O.htm

Core Knowledge Foundation. (2003d, December 1). Core Knowledge schools: How to get started. Retrieved July 20, 2004, from http://www.coreknowledge.org/CKproto2/schools/start.htm

Core Knowledge Foundation. (2003e). Annual report of the Core Knowledge Foundation. Charlottesville, VA: Author.

Core Knowledge Foundation. (2004a, March 10). Core Knowledge-TASA curriculum-referenced tests. Retrieved July 29, 2004, from http://www.coreknowledge.org/CKproto2/schools/testing.htm

Core Knowledge Foundation. (2004b, May 25). Core Knowledge K–8 schools list. Retrieved June 15, 2004, from http://www.coreknowledge.org

Core Knowledge Foundation. (2004c, July 16). Becoming a Core Knowledge K-8 school [breakdown of schools]. Retrieved July 20, 2004, from http://www.coreknowledge.org

Core Knowledge Foundation. (2004d). Core Knowledge teacher handbook, grade 1. Charlottesville, VA: Author.

Core Knowledge Foundation. (2004e). Home page. Available: http://www.coreknowledge.org

Core Knowledge Foundation. (2004f). Parent brochure. Retrieved March 31, 2005, from http://www.coreknowledge.org/CKproto2/schools/schools_parentbrochure.htm

Core Knowledge Foundation. (2004g). Share the knowledge: Core Knowledge national conference units and handouts. Charlottesville, VA: Author.

Core Knowledge Foundation. (2006a). Annual report of the Core Knowledge Foundation. Charlottesville, VA: Author.

Core Knowledge Foundation. (2006b). Board of trustees.Available: http://www.coreknowledge.org/CK/about/boardoftrustees.htm

Core Knowledge Foundation. (2006c). Home page. Available: http://www.coreknowledg.org

Core Knowledge Foundation. (2006d). Home school. Retrieved May 19, 2006, fromhttp://www.coreknowledge.org/CK/about/FAQ/FAQ_homeschool.htm

Core Knowledge Foundation. (2007a, March 6). Core Knowledge K–8 schools list. Retrieved July 9, 2007, from http://www.coreknowledge.org

Core Knowledge Foundation. (2007b). Core Knowledge articles. Retrieved July 17, 2007, from http://www.coreknowledge.org/CK/about/print/index.htm

Core Knowledge Foundation. (2007c). Core Knowledge bookstore. Available: http://www.coreknowledge.org/bookstore/index.php?main_page+index

Core Knowledge Foundation. (2007d). Core Knowledge preschool. Available: http://www.coreknowledge.org/CK/Preschool/preschool_sequence.htm

Core Knowledge Foundation. (2007e). Staff directory. Available: http://www.coreknowledge.org/CK/about/Directory.htm

Core Knowledge Foundation. (n.d.). Q&A: Core Knowledge testing program [brochure]. Charlottesville, VA: Author.

Cornbleth, C. (Ed.). (2000). *Curriculum politics, policy, practice: Cases in comparative context.* Albany: State University of New York Press.

Cornbleth, C., & Waugh, D. (1999). *The great speckled bird: Multicultural politics and education policymaking.* Mahwah, NJ: Erlbaum.

Crenshaw, K., Gotanda, N., Peller, G., & Thomas, K. (Eds.). *Critical race theory: The key writings that formed the* movement. New York: The New Press.

Crossman, R. H. (Ed.). (1949). *The god that failed.* New York: Columbia University Press.

Cruz, B. C. (1994). Stereotypes of Latin Americans perpetuated in secondary school history textbooks. *Latino Studies Journal, 1*(1), 51–67.

Cuban, L. (1993). *How teachers taught: Constancy and change in American classrooms.* New York: Teachers College Press.

Dahl, R. A. (1998). *On democracy.* New Haven, CT: Yale University Press.

Datnow, A., Borman, G., & Stringfield, S. (2000). School reform through a highly specified curriculum: Implementation and effects of the Core Knowledge sequence. *Elementary School Journal, 101*(2), 167–191.

Davis, M. (2002). Core Knowledge offers blueprint for content-rich teacher education. *Common Knowledge, 15*(3), 4.

Davis, M. (2003). An overview of research: How do we know Core Knowledge works? *Common Knowledge, 16*(1), 12–17.

Davis, M. (2005). *Reading instruction: The two keys.* Charlottesville, VA: Core Knowledge Foundation.

Davis, M. (2006). *Planet of slums.* New York: Verso.

Deckman, M. M. (2004). *School board battles: The Christian right in local politics.* Washington, DC: Georgetown University Press.

Dekker, J. J. H. (1996). A republic of educators: Educational messages in seventeenth-century Dutch genre painting. *History of Education Quarterly, 36*(2), 155–182.

Delfattore, J. (1992). *What Johnny shouldn't read: Textbook censorship in America.* New Haven, CT: Yale University Press.

Delgado, R., & Stefancic, J. (Eds.). (1997). *Critical white studies: Looking behind the mirror.* Philadelphia: Temple University Press.

Delgado Bernal, D. (2002). Critical race theory, Latino critical theory, and critical race-gendered epistemologies: Recognizing students of color as holders and creators of knowledge. *Qualitative Inquiry, 8*(1), 105–126.

Delgado Bernal, D. (2006). Rethinking grassroots activism: Chicana resistance in the 1968 East Los Angeles school blowouts. In M. W. Apple & K. L. Buras (Eds.), *The subaltern speak: Curriculum, power, and educational struggles* (pp. 141–162). New York: Routledge.

Delpit, L. (1995). *Other people's children: Cultural conflict in the classroom.* New York: The New Press.

deMarrais, K. (2006). "The haves and have mores": Fueling the conservative ideological war on public education (or tracking the money). *Educational Studies, 39*(3), 201–204.

Deyhle, D. (1995). Navajo youth and Anglo racism: Cultural integrity and resistance. *Harvard Educational Review, 65,* 403–444.

Dillard, A. D. (2001). *Guess who's coming to dinner now? Multicultural conservatism in America.* New York: New York University Press.

Dixson, A. D., & Rousseau, C. K. (Eds.). (2006). *Critical race theory in education: All god's children got a song.* New York: Routledge.

Dollinger, M. (2000). *Quest for inclusion: Jews and liberalism in America.* Princeton, NJ: Princeton University Press.

Donsky, P. (2005, February 27). Capitol View Elementary looks past poverty, employs classics to enrich students' world. *Atlanta Journal Constitution.*

Dorman, J. (2000). *Arguing the world: The New York intellectuals in their own words.* Chicago: University of Chicago Press.

Dorrien, G. (1993). *The neoconservative mind: Politics, culture, and the war of ideology.* Philadelphia: Temple University Press.

Douglass, F. (1845). *Narrative of the life of an American slave.* New York: Penguin Books.

Drury, S. B. (1999). *Leo Strauss and the American right.* New York: St. Martin's Press.

Drury, S. B. (2003). Saving America: Leo Strauss and the neoconservatives [electronic]. Evatt Foundation. Available: http://evatt.labor.net.au/publications/papers/112.html

Dyson, M. E. (2005). *Is Bill Cosby right? (Or has the black middle class lost its mind?)* New York: Basic *Civitas* Books.

Education Department. (n.d.). No child left behind: Proven methods. Retrieved September 23, 2003, from http://www.ed.gov/nclb/methods/whatworks/doing.html

Education Next. (2006). Education Next [past issues]. Available: http://www.educationnext.org/pastissues.html

Educational Testing Service. (1998). Financial report [Internet]. Available: http://www.ets.org/estar/arscr12.html.

Ehrman, J. (1999). *Commentary*, the *Public Interest*, and the problem of Jewish neoconservatism. *American Jewish History, 87*(2 & 3), 159–181.

Ellington, L. (1986). Blacks and Hispanics in high school economics texts. *Social Education, 50*(1), 64–67.

Ellington, L., & Eaton, J. S. (2003). Multiculturalism and social studies. In J. Leming, L. Ellington, & K. Porter (Eds.), *Where did social studies go wrong?* (pp. 70–93). Washington, DC: Thomas B. Fordham Foundation.

Ellington, L., & Rutledge, V. C. (2001). Core Knowledge: A content foundation for civic virtue? *International Journal of Social Education, 16,* 34–44.

Enterprise Foundation. (2000). Community Building in Partnership, Baltimore, Maryland: A case study from on the ground with comprehensive community initiatives. Available: http://www.enterprisefoundation.org/resources/ERD/browse.asp?c=35

Farmer, J. (1996). We are bound together. *Common Knowledge, 9*(1/2), 2.

Finn, C. (Ed.). (2003). *Terrorists, despots, and democracy: What our children need to know.* Washington, DC: Thomas B. Fordham Foundation.

Fiori, G. (1970). *Antonio Gramsci: Life of a revolutionary.* London: NLB.

Fisher, M. T. (2007). *Writing in rhythm: Spoken word poetry in urban classrooms.* New York: Teachers College Press.

Foner, E. (Ed.). (1997). *The new American history.* Philadelphia: Temple University Press.

Foner, E. (2002). *Who owns history?: Rethinking the past in a changing world.* New York: Hill and Wang.

Fraser, N. (1997). *Justice interruptus: Critical reflections on the "postsocialist" condition.* New York: Routledge.

Frazee, B. M. (1996). Hawthorne Elementary School: The university perspective. *Journal of Education for Students Placed at Risk, 1*(1), 25–31.

Free Congress Foundation. (2004a). Declaration of cultural independence. Retrieved June 22, 2004, from http://www.freecongress.org/centers/cc/culturalindependence.asp

Free Congress Foundation. (2004b). Home page. Retrieved June 22, 2004, from http://www.free congress.org/about/index.asp

Freire, P. (1993). *Pedagogy of the oppressed.* New York: Continuum.

Friedman, M. (1999). Opening the discussion of American Jewish political conservatism. *American Jewish History, 87*(2 & 3), 101–122.

Friedman, M. (Ed.). (2005a). Commentary *in American life*. Philadelphia: Temple University Press.

Friedman, M. (2005b). *The neoconservative revolution: Jewish intellectuals and the shaping of public policy*. New York: Cambridge University Press.

Gabler, M., & Gabler, N. (1985). *What are they teaching our children?* Wheaton, IL: Victor Books.

Garcia, J., & Sadoski, M. (1986, April). The treatment of minorities in nine recently published basal series. Paper presented at the American Educational Research Association annual meeting, San Francisco, CA.

Garcia, J., & Tanner, D. E. (1985). The portrayal of Black Americans in U.S. history textbooks. *The Social Studies, 76*(5), 200–204.

Garvin-Kester, B. (2006a). Core Knowledge: A multicultural experience [electronic]. *Common Knowledge, 19*(1).

Garvin-Kester, B. (2006b). First ever Core Knowledge national sales conference [electronic version]. *Common Knowledge, 19*(2).

Gates, H. L., Jr. (1992). *Loose canons: Notes on the culture wars*. New York: Oxford University Press.

Gee, J. P. (1999). *An introduction to discourse analysis*. New York: Routledge.

Gerson, M. (Ed.). (1996). *The essential neoconservative reader*. New York: Addison-Wesley.

Gerson, M. (1997). *The neoconservative vision: From the cold war to the culture wars*. New York: Madison Books.

Giroux, H. A. (1995). Insurgent multiculturalism and the promise of pedagogy. In D. T. Goldberg (Ed.), *Multiculturalism: A critical reader* (pp. 325–343). Oxford: Blackwell.

Glazer, N. (1997). *We are all multiculturalists now*. Cambridge, MA: Harvard University Press.

Glazer, N. (2005). Neoconservatism from the start [electronic]. *The Public Interest, 159*.

Goldberg, M. F. (1997). An interview with E. D. Hirsch, Jr.: Doing what works. *Phi Delta Kappan, 79*(1), 83–85.

Goldstein, E. L. (2006). *The price of whiteness: Jews, race, and American identity*. Princeton, NJ: Princeton University Press.

Goodlad, J. I. (1984). *A place called school*. New York: McGraw-Hill.

Goodman, J. (1986). University education courses and the professional preparation of teachers: A descriptive analysis. *Teaching and Teacher Education, 2*, 341–353.

Gould, S. J. (1996). *The mismeasure of man*. New York: W. W. Norton.

Graff, G. (1992). *Beyond the culture wars: How teaching the conflicts can revitalize American education*. New York: W. W. Norton.

Grant, S. G. (2001). An uncertain lever: Exploring the influence of state-level testing in New York State on teaching social studies. *Teachers College Record, 103*(3), 398–426.

Gutstein, E. (2006). *Reading and writing the world with mathematics: Toward a pedagogy for social justice*. New York: Routledge.

Haggard-Gilson, N. (1998). Against the grain: Black conservatives and Jewish neoconservatives. In V. P. Franklin (Ed.), *African Americans and Jews in the twentieth century: Studies in convergence and conflict* (pp. 165–190). Columbia: University of Missouri Press.

Hahn, C. L., & Blankenship, G. (1983). Women and economics textbooks. *Theory and Research in Social Education, 11*(3), 67–76.

Hammock, C. S. (Ed.). (2004, March). American Horse School newsletter. Allen, South Dakota: Author.

Harris, C. (1995). Whiteness as property. In K. Crenshaw, N. Gotanda, G. Peller, & K. Thomas (Eds.), *Critical race theory: The key writings that formed the movement* (pp. 276–291). New York: The New Press.

Harvey, D. (2005). *A brief history of neoliberalism*. New York: Oxford University Press.

Hawthorne Elementary School. (1998). Home page. Available: http://www.trinity.edu/departments/education/haw.htm

Heilman, S. C. (1995). *Portrait of American Jews: The last half of the 20th century*. Seattle: University of Washington Press.

Himmelfarb, G. (2004). *The new history and the old: Critical essays and reappraisals*. Cambridge: Harvard University Press.

Hirsch, E. D., Jr. (1983). Cultural literacy. *The American Scholar, 52*, 159–169.

Hirsch, E. D., Jr. (1987). *Cultural literacy: What every American needs to know*. New York: Vintage Books.

Hirsch, E. D., Jr. (1991). *What your first grader needs to know: Fundamentals of a good first-grade education* (1st ed.). New York: Doubleday.

Hirsch, E. D., Jr. (1992a). Fairness and Core Knowledge. Charlottesville, VA: Core Knowledge Foundation.

Hirsch, E. D., Jr. (1992b). Toward a centrist curriculum: Two kinds of multiculturalism in elementary school. Charlottesville, VA: Core Knowledge Foundation.

Hirsch, E. D., Jr. (1993). Common misconceptions about Core Knowledge. Charlottesville, VA: Core Knowledge Foundation.

Hirsch, E. D., Jr. (1996). *The schools we need and why we don't have them*. New York: Doubleday.

Hirsch, E. D., Jr. (1997a, March/April). Why traditional education is more progressive. Available:http://www.taemag.com/

Hirsch, E. D., Jr. (1997b). An address to the California State Board of Education. *Common Knowledge, 10*(1/2), 4–8.

Hirsch, E. D., Jr. (Ed.). (1998a). *What your second grader needs to know: Fundamentals of a good second-grade education* (rev. ed.). New York: Doubleday.

Hirsch, E. D., Jr. (1998b). Why general knowledge should be a goal of education in a democracy. *Common Knowledge, 11*(1/2), 1, 14–16.

Hirsch, E. D., Jr. (1999a). Education: The new civil rights frontier [weekly essays]. Available: http://www.hoover.org/publicaffairs/we/current/hirsch_1199.html

Hirsch, E. D., Jr. (1999b). Why Core Knowledge promotes social justice [electronic]. *Common Knowledge, 12* (4).

Hirsch, E. D., Jr. (2001a). Breadth versus depth: A premature polarity. *Common Knowledge, 14*(4), 3–4.

Hirsch, E. D., Jr. (2001b). Curriculum and competence. In T. M. Moe (Ed.), *A primer on America's schools* (pp. 185–204). Stanford, CA: Hoover Institution Press.

Hirsch, E. D., Jr. (Ed.). (2002). *Pearson Learning-Core Knowledge history and geography textbooks, grades K-6.* Parsippany, NJ: Pearson Learning Group.

Hirsch, E. D., Jr. (2003). Moral progress in history. In C. E. Finn (Ed.), *Terrorists, despots, and democracy: What our children need to know* (pp. 72–73). Washington, DC: Thomas B. Fordham Foundation.

Hirsch, E. D., Jr. (2005). Education reform and content: The long view. In D. Ravitch (Ed.), *Brookings papers on education policy* (pp. 175–186). Washington, DC: Brookings Institution Press.

Hirsch, E. D., Jr. (2006). *The knowledge deficit: Closing the shocking education gap for American children.* New York: Houghton Mifflin Company.

Hirsch, E. D., Jr., & Holdren, J. (Eds.). (2001). *Lo que su alumno de kindergarten necesita saber* [field copy]. Charlottesville, VA: Core Knowledge Foundation.

Hirsch, E. D., Jr., Kett, J. F., & Trefil, J. (1988). *The dictionary of cultural literacy: What every American needs to know.* New York: Houghton Mifflin Company.

Hitchcock, S. T. (2002). Teaching the teachers: New education school programs promise to help Core Knowledge teachers. *Common Knowledge, 15*(1), 4–6.

Hitchens, C. (1990, May 13). Why we don't know what we don't know: Just ask E. D. Hirsch. *New York Times* [Late Edition], A32.

Hoare, Q., & Nowell Smith, G. (Eds.). (1971). *Selections from the prison notebooks of Antonio Gramsci.* New York: International Publishers.

Hoff, D. J. (2002). Bush to push for math and science upgrade. *Education Week, 22*(12), 19, 24.

hooks, b. (1994). *Teaching to transgress: Education as the practice of freedom.* New York: Routledge.

Hoover Institution. (2002). E. D. Hirsch, Jr. [profile]. Retrieved November 12, 2003, from http://www.hoover.stanford.edu/BIOS/Hirsch.html

Hoover Institution. (2006). Hoover Institution home page [fellows]. Available: http://www.hoover.org

Houghton Mifflin. (2007). Elementary education [social studies]. Retrieved July 17, 2007, from http://www.hmco.com/products/products_elementary.html

Howe, I. (1976). *World of our fathers: The journey of the East European Jews to America and the life they found and made.* New York: Harcourt, Brace, Jovanovich.

Huntington, S. P. (2005). *Who are we?: The challenges to America's national identity.* New York: Simon & Schuster.

Ibbett, J. (2003). Our obligation to the past: A response to Keith Jenkins. *Rethinking History, 7* (1), 51–67.

Irvine, J. J. (2003). *Educating teachers for diversity: Seeing with a cultural eye.* New York: Teachers College Press.

Jaworski, A., & Coupland, N. (Eds.). (1999). *The discourse reader.* New York: Routledge.

Jenkins, K. (1997). Why bother with the past?: Engaging with some issues raised by the possible "end of history as we have known it." *Rethinking History, 1*(1), 56–66.

Jenkins, K. (1999). "After" history. *Rethinking History, 3*(1), 7–20.

Jones, C. (1991). *A school's guide to Core Knowledge: Ideas for implementation.* Charlottesville, VA: Core Knowledge Foundation.

Jones. C. (1996). School clips. *Common Knowledge, 9*(4), 6–7.

Jones, C. (1997a). School clips. *Common Knowledge, 10*(1/2), 10, 16.

Jones, C. (1997b). School clips. *Common Knowledge, 10*(3), 6, 12.

Jones, C. (1997c). School clips. *Common Knowledge, 10*(4), 6, 12.

Judis, J. B. (1988). *William F. Buckley, Jr.: Patron saint of the conservatives.* New York: Simon & Schuster.

Kaestle, C. F. (1983). *Pillars of the republic: Common schools and American society, 1780–1860.* New York: Hill & Wang.

Kaestle, C. F. (1992). Standards of evidence in historical research: How do we know when we know? *History of Education Quarterly, 32*(3), 361–366.

Kantrowitz, B., Chideya, F., & Wingert P. (1992, November 2). What kids need to know: Putting cultural literacy into elementary school. *Newsweek,* 80.

Kelley, R. D. G. (1993). "We are not what we seem": Rethinking Black working-class opposition in the Jim Crow South. *Journal of American History, 8*(1), 75–112.

Kelley, R. D. G. (1998). *Yo' mama's disfunktional: Fighting the culture wars in urban America.* Boston, MA: Beacon Press.

Kelley, R. D. G. (2002). *Freedom dreams: The black radical imagination.* Boston: Beacon Press.

Kissen, R. M. (1993). Listening to gay and lesbian teenagers. *Teaching Education, 5,* 57–68.

Klee, M. B. (1995). Wisdom on woe: How to teach the worst in world history. Retrieved on October 12, 2003, from http://www.coreknowledge.org/CKproto2/about/nwsltr/WisdomWoe.htm

Klee, M. B. (1999). History from K–4: What can we really do? *Journal of Education of Boston University, 180*(1), 33–53.

Klee, M. B. (2003). What schools should do on September 11. In C. Finn (Eds.), *Terrorists, despots, and democracy: What our children need to know* (pp. 56–57). Washington, DC: Thomas B. Fordham Foundation.

Kliebard, H. M. (1995). *The struggle for the American curriculum, 1893–1958.* New York: Routledge.

Klug, B. J., & Whitfield, P. T. (2003). *Widening the circle: Culturally relevant pedagogy for American Indian children.* New York: RoutledgeFalmer.

Koret Task Force. (2006). Members. Available: http://www.korettaskforce.org/members.html

Kovacs, P., & Boyles, D. R. (2005). Institutes, foundations, and think tanks: Conservative influence on U.S. public schools. *Public Resistance, 1*(1), 24–41.

Kramer, H., & Kimball, R. (Eds.). (1997). *The future of the European past.* Chicago: Ivan R. Dee.

Kretman, K. P., & Parker, B. (1986). New U.S. history texts: Good news and bad. *Social Education, 50*(1), 61–63.

Kristol, I. (1952). "Civil liberties," 1952—A study in confusion. *Commentary, 13*(3).

Kristol, I. (1995). *Neoconservatism: The autobiography of an idea.* Chicago: Ivan R. Dee.

Kristol, I. (1996). A conservative welfare state. In M. Gerson (Ed.), *The essential neoconservative reader* (pp. 283–287). New York: Addison-Wesley.

Kristol, I. (2005). Forty good years [electronic]. *The Public Interest, 159.*

Kristol, I. (n.d.). American conservatism, 1945–1995 [electronic]. *The Public Interest.* Available: http://www.thepublicinterest.com/notable/article2.html

Kumashiro, K. K. (Ed.). (2001). *Troubling intersections of race and sexuality: Queer students of color and anti-oppressive education.* New York: Rowman & Littlefield.

Ladson-Billings, G. (1994). *The dreamkeepers: Successful teachers of African American students.* San Francisco: Jossey-Bass.

Ladson-Billings, G. (2005). *Beyond the big house: African American educators on teacher education.* New York: Teachers College Press.

Ladson-Billings, G. (2006). From the achievement gap to the education debt: Understanding achievement in U.S. schools. *Educational Researcher, 35*(7), 3–12.

Ladson-Billings, G., & Gillborn, D. (Eds.). (2004). *The RoutledgeFalmer reader in multicultural education.* New York: RoutledgeFalmer.

Ladson-Billings, G., & Tate, B. (2006). Toward a critical race theory of education. In A. D. Dixson & C. K. Rousseau (Eds.), *Critical race theory and education: All god's children got a song* (pp. 11–30). New York: Routledge.

Leming, J., Ellington, L., & Porter, K. (Eds.). (2003). *Where did the social studies go wrong?* Washington, DC: Thomas B. Fordham Foundation.

Leonardo, Z. (Ed.). (2005). *Critical pedagogy and race.* Malden, MA: Blackwell Publishing.

Levine, D., Lowe, R., Peterson, B., & Tenorio, R. (1995). *Rethinking schools: An agenda for change.* New York: The New Press.

Levstik, L. S., & Barton, K. C. (2001). Committing acts of history: Mediated action, humanistic education, and participatory democracy. In W. B. Stanley (Ed.), *Social studies research for the 21st century* (pp. 119–147). Greenwich, CT: Information Age Publishing.

Lindsay, D. (2001, November 11). Against the establishment: How a U-VA professor, denounced as elitist and ethnocentric, became a prophet of the school standards movement. *Washington Post*, W24.

Locke, P. (2002). Core Knowledge takes root outside the United States. *Common Knowledge, 15*(3), 14–17.

Mackley, T. A. (1999). *Uncommon sense: Core Knowledge in the classroom.* Alexandria, VA: Association for Supervision and Curriculum Development.

Marshall, M. (Ed.). (1997a). Baltimore lessons are on the net. *Common Knowledge, 10*(3), 2.

Marshall, M. (Ed.). (1997b). Hirsch receives AFT's Quest Award. *Common Knowledge, 10*(3), 1.

Marshall, M. (1997c). In Polk County, Florida: Going for Core in a big way. *Common Knowledge, 10*(3), 1, 7, 11.

Marshall, M. (Ed.). (1997d). Preschool sequence now available. *Common Knowledge, 10*(3), 3.

Marshall, M. (Ed.). (1997e). Sequence for 7th and 8th finalized. *Common Knowledge, 10*(3), 4.

Marshall, M. (1997f). What math book to use? *Common Knowledge, 10*(3), 1, 8, 11.

Marshall, M. (1998a). Feldman joins Core Knowledge Foundation board of trustees. *Common Knowledge, 11*(3), 2.

Marshall, M. (1998b). The bad news about discovery learning: A nugget from the annals of research. *Common Knowledge, 11*(3), 6–7.

Marshall, M. (Ed.). (1999a). Minnesota's Lt. Governor is a Core Knowledge teacher. *Common Knowledge, 12*(1/2), 3.

Marshall, M. (Ed.). (1999b). Pearson Learning to publish Core Knowledge materials for K-6. *Common Knowledge, 12*(1/2), 2.

Marshall, M., & Hirsch, E. D., Jr. (Eds.). (1997). *Core classics series.* Charlottesville, VA: Core Knowledge Foundation.

Martinez, G. (2006). "In my history classes they always turn things around, the opposite way": Indigenous youth opposition to cultural domination in an urban high school. In M. W. Apple & K. L. Buras (Eds.), *The subaltern speak: Curriculum, power, and educational struggles* (pp. 121–140). New York: Routledge.

Masur, L. P. (1998). "Pictures have now become a necessity": The use of images in American history textbooks. *Journal of American History, 84*(4), 1409–1424.

Mathematically Correct. (1996, November 20). A letter to the president. Retrieved July 14, 2004, from http://www.mathematicallycorrect.com/clinton.htm

McCarthy, C. (1993). After the canon: Knowledge and ideological representation in the multicultural discourse on curriculum reform. In C. McCarthy & W. Crichlow (Eds.), *Race, identity, and representation in education* (pp. 289–305). New York: Routledge.

McCarthy, C. (1998). *The uses of culture: Education and the limits of ethnic affiliation.* New York: Routledge.

McCoy, D. R. (1980). *The elusive republic: Political economy in Jeffersonian America.* Chapel Hill: University of North Carolina Press.

McGraw-Hill. (2006). Adventures in time and place. Retrieved July 17, 2007, from http://www.mhschool.com/socialstudies/2000/student/index.html

McNeil, L. M. (2000a). Creating new inequalities: Contradictions of reform. *Phi Delta Kappan, 81*(10),729–734.

McNeil, L. M. (2000b). Sameness, bureaucracy, and the myth of educational equity: The TAAS system of testing in Texas public schools. *Hispanic Journal of Behavioral Sciences, 22* (4), 508–523.

McNeill, W. H. (1986). *Mythistory and other essays.* Chicago: University of Chicago Press.

McPike, E. (Ed.). (1996–1997). Teacher welcomes defined, rich curriculum. *American Educator, 20*(4), 14–15.

Media Transparency. (2006). Grants to Core Knowledge Foundation. Available: http://www.mediatransparency.org/recipientgrantsprint.php?recipientID=2204

Meier, D., & Schwartz, P. (2007). Central Park East secondary school: The hard part is making it happen. In M. W. Apple & J. A. Beane (Eds.), *Democratic schools* (2nd ed., pp. 130–149). Portsmouth, NH: Heinemann.

Meier, D., & Wood, G. (Eds.). (2004). *Many children left behind: How the No Child Left Behind Act is damaging our children and our schools.* Boston: Beacon Press.

Mentzer, D., & Shaughnessy, T. (1996). Hawthorne Elementary School: The teachers' perspective. *Journal of Education for Students Placed at Risk, 1*(1), 13–23.

Meyer, P. (1991, September). Getting to the Core. *Life, 14*(11), 36–39.

Michels, T. (2000). Socialism and the writing of American Jewish history: *World of our fathers* revisited. *American Jewish History, 88*(4), 521–546.

Michie, G. (1999). *Holler if you hear me: The education of a teacher and his students.* New York: Teachers College Press.

Mills, N., & Walzer, M. (Eds.). (2004). *50 years of Dissent.* New Haven, CT: Yale University Press.

Molnar, A. (1996). *Giving kids the business: The commercialization of America's schools.* Boulder, CO: Westview Press.

Molnar A. (2005). *School commercialization: From democratic ideal to market commodity.* New York: Routledge.

Moloney, W. (1998). The place of Core Knowledge in American school reform. *Common Knowledge, 11*(1/2), 5–6, 12–13.

Morris, G. (1992, September 14). Whittling at the wall: Chris Whittle's Edison Project to create profit-oriented schools. *National Review, 44*(18), 50–51.

Morris, P. (Ed.). (1994). *The Bakhtin reader.* New York: Edward Arnold.

Moynihan, D. P. (1996). The negro family: The case for national action. In M. Gerson (Ed.), *The essential neoconservative reader* (pp. 23–37). New York: Addison-Wesley Publishing.

Munslow, A. (1997). *Deconstructing history.* New York: Routledge.

Nagin, R. (2006, January 16). Transcript of Nagin's speech. *Times Picayune.* Available at http://www.nola.com

Nash, G. H. (2005). Joining the ranks: *Commentary* and American conservatism. In M. Friedman (Ed.), Commentary *in American life* (pp. 151–173). Philadelphia: Temple University Press.

National Association of Scholars. (2004). Conference schedule of activities and registration form. Available: http://www.nas.org/conferences/conf_sched_reg04.htm

National Association of Scholars. (2006). Home page. Available: http://www.nas.org

National Core Knowledge Coordinator of Colorado. (2004). Home page. Available: http://www.ck colorado.org

New. (2003). New K-8 director in Arkansas [electronic]. *Common Knowledge, 16*(2).

Oakes, J. (2005). *Keeping track: How schools structure inequality* (2nd ed.). New Haven, CT: Yale University Press.

Ozick, C. (1999). The rights of history and the rights of imagination. *Commentary, 107*(3), 22–27.

Pearson Learning. (2004). Pearson Learning Group catalog: Pre-K–12 supplemental educational materials [social studies and economics]. Retrieved July 17, 2007, from http://plgcatalog.pearson.com/subject_area_listing.cfm?site_id=2&discipline_id=809

Peden, W. (Ed.). (1982). *Thomas Jefferson: Notes on the state of Virginia.* Chapel Hill: University of North Carolina Press.

Pedroni, T. C. (2007a). Conservatism. In D. Gabbard (Ed.), *Knowledge and power in the global economy: The effects of school reform in a neoliberal/neoconservative age* (2nd ed.). Mahwah, NJ: Erlbaum.

Pedroni, T. C. (2007b). *Market movements: African American involvement in school voucher reform.* New York: Routledge.

Pellerano, C., Fradd, S. H., & Rovira, L. (1998). Coral Way Elementary School: A success story in bilingualism and biliteracy. Retrieved November 10, 1999, from http://www.ncbe.gwu.edu/ncbepubs/ discover/03coral.htm

Perry, C. (1994, October). Maverick principal. *Reader's Digest*, 134–138.

Plank, D. N., & Sykes, G. (Eds.). (2003). *Choosing choice: School choice in international perspective*. New York: Teachers College Press.

Podair, J. E. (2002). *The strike that changed New York: Blacks, whites, and the Ocean Hill-Brownsville crisis*. New Haven, CT: Yale University Press.

Podhoretz, N. (1967). *Making it*. New York: Harper & Row Publishers.

Podhoretz, N. (1979). *Breaking ranks: A political memoir*. New York: Harper & Row.

Podhoretz, N. (1996). My negro problem—and ours. In M. Gerson (Ed.), *The essential neoconservative reader* (pp. 5–22). New York: Addison-Wesley.

Pollock, M. (in press). *Because of race: How Americans debate harm and opportunity in our schools*. Princeton, NJ: Princeton University Press.

Potter, E. F., & Rosser, S. V. (1992). Factors in life science textbooks that may deter girls' interest in science. *Journal of Research in Science Teaching*, *29*(7), 669–686.

Powers, R. G. (2005). Norman Podhoretz and the cold war. In M. Friedman (Ed.), *Commentary in American life* (pp. 134–150). Philadelphia: Temple University Press.

Pritchett, W. (2002). *Brownsville, Brooklyn: Blacks, Jews, and the changing face of the ghetto*. Chicago: University of Chicago Press.

Prum, D. M. (1999). *Rats, bulls, and flying machines*. Charlottesville, VA: Core Knowledge Foundation.

Putka, G. (1991, September 5). Florida schools to put cultural literacy to test. *Wall Street Journal*, B1.

Ravitch, D. (1995). *National standards in American education: A citizen's guide*. Washington, DC: Brookings Institution Press.

Ravitch, D. (1996). Why we need a literate core curriculum. *Common Knowledge*, *9*(1/2), 1, 6–11.

Ravitch, D. (2000a). *Left back: A century of failed school reform*. New York: Simon & Schuster.

Ravitch, D. (2000b). *The great school wars: A history of the New York City public schools*. Baltimore, MD: Johns Hopkins University Press.

Ravitch, D. (2004). *The language police: How pressure groups restrict what students learn*. New York: Vintage Books.

Ravitch, D. (Ed.). (2005). *Brookings papers in education policy*. Washington, DC: Brookings Institution Press.

Real Utopias Project. (2007). Real utopias project. Available: http://www.ssc.wisc.edu/~wright/RealUtopias.htm

Reed, R. (1996). *After the revolution: How the Christian Coalition is impacting America*. Dallas, TX: Word.

Robinson, J. H. (1912/1965). *The new history*. New York: The Free Press.

Rodriguez, R. (1997). Assimilation happens. *Common Knowledge*, *10*(1/2), 12–13.

Roeder, G. H., Jr. (1994). Coming to our senses. *Journal of American History*, *81*(3), 1112–1122.

Roeder, G. H., Jr. (1998). Filling in the picture: Visual culture. *Reviews in American History, 26* (1), 275–293.

Roediger, D. R. (1991). *The wages of whiteness: Race and the making of the American working class.* New York: Verso.

Rounds, S. (2004, February). Hobbs Municipal Schools: Comprehensive K–12 reform programs—the Core Knowledge sequence. Hobbs, NM: Hobbs Municipal Schools.

Ruenzel, D. (1996–97). Washington Core Knowledge school: Fort Collins, Colorado. *American Educator, 20*(4), 8, 24–26, 28–29.

Said, E. (1988). Foreword. In R. Guha & G. C. Spivak (Eds.), *Selected subaltern studies* (pp. v–x). New York: Oxford University Press.

Saltman, K. (Ed.). (2007). *Schooling and the politics of disaster.* New York: Routledge.

Sarna, J. D. (1999). American Jewish political conservatism in historical perspective. *American Jewish History, 87*(2 & 3), 113–122.

Scatamburlo-D'Annibale, V., & McLaren, P. (2005). Class dismissed? Historical materialism and the politics of "difference." In Z. Leonardo (Ed.), *Critical pedagogy and race* (pp. 141–157). Malden, MA: Blackwell Publishing.

Scherer, M. (1996). On better alternatives for urban students: A conversation with Sylvia Peters. *Educational Leadership, 54*(2), 47–52.

Schlesinger, A. M, Jr. (1992). *The disuniting of America: Reflections on a multicultural society.* New York: W. W. Norton.

Schweber, S. A. (2004). *Making sense of the Holocaust: Lessons from classroom practice.* New York: Teachers College Press.

Selden, S. (2004). The neo-conservative assault on the undergraduate curriculum. In M. Walker & J. Nixon (Eds.), *Reclaiming universities from a runaway world* (pp. 51–66). New York: Open University Press.

Shapiro, E. S. (1999). Jews and the conservative rift. *American Jewish History, 87*(2 & 3), 195–215.

Shavelson, R. J., & Towne, L. (2002). Scientific research in education. Washington, DC: National Academy Press.

Shaver, J. P., Davis, O. L., & Helburn, S. W. (1978). An interpretive report on the status of pre-college social studies education based on three NSF-funded studies. Washington, DC: National Council for the Social Studies. (ERIC Document Reproduction Service No. ED 164 363)

Sheets, R. H. (1995). From remedial to gifted: Effects of culturally centered pedagogy. *Theory Into Practice, 34,* 186–193.

Shields, C. J. (2003b). Interview with CSR coordinator Yolanda Van Ness [electronic]. *Common Knowledge, 16* (4).

Siddle Walker, V. (1996). *Their highest potential: An African American school in the segregated south.* Chapel Hill: University of North Carolina Press.

Siler, J. N. (1997). Report on the sixth national Core Knowledge conference: Bigger is still better. *Common Knowledge, 10*(1/2), 1, 8–9.

Siler, J. N. (1998). Atlanta '98: Core content with southern hospitality. *Common Knowledge, 11*(1/2), 10–11.

Siler, J. N. (1999). Coast to coast, trainers spread Core Knowledge with enthusiasm. *Common Knowledge, 12*(4), 5, 9.

Siler, J. N. (Ed.). (2001a). Gerald Terrell joins foundation staff in Charlottesville. *Common Knowledge, 14*(3), 3.

Siler, J. N. (Ed.). (2001b). It's the principal of the thing! *Common Knowledge, 14*(3), 14.

Siler, J. N. (Ed.). (2001c). National Core Knowledge coordinators replace regional centers. *Common Knowledge, 14*(3), 3.

Sleeter, C. E., & Grant, C. A. (1991). Race, class, gender, and disability in current textbooks. In M. W. Apple & L. K. Christian-Smith (Eds.), *The politics of the textbook* (pp. 78–110). New York: Routledge.

Smith, M. L., with Miller-Kahn, L., Heinecke, W., & Jarvis, P. F. (2004). *Political spectacle and the fate of American schools*. New York: RoutledgeFalmer.

Solórzano, D., & Yosso, T. J. (2002). Critical race methodology: Counter-storytelling as an analytical framework for education research. *Qualitative Research, 8*(1), 23–44.

Southgate, B. (2001). *History: What and why?* (2nd ed.). New York: Routledge.

Sowell, T. (1984). *Civil rights: Rhetoric or reality?* New York: William Morrow.

Spencer, L. C. (1999). Spencer responds to Buras [correspondence]. *Harvard Educational Review, 69*(4), 467–468

Stearns, P. N. (1993). The old social history and the new. In M. K. Cayton, E. Gorn, & P. W. Williams (Eds.), *Encyclopedia of American social history* (pp. 237–250). New York: Macmillan.

Steele, S. (1998). *A dream deferred: The second betrayal of black freedom in America*. New York: HarperPerennial.

Steinfels, P. (1979). *The neoconservatives: The men who are changing America's politics*. New York: Simon & Schuster.

Stern, S. M. (2003). *Effective state standards for U.S. history: A 2003 report card*. Washington, DC: Thomas B. Fordham Foundation.

Stotsky, S. (2004). *The stealth curriculum: Manipulating America's history teachers*. Washington, DC: Thomas B. Fordham Foundation.

Stringfield, S., Datnow, A., Borman, G., & Rachuba, L. (1999). National evaluation of Core Knowledge sequence implementation: Final report. Baltimore: Center for Social Organization of Schools, Johns Hopkins University.

Stuckey, S. (1987). *Slave culture: Nationalist theory and the foundations of Black America*. New York: Oxford University Press.

Summers, M. (1999, July 26). Defining literacy upward. *Forbes*, 70, 72.

Symcox, L. (2002). *Whose history? The struggle for national standards in American classrooms*. New York: Teachers College Press.

TASIS Staff. (2007). Core Knowledge hits the Alps [electronic]. *Common Knowledge, 20*(1).

Tate, W. (1995). Returning to the root: A culturally relevant approach to mathematics pedagogy. *Theory Into Practice, 34,* 309–331.

Telling. (2003). Telling your story with test data [electronic]. *Common Knowledge, 16*(3).

Tetreault, M. K. (1984). Notable American women: The case of United States history textbooks. *Social Education, 48*(7), 546–550.

Thomas B. Fordham Foundation. (2003a). E. D. Hirsch: The unexpected crusader. Available: http://www.edexcellence.net/foundation/global/page.cfm?id=32

Thomas. B. Fordham Foundation. (2003b). The Thomas B. Fordham Foundation prize 2003 winners for excellence in education. Available: http://www.edexcellence.net/foundation/global/page.cfm?id+40

Torres, C. A. (1998). *Democracy, education, and multiculturalism: Dilemmas of citizenship in a global world.* New York: Rowman & Littlefield.

Trachtenberg, A. (1989). Illustrious Americans. In A. Trachtenberg, *Reading American photographs: Images as history* (pp. 21–70). New York: Hill and Wang.

Tryneski, J. (Ed.). (1997). *Requirements for certification.* Chicago: University of Chicago Press.

Vail, K. (1997). Core comes to Crooksville. *The American School Board Journal, 184*(3), 14–18.

Valenzuela, A. (Ed.). (2004). *Leaving children behind: How Texas-style accountability fails Latino youth.* New York: State University of New York Press.

Vansledright, B. (2002). *In search of America's past: Learning to read history in elementary school.* New York: Teachers College Press.

Villanueva, V. (1993). *Bootstraps: From an American academic of color.* Urbana, IL: National Council of Teachers of English.

Wade, R. C. (1993). Content analysis of social studies textbooks: A review of ten years of research. *Theory and Research in Social Education, 21*(3), 232–256.

Wang, M. C., Haertel, G. D., & Walberg, H. J. (1997). *What do we know?: Widely implemented school improvement programs.* Philadelphia: Temple University Center for Research in Human Development and Education.

Warren, E. (1954). *Brown v. Board of Education.* Available: http://www.nationalcenter.org/brownhtml

West, C. (1993). *Race matters.* New York: Vintage Books.

Wexler, L. (2000). Black and white and color: The Hampton album. In L. Wexler, *Tender violence: Domestic visions in an age of U.S. imperialism* (pp. 127–176). Chapel Hill: University of North Carolina Press.

White, J. J. (1988). Searching for substantial knowledge in social studies texts. *Theory and Research in Social Education, 16*(2), 115–140.

Whitty, G. (1985). *Sociology and school knowledge: Curriculum theory, research and politics*. London: Methuen.

Wiener, J. M. (1989). Radical historians and the crisis in American history, 1959–1980. *Journal of American History, 76*, 399–434.

Wildavsky, A. (1996). Government and the people. In M. Gerson (Ed.), *The essential neoconservative reader* (pp. 76–92). New York: Addison-Wesley Publishing.

Williams, R. (1989). *Resources of hope*. New York: Verso.

Willingham, D. B. (1999). What do scientists know about how we learn? A brief summary of the most important principles of learning and memory. *Common Knowledge, 12*(1/2), 6–7.

Willis, A. (1995). Reading the world of school literacy: Contextualizing the experience of a young African American male. *Harvard Educational Review, 65*, 30–49.

Willis, P. (1977). *Learning to labor: How working class kids get working class jobs*. New York: Columbia University Press.

Wilson, J. Q. (1996). The rediscovery of character: Private virtue and public policy. In M. Gerson (Ed.), *The essential neoconservative reader* (pp. 291–304). New York: Addison-Wesley Publishing.

Wineberg, S. (2001). Historical thinking and other unnatural acts: Charting the future of teaching the past. Philadelphia: Temple University Press.

Wolfe, A. (2005). The great Jewish-American synthesis. *The Chronicle Review, LI* (39), B9–B11.

Woodson, C. G. (1933/2000). *The mis-education of the Negro*. Chicago, IL: African American Images.

Wright, D. R. (1993). *African Americans in the early republic, 1789–1831*. Wheeling, IL: Harlan Davidson.

Yosso, T. J. (2006). *Critical race counterstories along the Chicana/Chicano educational pipeline*. New York: Routledge.

Zimmerman, J. (2002). *Whose America: Culture wars in the public schools*. Cambridge: Harvard University Press.

Zinn, H. (1995). *A people's history of the United States*. New York: Harper Perrenial.

INDEX

213